VISITING
HISTORIC
BEIJING

"Une Rue de Pékin — A Street of Peking," postcard, anonymous

VISITING HISTORIC BEIJING

A Guide to Sites and Resources

Robert L. Thorp

FLOATING WORLD EDITIONS

First edition, 2008

Published by Floating World Editions, Inc., 26 Jack Corner
Road, Warren, CT 06777. Protected by copyright under the
terms of the International Copyright Union; all rights reserved.
Except for fair use in book reviews, no part of this book may be
reproduced for any reason by any means, including any method
of photographic reproduction, without the permission of the
publisher. Printed in the U.S.A.

ISBN 978–1–891640–53–7

Front cover photograph by Ellen Kaplowitz.

Library of Congress Cataloging-in-Publication data available.

Contents

Box Features

Preface

The first published guides to Beijing appeared during the Ming (1368–1644) period, written by Chinese scholars whose careers brought them to the seat of imperial power (see Box, p. 10). Accounts by foreigners have a long history as well—the most famous being that of the Venetian Marco Polo, who left a remarkably clear and detailed description of the city he may have roamed in the late thirteenth century (Ch. 1). Thus this guide falls into a long tradition of writings about the city with the needs of visitors in mind. What are this guide's goals and limits? How does it complement the larger literature on Beijing?

Contents and Organization

Visiting Historic Beijing introduces the major sites of the Ming and Qing periods with attention to cultural context, history, and architecture. The bulk of the text (Ch. 2–7) covers the period from the early fifteenth century through the early twentieth century, with scant attention to anything earlier or later. In order to cover this ground in a compact package, I observe the following limits:

I focus on the area once enclosed by the city walls, roughly today's Second Ring Road (Er Huan Lu). Exceptions are the Ming Valley and Great Wall, and imperial garden-palaces of the near northwest suburbs. A few more distant sites—the Qing tombs and additional segments of the Great Wall—warrant brief discussions. Chengde is not included.

After a chapter on Beijing before the Ming, sites are grouped by generic or functional categories. The main text of each chapter contains general information; numbered items followed by an arrowhead [1 ▶] indicate specific sites treated in detail. Sometimes placement in one category rather than another is arbitrary. The Confucian Temple [17 ▶], here grouped with Altars and Tombs (Ch. 4) because of its status in state rites, could as logically be grouped with other temples devoted to gods and buddhas (Ch. 5).

Although I have been visiting the city regularly since 1979, the guide was researched and written in 2006 and 2007, and most entries are based on several visits during that time. However, a few sites were closed or partially shut down for renovations, and visitors may encounter changes when these sites reopen.

The illustrations are a mixture of historic photographs (most postcards from the early twentieth century) and contemporary views. The former show the look of things lost or much changed; you should recognize your destination by consulting the latter.

SIGHTS OF THE CAPITAL

Our oldest map of Beijing (opposite) represents the capital after construction of the Southern City outer wall in the 1550s. It complemented Zhang Jue's text on the "neighborhoods and alleys of the capital's five districts." Zhang's work enumerates many of the city's landmarks and sights for visitors; it may be the first true guide to the city.

In the map we see the Palace [10–12 ▶] bisected by a stack of tile roofs that resembles a pagoda, and the larger Imperial City with the scalloped waves of Bei Hai [30 ▶] filling the walled areas on the left. Both the Palace and Imperial City are drawn as rectangles stretching east-west. The shape of both city walls is similarly distorted. All city gates—nine on the north (see Box, p. 83) and seven on the south—however, are correctly labeled.

What this map lacks in visual accuracy it makes up for with abundant landmarks, both inside the walls and in the suburbs. Dong Si and Xi Si (the four *pailou*—wooden arches—on the east and west sides of the city) are shown, as are Dong Dan and Xi Dan (each a single *pailou*) below them (see Box, p. 186). Note the Altar to Heaven [16 ▶] in two circles at bottom right balanced by an incongruously named Altar to Earth in a double rectangle at bottom left. Thirty-three residential neighborhoods (*fang*) of sixteenth-century Beijing are labeled in relation to these walls, gates, and landmarks. Famous sights include several of the canonical "Eight Views:" Lugou Bridge [2 ▶] in the lower left corner, the Western Hills at top left, the Golden Terrace at top right (see Box, p. 50).

Like this early map, this guide attempts both to see the city whole and to focus on its major landmarks, the architectural monuments of the Ming and Qing periods that survive today.

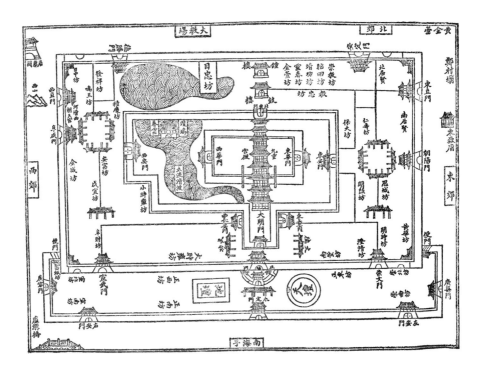

The information presented in this guide relies almost exclusively on Chinese-language sources, especially scholarship by Fu Xinian, Hou Renzhi, Luo Zhewen, Ma Bingjian, Shan Shiyuan, Wang Shiren, Xiao Mo, Xu Pingfang, and Yu Zhuoyun, as well as older studies by Liang Sicheng and Liu Dunzhen. I have tried not to rehearse misinformation, and to make judicious choices from among competing scholarly opinions.

Map of the Capital, ca. 1560, from Zhang Jue, *Jingshi wucheng fangxiang hutong ji* (Beijing Guji, 1983)

How to Use This Guide

Entries describe the plan of each site and its major buildings with other topics introduced as relevant. Readers need not read in sequence. Each entry was written as a stand-alone essay, and many cross references are provided.

MODERN MISCONCEPTIONS

Three misconceptions plague attempts to write a modern guide to the city. Some of these ideas developed in the late nineteenth and early twentieth centuries when large numbers of foreign (European and American) visitors first came to the city. Others date from the 1970s, when China opened itself to the world after a long hiatus. The ignorance of the early visitors (opposite)—only a few of whom had any command of Chinese—all too often is perpetuated in recent writings. And the impressions of tourists in the 1970s still circulate as truths about the city.

1 Of the historic city: *"Old Peking is lost; they've torn it all down."*

No one doubts that destruction (see Introduction and Ch. 7) has played a large part in the modern history of the city. But this misconception, fueled by egregious examples of recent urban development (see Jasper Becker), ignores major efforts by the government, both national and municipal, since the 1930s to identify and protect the city's architectural heritage. Far more sites still survive than I can include in this guide, and some of them will come "on line" in years hence. There is more to see now than ever.

2 Of late imperial architecture: *"The level of interest is relatively low."*

This bias against later buildings (quoted from Alexander C. Soper, ca. 1956) is an historical by-product of: (a) attitudes of the first European visitors who found no monuments to match their own Greek temples or European cathedrals; (b) enthusiasm for the monuments of earlier eras identified by the pioneers of architectural history in the 1930s; and (c) anti-Manchu prejudice, a bias against the dynasty that presided over the collapse of imperial China, ushering in the disasters of the first half of the twentieth century. Ming and Qing imperial architecture is a rich and diverse corpus of many types and great interest. Serious studies of later architecture are now flourishing among Chinese and foreign scholars alike and their efforts promise more enlightenment in years to come.

3 Of the modern city: *"There is nothing to do there."*

As one who first encountered Beijing in the days when this generalization seemed true, the persistence of this opinion is a great disappointment. Beijing today offers myriad attractions and diversions. Any issue of several local magazines, like *Time Out Beijing*, lists hundreds of things to do by many categories (Around Town, Art, Books, Film, Music, Nightlife, Performance, and Sport). The days when an evening's great excitement was a scoop of vanilla ice cream in the hotel lobby and a soak in the tub are long gone. Today's Beijing is a great international capital city.

All of these sites should be easy to find using commonly available maps or conventional travel guides. Chinese characters will also help when consulting a taxi driver or people on the street; a list is provided on pages 320–23, with street addresses. Practical information such as hours, phone numbers, admission prices, and the like change frequently and so are omitted.

Acknowledgments

I have had the pleasure and stimulation of staying in Beijing with Freda and Chris Murck for many years. This guide is dedicated to them as a small token of my gratitude. Karen Brock jumped into this project with

"Western Gate, Peking, China," steel engraving by Thomas Allom, *China Illustrated*, ca. 1842; author's collection. Allom's sweeping roofs, one of the enduring stereotypes of Chinese architecture, were not a feature of the walls and gates of Peking. The representation hovers between pictorial accuracy and Orientalist fantasy.

two feet, scanning images as well as giving the text a stiff editing. Everything about this guide is better for her attention. Most of all, credit goes to Ray Furse of Floating World Editions. Ray let me go my own way, and then took on the hard work of turning manuscript into book. No simple task but a writer's dream.

SUGGESTED
READING

The best historical treatment of Beijing in English is Susan Naquin's *Peking: Temples and City Life, 1400–1900* (2000). I have followed her lead in many matters, including translations of names and terms. I would be pleased if this guide serves as a supplement to her far more important work. Evelyn Rawski's *The Last Emperors: A Social History of Qing Imperial Institutions* (1998) is indispensable for all matters imperial. Parenthetical references to both volumes will be found in several chapters. For the full sweep of the city's history, see Lillian M. Li, Alison J. Dray-Novey, and Haili Kong, *Beijing: From Imperial Capital to Olympic City* (2007).

Anyone with access to a large library can find many accounts of the city written by early visitors, missionaries, participants in the siege of the Legations, and expatriates who lived in the city before 1949. Many of these accounts are charming, but too often they retell various urban myths and folk tales about the city and its sights. Take them with the requisite large grain of salt. (Some more recent writers perpetuate these dubious remarks.) Reliable readings arranged by topic are suggested at the end of each chapter and gathered in the Bibliography.

Introduction

Seen from a little distance with its walls and gate towers sharply defined against a background of hills, the city still appears what it was when it first became the capital of China in the Middle Ages, a Tartar encampment in stone, "a fortified garrison of nomad bannermen surrounding the palace of the Great Khan."

Many of the oldest monuments have disappeared . . . because the Chinese have been too indifferent to preserve them.

But let us not forget that in its best days all that was most worth seeing was rigorously forbidden to the public.

JULIET BREDON, *PEKING* (1931), 14–15

My decision to write a guide to historic Beijing presupposes the survival of such a thing. Like many others, including citizens of the capital, I have watched with dismay as large portions of Beijing's pre-modern urban fabric have disappeared in clouds of dust over the last thirty years, lately accelerated by preparations for the 2008 Olympic Games. Yet, through the efforts of the same national and municipal governments that presided over this destruction, enough of the old city has been protected that this guide is not entirely an exercise in evoking a vanished past.

Destruction and Preservation

Destruction has been commonplace in the history of Beijing, and was usually a prelude to new building, as today. The Liao and Jin rulers reused the old Tang city as the core of their capitals, preserving some of it, but Genghis Khan did his best to decimate the Jin capital (Zhongdu) in 1215. The Mongols returned about sixty years later to build a grand new city just north of the ruins of Zhongdu. Like the Liao and Jin capitals, Dadu their capital (Cambaluc to Marco Polo) was short-lived. Scholars debate how much of the Yuan capital was leveled in the Ming conquest and how much survived. Nonetheless, Dadu left an enduring imprint still detectable today. After the Ming founder's fourth son, Zhu Di, was enfoeffed as Prince of Yan, the city came back to life. Zhu Di's builders utilized the Yuan capital, again preservation of a sort, as they created what we call Beijing. Their city served for about five hundred years (ca. 1421–1911) as the imperial capital, a long run. Moreover its Qing masters were especially good custodians of their captured city, again preservationists in a sense.

Remarkably, much of that old city—a Qing version of a Ming original based on a Yuan footprint—still stood in the early twentieth century when Juliet Bredon wrote. Unlike London, Paris, or Rome, Beijing's urban form remained frozen from the fifteenth century to 1900. The city did not abandon its walls or burn in catastrophic fires. No Napoleon III or Baron Haussmann renovated the old city into a grand metropolis of new boulevards. Nor did Beijing experience the kind of economic and social change during the eighteenth and nineteenth centuries that created the institutions of the modern city across Europe and in America. No parliament, train stations, lighting and sewers, department stores, parks, museums, or omnibuses appeared inside the walls of the Tartar and Chinese cities until after 1900. In many ways, this late medieval city continued to function into the early twentieth century, especially in terms of the daily life of its residents. Even the twentieth century arrived slowly, haltingly, sometimes inconclusively prior to 1949. As modernization accelerated in Europe and America during the pre-war decades, Beijing remained only modestly affected. A few trolley lines, shopping avenues, imperial precincts opened as parks, and a smattering of modern institutions in good looking campuses dotted the city. Prior to the Japanese occupation (1937–45), the pre-modern capital had changed only on a limited scale.

The persistence of the past, of the fifteenth century in the twentieth, largely resulted from acts of omission. However, the idea that the past had value and should be protected took hold gradually as young people, most educated abroad, returned to pursue careers and to create new pursuits like the study of Chinese architecture. Indeed, the first efforts at historic restoration took place in the 1930s under the aegis of the Society for the Study of Chinese Architecture (Zhongguo Yingzao Xueshe). Local government rationalized these efforts as adding to Peking's value as an international tourist destination, an attitude echoed today.

Extensive modernization came to the city only after 1950. In the 1920s and 30s piecemeal efforts improved train and street traffic by punching through the Ming walls or tearing some down. More concerted efforts to integrate a modern transportation grid after 1949 culminated in the near-total destruction of the city walls in the 1960s and 70s with the creation of the ring roads that now define the old city. Large swaths of residential alleys (hutong) disappeared with the building of the great projects completed for the 1959 ten-year anniversary of the People's Republic of China. These new edifices in the heroic and colossal Soviet idiom displayed tile cornices or roofs in Chinese style as icing on the cake. Industries mostly grew outside the city, as did tracts of housing. But efforts at "basic construction" were constrained by the Korean War and many "anti" campaigns, the Great Leap Forward and famine, the Great Proletarian Cultural Revolution and Tangshan earthquake. By the late 1970s, as the city emerged from "ten years of chaos," Beijing was still small in scale, its infrastructure and public institutions modest by international standards. Major avenues were mostly empty, except for bicycles, the outskirts remained largely rural, and the city's skyline was non-existent.

Some of the preservation characteristic of the era after 1949 resulted from neglect. For example party or state work units (*danwei*) occupied major sites like Dong Yue Miao [26 ▶], while an elementary school took over Pudu Si (below). Saved from wholesale destruction, traditional compounds like these were retrofitted as offices, schools, workshops, and warehouses. This adaptive reuse, to put a positive spin on it, could be more or less severe as many site plans attest. Many monuments introduced in this guide lived through decades of such treatment prior to being reclaimed for the Cultural Heritage system.

The current situation presents the most widespread challenge to historic preservation in Beijing yet. The dangers posed skirt around major sites that have been accorded recognition and protection since 1961 via the national and municipal historic registers. However, contemporary development lays waste to ever larger tracts, wiping out whatever assets they may have had: not just picturesque alleys, but also small temples, commercial facades, old theaters and native place lodges, small bridges, old trees, and the myriad sights that once formed part of the urban experience. Rarely can parts of this fabric be saved when a developer proceeds with an office tower, shopping mall, or residential high rises (opposite). As new super blocks rise, older sites accorded protection may survive incongruously as islands amid a modern cityscape.

Pudu Si before restoration. The Mahakala Temple, as it was known to foreign visitors, was a useful property for the new government after 1949. The historic grounds, once the residence of Dorgon, the Manchu general who occupied the Ming capital in 1644, became an elementary school. Later turned over to the cultural heritage authorities, the gate now houses a display on the history of the site.

The present plan for the historic conservation of the old city, which was announced in 2002, is nonetheless admirably ambitious. The plan identifies forty conservation districts, of which thirty lie within the walls of the Ming–Qing city (see fig. p. 22). Virtually the entire area of the former Imperial City is designated for conservation, as are contiguous areas to the north and several large patches on the east, west, and south. When these are combined with current historic register sites, the total area that will come under protection exceeds 40 percent of the 62 square km within the walls. Plans for these districts include restoration of additional heritage sites, improvements to amenities such as strip parks, attention to historic water channels, and general upgrading of infrastructure such as electricity, sewers, telephone, gas, and street lights. While master plans like this one are unavoidably fraught with pitfalls and challenges (such as how to persuade tenants to move out, how to work with developers and government agencies), some of these projects are already bearing fruit, such as the strip park that runs along the path of the east wall of the Imperial City (Nan and Bei Heyan streets) and the sunken plaza that reveals parts of the Dong'an Men near the intersection with Dong Hua Men Dajie (see p. 105).

Nan Xin Cang, Ping'an Dadao, near Dongsi Shitiao Bridge. Located near the former east city wall, this site once had seventy-six granaries (*cang*) for storing grain brought by canal from the south, each capable of holding 12,000 *shi* (equivalent to 33,000 bushels). These structures have been put to new uses by Beijing developers, housing high-end shops, galleries, and even an "Imperial Granary Bar."

NATIONAL REGISTER SITES IN BEIJING

Even as Beijing was being remade into the People's Capital, the new government created an historic preservation law and administrative system. Provisional legislation recognizing historic structures as "cultural relics" (wen wu) was written during the 1950s, and by 1961 the State Council had promulgated an historic register, the "National Important Cultural Relics Protected Units" (Quanguo zhongdian wenwu baohu danwei). The listing found enduring historic, scientific or aesthetic value in archaeological sites, Buddhist temples, and imperial altars, as well as places associated with the Communist Revolution. On a list of 180 units, Beijing boasted twelve (of seventy-seven) architectural sites and four (of thirty-three) revolutionary ones, as well as the cave home of Peking Man (Zhoukoudian, Fangshan) and the Ming Valley (Changping).

A comparable city register and district listings complemented the national list. Over the years, the State Council has announced five additions to the national list, in 1982, 1988, 1996, 2001, and 2006. With the latest cohort, a total of 2352 sites are now enrolled

Ancient Architecture		
Yunju Si, Fangshan	Sui-Jin	
Bai Ta	Yuan	[23 ▶]
Wu Ta Si, Haidian	Ming	[24 ▶]
Cloud Terrace, Juyong Guan	Yuan	[3 ▶]
Forbidden City	Ming-Qing	[10–12 ▶]
Badaling Great Wall	Ming	
Altar to Heaven	Ming	[16 ▶]
Bei Hai	Ming-Qing	[30 ▶]
Zhihua Si	Ming	[22 ▶]
Guozijian	Qing	
Yonghe Gong	Qing	[25 ▶]
Yihe Yuan, Haidian	Qing	
Revolutionary Sites		
Red Building, Peking University		
Marco Polo Bridge	Jin	[2 ▶]
Tian'an Men	Ming	[8 ▶]
Monument to People's Martyrs		
Archaeological Sites		
Zhoukoudian (Peking Man)	Paleolithic	
Tombs		
Thirteen Ming Tombs	Ming	[18–19 ▶]

Source: Qiu Fuke, *Zhongguo wenwu luyou tu ce* (Wenwu, 2003).
Entries with bracketed numbers refer to sites discussed in this book.

on the national register. In Beijing, the additions have generally advanced the status of pre-viously recognized city- or district-level sites. Moreover, cultural heritage administrators vie in soliciting UNESCO World Heritage status for sites. Beijing claims the Forbidden City, Zhoukoudian, and the Great Wall (all designated 1987), Yihe Yuan and Tian Tan (both 1998), and Ming and Qing imperial tombs (2000). (On the other hand, the State Administration of Cultural Heritage itself calculates that only 17% of the nation's 400,000 cultural relic sites identified by surveys are protected. Much remains to be done.)

In principle, protected sites are researched and documented, and an archive created. They are restored and maintained by a permanent staff that act as caretakers and serve the public. Ideally over time facilities are upgraded, offering new displays and publications. Yet despite legal recognition, some sites have indeed been damaged, even destroyed. Just as many American towns and cities have a lamented lost movie palace or court house, so too many districts of Beijing have watched old houses and temples disappear.

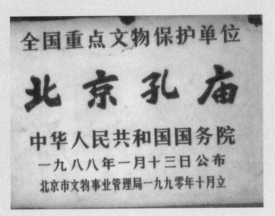

Historic Register marker. The text follows a standard format: (top line) National Important Cultural Relics Protected Unit; (second line) Beijing Confucian Temple; (third line) State Council of the People's Republic of China; (fourth line) Announced January 13, 1988; (fifth line) Erected by the Beijing Cultural Relics Bureau, October 1990.

Residents and frequent visitors should avail themselves of programs organized by the Friends of Old Beijing (Lao Beijing zhi You). An NGO dedicated to raising awareness of Beijing's heritage and conservation issues more generally, the Friends offer a variety of lectures and other activities. They can be contacted at:

Beijing Cultural Heritage Protection Center
Bailin Si, Dongcheng
Phone: (86 10) 6403 4932
Website: www.bjchp.org

Friends of Beijing

Conservation Districts, 2002, from *Beijing lishi wenhua ming cheng*, 157. The dark areas designate the first twenty-five conservation districts announced in 2002, to which fifteen more have been added. Areas targeted here include Qian Men, the Legation Quarter, and tracts surrounding the Forbidden City, the Bell and Drum Towers, and Hou Hai.

Another way to stay on top of heritage issues is the *China Heritage Quarterly*, produced online by editors Bruce Doar and Geremie Barmé at the Australian National University (www.chinaheritagenewsletter.org).

Ming and Qing Imperial Architecture

Most of the extant historic monuments of Beijing were produced by and for the imperial institution. They comprise a remarkably homogeneous and internally consistent system for organizing space and constructing shelter. This should not be surprising. Almost all of the thirty-two sites featured in this guide were built and rebuilt during the Ming and Qing periods (exceptions being [1–3, 21, 23 and 32 ▶]). Most of these structures were designed and assembled by a cohort of specialist craftsmen employed by the Ministry of Works or similar bureaus either for use by the court or as objects of court patronage. The construction materials derived from factories and workshops established to build and maintain the palace and other imperial sites. In visiting these buildings, moreover, we are investigating the late stages of a sophisticated architectural tradition, one rigorously standardized to serve the needs of patrons, bureaucrats, artisans, and users. The overview below is designed as a primer for the concepts and vocabulary of Chinese architecture.

Courtyard Plans

Natives of Beijing seem to have an unerring sense of the compass. Ask for directions and the response is likely to be: "Go north and turn west at the intersection." Not only do all major avenues run along compass lines in parallel with other thoroughfares and, originally, city walls (see figs. 1.8, 2.7), but major sites are also laid out as regular, four-sided plots, usually rectangles aligned on a north-south axis. With few exceptions the approach to a building is from the south, and the other walls of the site face the cardinal directions. Thus the entire city—its thoroughfares, the large blocks that make up urban cells, and individual sites, large and small—is consistently oriented to the points of the compass and the path of the sun. Of course, a few sites could not be placed on a north-south axis. Mosques in Beijing and elsewhere were aligned so the faithful can face Mecca (west) at prayer. Temples nestled in the Western Hills or tombs in the foothills of the Ming Valley also vary from a strict orientation to utilize available terrain.

Both the vast Forbidden City [10-12 ▶] and the humble abode of Mei Lanfang [29 ▶] share a common plan: the courtyard (p. 25). Historically, the courtyard design is documented from the early Bronze Age. The following traits are typical across time: square or rectangular shape, entrance on the south, perimeter walls to screen within from without, courtyards disposed from south to north, buildings oriented to the interior of yards, well-defined paths for moving both on axis or off. By custom we describe such sites as having one or more "routes" (*lu*); larger sites have both a central axis and others in parallel to either side. Plans are also described as being so many "steps or enclosures" (*jin*) in depth along each route. A modest residence may be no more than one route and one or two enclosures. The Forbidden City comprises three main routes and dozens of enclosures. A site comprised of such yards may be easily enlarged, both in depth and side to side. Moreover, from the exterior, the scale of the total site cannot be discerned unless one goes to the trouble to trek around the perimeter.

Functionally, courtyard plans could serve every purpose: from domestic to governmental, religious to mortuary. Thus sites were distinguished more by scale, the number of routes and yards, than by distinctive features. Walls, gates, galleries, and halls are common to all types. A tomb mound is a rare example of a specific feature adapted to a function not found at other sites. Only rarely do building plans take advantage of unusual terrain or respond to the whims of a patron. The foremost examples of such variations are the imperial gardens, and even then courtyards within a garden precinct strictly follow norms.

The details of courtyard plans were choices enshrined in custom from early times. A main gate (*da men*) was usually centered on the south wall, but in courtyard houses (*sihe yuan*) entries appear at the southeast or northwest corners (see fig. 6.9). A screen wall (*zhaobi*) often blocked the entrance, requiring a visitor to step around. This wall masks the interior from an outsider's gaze, but was only sensible with relatively light traffic, as at a residence. In the Forbidden City, screen walls on axis are found at the entrance to residential yards, for example the Hall of Mental Cultivation or East and West Six Palaces, but not in the Outer Court.

Gate house, yard, and principal halls were by custom laid across the central axis. By virtue of this orientation, yards and all south-facing structures enjoy optimum sunlight and warmth in the winter months

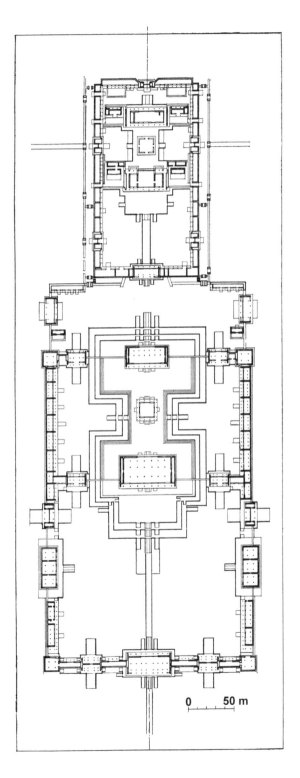

Courtyards of the Inner
and Outer Courts, from
Fu, *Lunwenji*, 361. Careful
measurements led Fu
Xinian to conclude that the
compound containing the
rear residential palaces
(top) served as a module
for laying out the grand
spaces of the outer court
(bottom) at a ratio of 1:4.
In each compound, the
emperor's throne sat at the
crossing of diagonals drawn
from the corners.

0 ___ 50 m

and good shade in the summer season. Gates and halls (*dian*, *tang*) likewise are rectangular in plan, their long dimension running side to side. One does not approach a hall from the end like a Greek temple but rather at the center of its broad façade. Like a Greek temple, exteriors may appear uniform on all sides: most commonly a perimeter of columns under an overhanging eave. A placard over the central doorway announces the name of the building.

Stone-clad terraces (*tai*) elevated major gates and halls above the level of the courtyard. Thus any large yard at the palace or a temple has a front gate that must be ascended and crossed over before descending to the level of the interior. Admission to the hall for an audience or for worship in turn required ascending its steps, leaving those not so privileged behind, gathered on the lower pavement. Surrounding galleries (*lang*), covered walkways inside perimeter walls, and the porches of flanking halls permitted one to circulate under shelter off axis. A modest temple or courtyard residence retains this topography, even if the difference in elevation between yard and platform is no more than a step or two.

As described in chapters on the palaces (Ch. 3) and the imperial altars (Ch. 4), builders designed the most important courtyards quite self-consciously as performance spaces. They were essentially open air theaters in which the primary actors held the stage— the central, elevated, south-facing positions—and the supporting cast occupied flanking, lower, north-facing places. Thus when on occasion the emperor turned to face north, he lowered himself in obeisance vis à vis the spirits of the ancestors or Heaven or even, on her birthday, his mother. As ritual theaters, officials dressed these yards for events in a way we rarely see them today. Curtains, carpets, smoking incense, and attendants with pennants all became part of the setting.

The sequence of gates and yards at any large site imposes a regimen for experiencing that ensemble. At the Forbidden City, one enters the Outer Court only after penetrating the massive Noon Gate [10 ▶], crossing marble bridges over the Golden Water, and finally crossing up and over the Gate of Supreme Harmony to take up positions on the pavement before the Hall of Supreme Harmony (see figs. 3.16–3.19). (Gates and their counterpart main halls have the same name.) Progress from outside to inside is measured, strictly predetermined, and during a court gathering was monitored by officials of the Ministry of Rites, who noted inappropriate deportment. The cracking of whips and playing of musical instruments regulated each step in a process that was meant to embody dignity and instill reverence. Much the same ambiance informs a temple, altar, or tomb ritual, or household rites. Ritual requirements regulated social interaction, and all the spaces where interaction took place as well.

Unlike the niceties of timber-frame carpentry and the other crafts that went into a building, the practices designers followed when laying out a site were not recorded in manuals for posterity. The contemporary scholar Fu Xinian has devoted himself to this topic in recent years. Based on careful analysis of intact Ming and Qing sites for which modern surveys are available, Fu's work reveals important conclusions about site planning. For example, in his study of the Forbidden City, Fu discovered that the basic module for the palaces and halls on the main axis was a rectangle that circumscribed the three residential palaces, the present Qianqing Gong, Jiaotai Dian, and Kunning Gong (see p. 25). Hence the Three Great Halls of State, the Outer Court, occupy an area four times that of the inner court palaces (e.g. four modules). Similarly, the spacing of the several gates from the Da Ming Men (the south gate of the Imperial City) to the Gate of Heavenly Peace is derived from this module (see p. 107). Just as the geometric center of the emperor's palace (Qianqing Gong) is the crossing of diagonals from each corner of the inner court rectangle-module, so too the center of the Outer Court, the throne within the Taihe Dian, is at the crossing of identical diagonals within a unit of four modules.

The modules employed for each site were generated from squares measured in units of ten feet (one *zhang*). Thus high status sites might be based on a module using 50 zhang squares, while lesser sites used 10 zhang, 5 zhang, or 3 zhang squares. Specific examples of these modules in play are given in several entries below. Fu's discoveries affect our understanding of city planning as well as the elevations of structures (see below). The many symmetries and strong sense of order at any large site are no accident.

Anatomy of Timber-frame Structures

Timber-frame buildings found in Beijing's historic sites and elsewhere embody a short list of common structural principles. Although masonry structures—for example walls, gates, and bridges—played important roles in the city as a whole, timber construction accounted for most occupied spaces. (The Bell Tower [6 ▶] and Imperial Archives [9 ▶] are local exceptions.) For purposes of analysis, scholars divide timber structures into three tiers: (a) the foundation and column grid, (b) the layer of bracket clusters, and (c) the roof frame (see opposite).

A foundation began as a block of pounded earth. For a large building, this thick earthen block was built up from an excavated trench well below ground level. Sometimes the earth was mixed with other material such as broken tiles. Sometimes the block itself was given additional support by wooden pilings and layers of brick. The greatest halls of the imperial palace stand upon elevated foundation platforms supported by masses of pounded earth extending as deep below ground level as the foundation platform rises above. Large stone blocks set in the earth supported the timber columns. Ceramic tile generally covered the top surface of the platform and dressed stone faced the terrace. Balustrades, ramps, and steps were also made from stone. Good examples of foundation platforms left with some of their stone work in place after a gate or hall disappeared are the foundation of the Wu Ta Si front hall (see fig. 5.20) or the gates and hall of the Dingling, the tomb of the Ming Wanli emperor.

Timber-frame buildings are described in terms of their spans or bays (*jian*). This can be thought of as the interval between two columns when describing an elevation, or as a set of four adjacent columns that define the corners of a square or rectangular space when describing a plan. Columns were disposed in regular rows side to side (width) and front to back (depth). Ming and Qing buildings always present an odd number of bays across their facades (3-5-7-9-11). The custom of displacing columns or of eliminating them, found in sophisticated structures of Song and Yuan date, was not perpetuated in Ming and Qing halls. Seen from the front, the wide central bay (*ming jian*) of a façade is flanked by slightly narrower bays (*ci jian*), with the terminal (outermost, *shao jian*) bays generally narrower still. Likewise, viewed from either end the bays under the front and rear eaves are shallow, functioning as porches, while interior bays were deeper.

Columns (*zhu*) stood on their stone bases (*chu*) without attachment. Sheer dead weight held them in

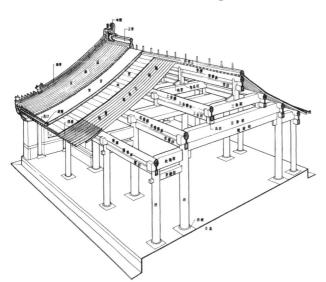

Structural diagram of a Qing hall, from Liu, *Gudai jianzhu*, 4. This diagram exposes three bays of a hall; the building is also three bays in depth. Sturdy columns and tie-beams carry a tile roof, here peeled back to reveal (right to left) rafters, boards and mud, and tile surface.

place, and this conferred a specific advantage: they could shift in response to seismic tremors. In the Hall of Supreme Harmony and the Offering Hall of the Changling in the Ming Valley, columns might reach 13 m in height with spans of 8.5 to 11 m at the center bays. By the Song period, if not earlier, columns had been given features to enhance the visual impression of stability and grace. Across the façade, eave columns were slightly taller as they moved out from the central bay (called rise), and were angled slightly inward from true vertical at their heads (batter). Shafts gradually tapered and were shaped at top. By Ming and Qing times, however, these refinements had been eliminated, although very slight batter persisted. Absent these touches, the façades appear stiff.

Around the perimeter, columns were tied together both at their bases (hence the need to step over thresholds) and at their heads using heavy beams or lintels (*liang*). This of course strengthened the grid both side-to-side and in depth. A sturdy column grid carries the enormous weight of roof frame and tile, while also resisting strong winds. While the column grids of Ming and Qing structures are regular, this structural system still allowed flexibility in the placement of partitions to define either exterior walls or interior divisions. For example, small buildings such as gates have three parallel rows (four columns across and three in depth) with tie-beams that span the column heads at ceiling level. In a gate, door panels and partitions were mounted in the center row (*jin zhu*) under the roof ridge, creating both the necessary barrier and deep shelter both outside and inside. In large halls, the spacing of rows of columns in depth often created a shallow porch. Typically, a line of door panels flanked by windows above masonry half walls one step (row) inward runs parallel to the eave row (*yan zhu*). Alternatively, a porch under its own eave could be added to a building by having a row of columns of lesser height encircle the

THE OLDEST BUILDINGS IN BEIJING

This listing enumerates the oldest surviving structures in and around the city (those built prior to 1550). Masonry generally outlives timber, so it is no surprise the oldest standing structures are all brick and stone:

Period	Structure	Date
Liao	Tianning Si Pagoda [21 ▶]	1119–20
Jin	Marco Polo Bridge [2 ▶]	1188–92
Yuan	Bai Ta Si Dagoba [23 ▶]	1271–79
	Cloud Terrace [3 ▶]	1343–45
Ming	Wu Ta Si Stupa [24 ▶]	1473
	Imperial Archives [9 ▶]	1536

Timber-frame buildings also survive through good fortune enhanced perhaps by a position separated from gates, galleries, and halls that were most often subject to fires (see Box, p. 118 for a list of fires in the Forbidden City). Both lightning and man-made causes were common; fires often spread via the roof frames from one building to another. Thus the Qin'an Dian (1535), which stands in the middle of the Imperial Flower Garden, and the main hall of the She Ji Tan (1420), are both isolated structures. The preservation of the Changling hall (ca. 1409–27) and Zhihua Si ensemble (1443–46) are even more remarkable.

Period	Site	Structure	Date
Yuan	Confucian Temple	Xianshi Men [17 ▶]	1302–06
Ming	Palace	Zhongcui Gong [12 ▶]	1417–20
		Shenwu Men	
		Xi Hua Men	1420
	She Ji Tan	Main Hall [13 ▶]	1420/1425
	Tai Miao	Ji Men [14 ▶]	1420/1545
	Tian Tan	Qi Nian Men [16 ▶]	1420
	Changling	Gate and Hall [18 ▶]	1409–27
	Zhihua Si	Ensemble [22 ▶]	1443–46
	Dong Yue Miao	Zhan Dai Men [26 ▶]	1447
	Bai Ta Si	Qi Fo Dian [23 ▶]	1505
	Xian Nong Tan	Taisui Dian	1532
	Palace	Qin'an Dian	1535
	Gulou	[6 ▶]	1541

Entries with bracketed numbers refer to sites discussed in this book.

perimeter of the hall. Thus a covered gallery surrounds many palace and temple buildings.

Brackets atop the columns are the most complex structural component of the timber frame (opposite). This layer of sets and tie-beams transmits the weight of the roof to the columns and stone bases set in the foundation. Bracket sets were usually pegged to the tops of columns or to horizontal tie-beams. One set consists of a large block (*dou*) cradling the lowest-level arms (*gong*), which cross at right angles in slots prepared to receive them. These short arms terminate with smaller blocks (*sheng*) with slots in one direction only that accept the next tier of arms or beams. One or two tiers of arms (called *qiao*) plus cantilever arms (called *ang*) are characteristic of the Ming and Qing periods. The individual elements are much smaller in scale than those found in older buildings, however. A Qing bracket cluster will be about one sixth the height of a column, whereas in earlier periods (Tang-Song) clusters might equal half the height of a column.

Compared to their predecessors, Ming-Qing bracket clusters contribute less functionality. They elevate tie-beams less above the column heads and do less to reduce the clear spans between columns. Nor do they project exterior eaves above and away from the eave columns as much as earlier large-scale clusters had done. In Qing sets, cantilever arms are not even functional. Moreover eave purlins are now carried by the ends of beams running through the building that rest atop the bracket clusters. All these functions were sacrificed while retaining the appealing decorative repetition of brackets under the eaves. Clusters range from four to nine (even eleven) in number spaced at regular intervals between columns. Cantilevered eaves protect the bases of columns and surrounding surfaces from the elements, although stone trim on platforms and the widespread use of brick and plaster walls both reduced this need.

Roof frames, the third layer in this structural analysis, consist of tiers of lateral and transverse tie-beams above the bracket sets. A roof frame consists of several steps ascending to and descending from the ridge. It is usually described accordingly, for example as "five frames" (*wu jia*) for five purlins (*lin*) including the ridge pole (*ji*). Depending on how their spans and heights are varied, a quite dramatic sweeping curvature in the roof line can be produced. Slopes became markedly steeper from Ming to Qing, with intervals moving upward toward the ridge becoming shorter, and their height differential greater. Superimposed transverse beams mount toward the ridge at both ends of the building, either at the eave (for a gabled roof) or one bay in if the roof is hipped (see below). A short kingpost (*gua zhu*) at the top usually carries the ridge pole (*ji lin*), which runs parallel to the facade. The purlins hold short rafters (*chuan*) placed at right angles; rafters do not run from

Qing bracket sets, from Ma, *Muzuo yingzao*, 241. Diagrams show: (a) elevation, three bracket clusters atop a lintel from the corner set (left) to intercolumnar set (middle) to column set (right); (b) plan view, same sequence emphasizing tiers of arms and tie-beams connecting the clusters; (c) side view, bracket set over column; and (d) side view, bracket set on lintel.

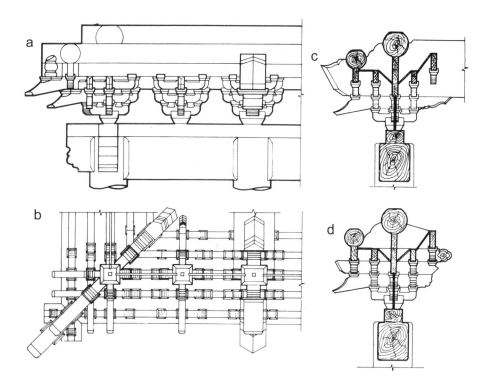

ridge to eave as a single length. When a ceiling was hung above the bracket level in the Ming period, the timbers above it could be left rough. By the Qing, however, roof frames have all timbers finished.

Impressive glazed tile roofs cover most imperial buildings. Boards were laid across the rafters to receive a thick coating of mud; tiles were set in this mud. The weight of mud and tile creates an enormous load that bears down on the roof frame, the bracket layer, and the columns. This has the practical benefit of keeping the roof and building in place during high winds. Roof tiles carry away rain water and snow. A special selection of ornamented tiles, in turn, was mounted on the ridges (see Box, p. 140).

Most roofs are simple two-slope structures (*ying shan* or *xuan shan*) with their tiles running perpendicular to the ridge toward the eave. Solid walls (*shan qiang*) rise under the roof at each end all the way to its gable. Such roofs are commonplace in residential courtyards as well as the secondary yards of large complexes. Free-standing gate houses and halls will often have a hipped roof (*wu dian*) with four slopes. Here the end roof slopes have a triangular shape descending from the ridge, while front and rear roof slopes flare outward as seen straight on. There are also roofs that combine a gable and hipped structure (*xie shan*). In such roofs the gables are exposed at each end, but the eave is continuous around four sides. In imperial sites, the kind of roof is correlated with the status of a hall or gate. The Hall of Supreme Harmony, the highest-ranking building of the Outer Court, has a hipped roof with two superimposed eaves (see fig. 3.19); the Hall of Preserving Harmony, of lesser status, has a hip-gable roof with two eaves (see fig. 3.21).

The timber-frame system allowed buildings to be constructed from hundreds, even thousands, of parts made from a common module. The earliest written exposition of this system appeared late in Northern

Song, the justly famous *Yingzao fashi* (*Building Standards*, ca. 1103) attributed to Li Jie, an imperial official. This text posits the height of a bracket arm as a standard unit or module (*cai*); this module could be rendered in any of eight grades. In each building project, every structure was assigned a grade from 1 to 8 based on its importance and position. The main hall was usually higher, side halls and gates lower. Measurements derived from the module were predetermined for each grade. Every timber was manufactured in appropriate quantities following these dimensions, probably with rulers carried by master carpenters. The module adjusted for grade also determined such basic features as the height and diameter of columns, the span of bays, the spacing of bracket sets on lintels, and the rise and pitch of the roof. Timber work for any structure was largely a matter of manufacturing enough components—columns, beams, blocks, and arms—to fulfill specifications.

In Ming and Qing times, this system remained intact but simplified in many particulars. An imperial manual dated to 1734, the *Gongcheng zuofa zeli* (*Structural Regulations*), now defined the module as the width of the mortise in a bearing block (*dou kou*). Using this module, a column was to be rendered as six *dou kou* in diameter and 60 *dou kou* in height (ten times the diameter). Bracket clusters (*zan*) were to be spaced at intervals of eleven *dou kou*. This rule thus determined the width and depth of a building (the spans). Inspection of Ming or Qing building frames also reveals that horizontal beams had become massive timbers, wider than the columns they surmounted, with a cross section of 5:4 or 6:5. Moreover, the spacing of purlins and pitch of rafters in a roof frame in this system yielded a steeper profile than earlier structures. Early architectural historians and critics, such as Liang Sicheng (1901–1972), deprecated the Qing system as excessively rigid for precisely these traits. The transition from earlier to later tendencies in Ming-Qing carpentry is visible in the Palace of Gathering Essence (Zhongcui Gong), one of the Six Eastern Palaces [12 ▶] of the Forbidden City.

Museum of Ancient Architecture

Unlike the Altar to Heaven, the large compound once occupied by the Altar to Agriculture (Xian Nong Tan) is no longer intact. However, the Hall of Jupiter (Taisui Dian, ca. 1532) now houses the informative Museum of Ancient Architecture (Zhongguo Gudai Jianzhu Bowuguan). The displays here include a scale model of Beijing in 1949, and fine models illustrating famous historic structures.

Address: 21 Dongjing Lu, south of Nanwei Lu, Xuanwu

SUGGESTED READING

On issues of historic preservation, see Anthony M. Tung, *Preserving the World's Great Cities* (2001), "Ideological Conflict with the Past," 131–68 (a study of Moscow and Beijing).

A lucid introduction to Chinese building is Liang Ssu-ch'eng's (Liang Sicheng's) *A Pictorial History of Chinese Architecture: A Study of the Development of Its Structural System and the Evolution of Its Types* (original 1946; re-published 1984). Also recommended is Fu Xinian, et al, *Chinese Architecture* (2002), especially the last two chapters on Ming and Qing topics by Pan Guxi and Sun Dazhang.

Before the Ming

1

The history of Peking is the history of China in miniature, for the town, like the country, has shown the same power of taking fresh masters and absorbing them. Both have passed through dark hours of anarchy and bloodshed. Happily both possess the vitality to survive them.

JULIET BREDON, PEKING (1931), 2

The present-day region of Beijing was the location of many cities before the Mongol conquest of North China in 1215. Prior to that calamitous event, the areas of Fengtai and Xuanwu Districts had sustained walled cities of regional importance continuously from the Eastern Han period (25–220). The southwest quadrant of the Ming-Qing city and its nearby suburbs comprise the most ancient sites, the ancestors of today's city.

Known then as Jicheng, the walled area was re-used by regimes in the post-Han, Sui-Tang, Liao, and Jin eras, more than one thousand years. The prominence of this particular area among all possible locales on the North China plain suggests assets that successive generations put to use. In spite of its long occupation, this environment was not exhausted by the population burden. The area had staying power and flourished until the Mongols established their new capital at a location further northeast, surrounding the modern Bei Hai [30 ▶].

Early Cities: Tang Youzhou and Liao Nanjing

ON THE NAME "PEKING"

In 1876, Emil Bretschneider, author of one of the first critical studies of the city by a European, wrote: "I must however remark, that the name "Peking," so familiar to every European, is hardly known by the Chinese of our days" (*Archaeological and Historical Researches*, 6).

Indeed, most of its pre-modern inhabitants simply called the city "the capital" (*jing shi* or a similar phrase). But when Matteo Ricci (1552–1610) and other Catholic fathers came north from Nanjing (Nanking) around 1600, they heard a word that sounded like Pacchino (Naquin, 479). This was the compound "northern capital," pronounced *bei jing* in Mandarin today. At the time of Ricci, the reigning Ming dynasty had designated two cities as capitals. The good fathers had moved from the southern one (Nanjing) to the northern (Beijing).

Over time this approximation of the sounds of Mandarin came to be spelled Pékin in French and Peking in English, rather crude renderings of the original. By the summer of 1861, members of the English and French legations thought of themselves as taking up residence in a city with this name. For an account of this early period, see D.G. Rennie's *Peking and the Pekingese* [1865]. Pékin and Peking appeared on maps and were also adopted by the postal services and some institutions in the capital. Even today both the Peking Hotel and Peking University retain this spelling, although Beijing is now regarded as the standard spelling. Most international publications have used Beijing since about 1980.

Through the long span of Chinese history, Beijing and the surrounding region have been known by a variety of appellations. Some of these names, used to evoke local history and identity, live on.

Period	City (Region)
High Antiquity	Youdu, Youzhou
Shang-Western Zhou	Ji, Yan
Eastern Zhou	Ji (Ji, Yan)
Qin	Ji (Yan)
Han	Ji (Youzhou, Guangyang)
Jin	Ji (Youzhou, Yan)
Northern Dynasties	Ji (Youzhou, Yan)
Sui	Ji (Zhuo)
Tang	Ji (Youzhou, Fanyang)
Liao	Nanjing, Yanjing
Jin	Zhongdu
Yuan	Dadu
Ming	Jingshi, Beijing
Qing	Jingshi
Republic	Beiping, Peking
People's Republic	Beijing, Peking

Source: Zhu Zuxi, *Ying guo jiang yi* (2007), 326–27

The primary water source for Jicheng was the Lotus Blossom Pond (Lianhua Chi) fed by a river of the same name that flowed from the Western Hills into today's Shijingshan District due west of the contemporary city. A pond with this name still exists as a park between the Second and Third Ring Roads. Presumably the early cities also drew water from the aquifer, as suggested by dozens of ancient wells with ceramic liners that have been excavated near Heping Men, Liulichang, and Xuanwu Men. Through the Liao period (907–1125), the cities here were regional centers. Even if the Liao population reached 300,000, the resources consumed and the areas occupied were modest by later standards. The Western Hills with their timber and wildlife were not far, and there was ample land in all directions for farming.

The walls of Tang-period Youzhou and its successor, Liao Nanjing, have been determined through ingenious deductions by Chinese archaeologists and historians. For example, the dozens of epitaphs from Tang, Liao, and Jin tombs customarily record not only a brief, laudatory biography of the deceased with dates of birth and death, but also the location of the tomb using contemporary landmarks. Thus an epitaph dated 781 for one Yao Zi'ang describes his tomb as "six *li* southeast of Youzhou wall." (A *li* is one-third of a kilometer.) By comparing such descriptions with knowledge of surviving sites such as early temples, archaeologists have been able to plot the approximate alignment of the early city walls. These inscriptions, as well as others dedicating pagodas or on stone steles, have also yielded a directory of the names of wards and rural districts. A Song writer, one Lu Zhen, described the Tang city of Youzhou as having twenty-six residential wards, each walled and gated in the fashion of the time. Inscriptions gathered by recent scholars confirm at least nineteen of those ward names and moreover suggest their relative locations. Likewise, the Tang city and its surrounding area was split into two counties, Ji and Youdu, for which the names of fourteen of thirty-four districts have also been documented.

Continuous occupation has meant continual recycling, especially of building material. City walls might be retained, improved, or, if necessary, cut down to ground level. Foundations, stone work, timbers, carpentry of all kinds, and tiles could be reused. Tang-period structures might incorporate elements from earlier ones, just as Liao buildings incorporated Tang elements, and so on into Jin times. But progressively more and more material from the earlier eras was used up or simply wore out. After the city's wholesale, intentional destruction by Genghis Khan's armies in 1215 (described below, p. 52), little from earlier ages would have remained. Little that is except those things buried deepest: the liners of water wells mentioned above, the brick chambers and durable contents of tombs, and the below-grade foundations of structures such as a water gate or pagoda. Caches, intentional deposits of valuables buried for safekeeping during an emergency, are a further exception that plays an important role in preserving ancient things. These deposits, never reclaimed by their owners, are discovered during modern construction as well as archaeological surveys. Dozens of deposits of metal coinage from the Liao and Jin eras (mostly Song issues) have been found throughout Beijing, sometimes hundreds of kilos in a single cache. With danger on the door step, well-to-do residents of Liao Nanjing and Jin Zhongdu evidently buried their bank accounts.

Today, remains from Youzhou and Nanjing are restricted to two types: Buddhist temples and elite tombs. The most important Tang temple in the city was the Minzhong Si (Grieving for the Loyal Ones Temple) founded in 645 by Taizong to commemorate the dead from his unsuccessful Korean campaigns. Later the local military commanders An Lushan and Shi Siming built a pair of pagodas on the site. The temple's oldest stele records this dedication, and Fu Xinian's restoration pictures the temple accordingly (fig. 1.1). Many later fires and rebuildings followed; today the temple plan dates to a fifteenth century revival and all structures are from the eighteenth century. Known as Fayuan Si [20▶], it is the seat of Chinese Academy of Buddhism. Fayuan Si offers a restful atmosphere amid the hustle and bustle of the Outer City, and displays an interesting collection of Buddhist images from temples in Beijing. The oldest structure in all modern Beijing proper is the brick Tianning Si pagoda of Liao date [21▶]. Suburban temple sites have other Liao and Jin era pagodas.

1.1
Minzhong Si (now Fayuan Si) in late Tang period, rendering by Fu Xinian from *Lunwenji*, 267

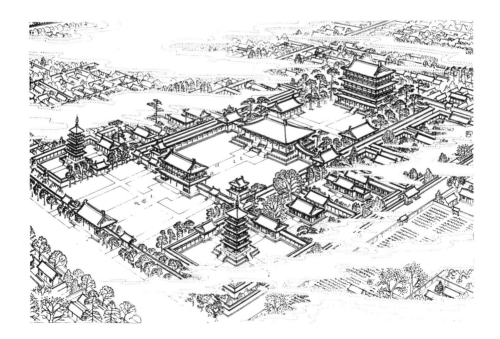

Tang and Liao tombs, on the other hand, are distributed across the entire west side of the city—Xicheng, Xuanwu, Fengtai, Shijingshan, Mentougou, and Haidian Districts—as well as in Changping, Daxing, and Shunyi Counties to the north. Most Tang tombs date from the eighth and ninth centuries. Notable from an historical viewpoint is the burial of Shi Siming (d. 761, Fengtai), co-conspirator with An Lushan in the great upheaval of the mid-eighth century that shook the Tang empire to its foundations. Shi was interred in a large tomb: 20 m in length with a chamber 5 m square. Several rare and valuable artifacts were recovered when it was opened in the 1960s: a gilt stirrup, a bronze dragon, and forty fragments of jade tablets with engraved text inlaid in gold, normally an imperial prerogative. Liao burials have yielded many fine ceramics as well as some wall paintings. Much of this material will be found at the Liao Jin City Walls Museum [1 ▶] as well as the Capital Museum.

The Jin Capital: Zhongdu (1153–1215)

For twenty-five years after the fall of the Liao in 1122, the city served as one of several secondary capitals for the successor Ruzhen Jin dynasty. Nanjing (then Yanjing) was overrun a few years before Bianliang (modern Kaifeng), the Song capital, one of the great turning points in later Chinese history. After the assassination of the Jin emperor Xizong in 1151, the new emperor promulgated an edict to make the Beijing site his primary capital. When new palaces modeled on those of Bianliang were ready, in 1153, the city officially became the Middle Capital (Zhongdu). For Beijing this was also a turning point: the first time a city in the region was a primary, national capital (if not for all of China Proper).

The Jin capital is also the first for which a modicum of relatively detailed information has been recovered, both through archaeology and by mining historical sources. In the 1950s, as Beijing began its post-war renewal, traces of the walls of Zhongdu could be surveyed, and recent work has filled in additional details. The city was roughly square (18.7 km around its perimeter), created by pushing the east, south, and west walls of the Liao capital outward about 1.5 km. The north wall stayed in the same position as in the Liao period, apparently because of a water channel. Traces of the west wall and its southwest corner were still standing in the 1950s, as were sections of the east and south walls. (Three portions of these walls are now protected by stone retaining walls.) Using the fragmentary walls and footings detected below ground level by probing, archaeologists determined the Jin city to be 4500 to 4900 m in length on each side. All thirteen city gates (four across the north, three on each other side) were located, as well as some street surfaces. Surveys demonstrated that Zhongdu had two grids. Inside the area of the old Liao walls (Tang Youzhou) neighborhoods were enclosed rectangular wards (*fang*) in the Tang manner. This area became the Jin Imperial City. Outside the Liao walls, on the other hand, residential areas were laid out as long alleys typical of Song and later cities.

The Jin Palace, the Tang-era prefectural government center occupying a southwest location in the Liao capital, was now west of center. It was built over the Liao palaces following Northern Song models. Parts of this Jin palace precinct now constitute Binhe Park at Guang'an Men Nan. The main hall, the Da'an Dian, was probed and found to be an imposing eleven bays across. The Fish Weed Pond (Yucao Chi) flanking the main axis of palace halls survives today as the lake and swimming pool in Qingnian (Youth) Park at Guang'an Men Wai Nanjie.

A visitor can experience several important Jin-period sites: the recently excavated Water Gate [1▶], and one of Beijing's oldest attractions, the bridge [2▶] known popularly from Marco Polo's description. The Jin imperial tombs should also be investigated.

1▶
Water Gate and Liao Jin City Walls Museum

YOU'AN MEN WAI
DAJIE, YULIN DONGLI,
FENGTAI

In fall 1990, construction of apartments north of the Liangshui River had to be halted. The contractors had uncovered a plot of well-made stone slabs, a water gate (*shui guan*; fig. 1.2) that once ran under the south city wall of Zhongdu. A full-scale excavation followed, and this exposure has now become the centerpiece of the Liao Jin City Walls Museum. The museum building mimics the appearance of a substantial, brick-faced city wall with a large arched stone portal suggesting the Water Gate as its façade. In addition to the archaeological site in the basement, the museum displays relics from a variety of excavations and finds around the city, stone sculpture, architectural carvings, and inscriptions that narrate the early history of the city.

Although the upper portions of the Jin Water Gate had been disassembled long ago, the stone-paved base of the channel and parts of its walls were intact. The channel was almost 8 m wide and 43 m from north to south (from inside to outside). This gate connected a channel that ran across Zhongdu from the northwest to the moat (the present Liangshui River channel). Some of this water was diverted to feed the lakes west of the imperial palaces. At the time of discovery, the depth of the channel was about 5 to 6 m. Sediments indicated abandonment in the 14th century.

The structure closely follows specifications known from the Northern Song *Imperial Building Standards* (ca. 1103). Like a Song design, the Jin Water Gate was built atop wooden pilings, 1800 pointed cypress timbers pounded deep into the ground. The pilings were

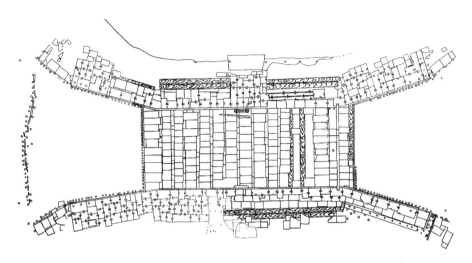

topped by dressed stones and then a stone paving 21 m long. Some 2500 cast iron cramps held the pavers together. More pilings and pounded earth backed the wall footings that carried the barrel vault. The city wall here would have been approximately 22 m wide at the base, 14 m wide at top and about 16 m tall assuming it also followed Song practices.

The Jin made serious efforts to improve the water supply for Zhongdu, a story still unfolding today. They attempted to link the city's channels and moats to the Grand Canal, which at that time terminated to the east at Tongzhou. Without this link, building materiel for the capital had to be shipped by land, an inefficient means of supply for any large pre-modern city. As a part of this plan, water from the Gaoliang River, which like the Lianhua River came out of the Western Hills, was channeled to a marshy area north of the city (present-day Bei Hai). Other new channels flowed south from that reservoir, one connecting to the north moat of Zhongdu, another reaching the canal on the east. However, the water volume was still inadequate to make canal transport feasible, and the problem remained unresolved until the Yuan period. The later

1.2
Plan of Jin Water Gate, from *Jin Zhongdu*, 6. The quantity and quality of materials invested in this water gate (especially 2500 iron cramps) are testimony to the high standards set for all imperial projects.

decision by the Mongols to locate their capital north-east of Zhongdu was motivated in part by the presence of this reservoir and then facilitated by their successful re-engineering of the Gaoliang River.

2 ▶
Marco Polo
Bridge
(Lugou Qiao)

JIN, 1189–92
NATIONAL
REGISTER, 1961
LUGOU QIAO EXIT,
JING-SHI EXPRESSWAY,
FENGTAI

Chapter XXXV: Here Begins the Description of the Interior of Cathay, and First of the River Pulisanghin

When you leave the City of Cambaluc [Dadu] and have ridden ten miles, you come to a very large river which is called Pulisanghin, and flows into the ocean, so that merchants with their merchandise ascend it from the sea. Over this River there is a very fine stone bridge, so fine indeed, that it has very few equals. The fashion of it is this: it is 300 paces in length, and it must have a good eight paces of width, for ten mounted men can ride across it abreast. It has 24 arches and as many water-mills, and 'tis all of very fine marble, well built and firmly founded. Along the top of the bridge there is on either side a parapet of marble slabs and columns, made in this way. At the beginning of the bridge there is a marble column, and under it a marble lion, so that the column stands upon the lion's loins, whilst on the top of the column there is a second marble lion, both being of great size and beautifully executed sculpture. At the distance of a pace from this column there is another precisely the same, also with its two lions, and the space between them is closed with slabs of grey marble to prevent people from falling over into the water. And thus the columns run from space to space along either side of the bridge, so that altogether it is a beautiful object.

YULE-CORDIER, *BOOK OF MARCO POLO*, II, 3-4

The major surviving monument from Jin Zhongdu is the bridge (fig. 1.3) now best known from this description in *The Book of Marco Polo*. The span crosses a major river 15 km southwest of Beijing. Prior to the reign of Kangxi (ca. 1698), the stream was known as the Wuding (Unsettled) River; thereafter it was renamed the Yongding (Eternally Settled) River. The section crossed by Polo's bridge, however, is also known as Reed Gully (Lugou) and this name has generally been applied to the structure and town that grew up near it. Above the bridge, the stream is called the Sanggan River, a name that Marco Polo seems to have known (as Pulisanghin). The bridge serves the major land route leading southwest from the capital toward the North China plain. Prior to the Jin, wooden bridges, perhaps of pontoon type, were used here.

The Jin history records an imperial command to construct a permanent span in 1189 and its completion by 1192. Numerous repairs and episodes of rebuilding are documented starting in the Ming. Local oral tradition has it that when the Guangxu emperor was transported to the Qing Western Tombs in 1909

1.3
Camels on Marco Polo Bridge, postcard by the Japanese Military Postal Service

（北 京）芦 溝 橋　マルコポーロの旅行記
◇ 靴 の 修 理　暴戻なる支那軍の不法射撃を端に發したる支那事變
◇ 驢馬の引き　昭和十二年七月八日午前零時
世界に紹介されたる有名の橋で北京西郊二十五支
里永定河に架せられ，暴戻なる支那軍の不法射撃を端に發したる支那事變又芦溝暁月は
發地としてはあまりにも有名な橋で乾隆帝御筆の碑があるが
北京八景の一つで橋の東に乾隆帝御筆の碑があるが。

for burial, the stone parapets were removed and additional road surface built with wooden scaffolding to accommodate the cortege with its huge coffin and many attendants. In modern Chinese history, the bridge is known as the site of a skirmish July 7, 1937, between Japanese troops, who had already occupied Beijing, and Chinese forces. This was the ostensible rationale for its listing on the first National Register in 1961. (A museum devoted to the Anti-Japanese War is located inside the re-constructed Wanping city walls opposite the bridge.)

The Marco Polo Bridge is the longest pre-modern bridge in North China (fig. 1.4), an eleven-span marble structure (not twenty-four as Polo claimed) with a total length of 267 m. Ten piers in the river bed carry the arches. The piers are spaced at wider intervals as they reach the center of the stream. Thus the central arch has a span of 13.42 m while the two smallest are 11.5 m. The pier design has elicited considerable admiration. Their upstream ends are pointed like the prow of a boat to funnel water around them. Iron fittings cover the leading edges to break up the river ice that rushes down stream each spring. These iron bars are called, poetically, "swords to slice the dragon." Each

1.4
Marco Polo Bridge, plan (top) and elevation (bottom), from *Wenwu* 1975.10: 74

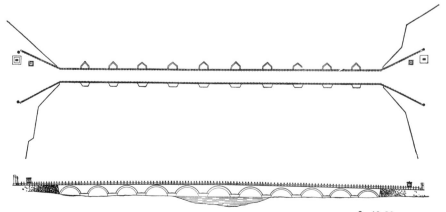

0 10 20 m

span is constructed from an array of parallel arches a single-stone wide, tied together by courses of masonry that run across the width of the bridge (compare the Jin Water Gate paving above). The voussoirs were further strengthened by metal cramps. Above the spans, a fill of rubble and several layers of stone supports the road bed. This type of construction was lighter and stronger than solid ashlar construction would have been. The road bed is 9 m wide, with 7.5 m for traffic (Polo's ten riders abreast). The road rises slightly in the middle, and flares dramatically at each end.

Writers of early Chinese tourist guides, like Marco Polo, marveled at the carved lions that adorn the parapet (fig. 1.5). Commonly said to be "too numerous to count," a careful survey in 1975 found 281 posts separating railings, each with a lion, plus 198 small lions (cubs?) with the former. In addition two large lions serve as buttresses at the east end of the bridge, and four more are associated with the stone columns (*huabiao*) nearby. Thus 485 would seem to be the winning number. The survey suggested the parapets had been renewed twice, and that the lions may have been carved at four different periods. A few lions are thought to be original, along with the elephants at

1.5
Lions on railing of Marco Polo Bridge

"EIGHT VIEWS OF YANSHAN"

This phrase (*Yanshan ba jing*) refers to a poetic sequence written in the Jin period (1115–1234) to celebrate the capital, using the old name Yan for the Beijing region. While the poems do not survive, the list of eight scenic views remains well known. The Qianlong emperor was especially devoted to this theme, and composed his own poems using the traditional titles. Several of his steles in praise of the "Eight Views" are still in place. The sequence runs as follows:

1 Layered Shades of Green at Juyong Pass

This historic approach to the capital from the north is commemorated today by a reconstructed portion of the Ming Great Wall, and the truly impressive and authentic Yuanperiod Cloud Terrace of 1345 [3 ▶]. The Qianlong stele has disappeared.

2 Cascading Rainbow at Jade Spring Hill

Jade Spring Hill is west of the Summer Palace (Yihe Yuan), and was commemorated by Qianlong as "the first spring under Heaven." This spring has been an important source of water for the city, and of drinking water for the palace, since Yuan times.

3 Crystal Clear Waves on Taiye Pond

This view is now within Nan Hai, and hence closed to the public.

4 Spring Clouds on Jasper Flower Island

The island forms the heart of Bei Hai [30 ▶]; the Qianlong stele stands on its eastern side (fig. 1.6).

5 Misty Trees at the Gate of Ji

The Qianlong stele has now been restored on a portion of the Yuan earthen wall along Xueyuan Road north of the Ming city wall. Ancient Jicheng, however, was in Xuanwu District, the southwest quadrant of the old city, not in this area.

1.6 Qianlong stele, Bei Hai

6 Clearing Snow in the Western Hills

This view is traditionally located in Qianlong's Garden of Peace and Harmony (Jingyi Yuan), now a part of Fragrant Hills Park (Xiang Shan).

7 Dawn Moonlight at Reed Gully Bridge

The locale is better known as Marco Polo Bridge [2 ▶]. Qianlong's stele stands at the east end.

8 Sunset at the Golden Terrace

This view was traditionally located east of the Inner City wall Chaoyang Men.

the west end and dragon heads on the keystones of three spans.

Recent publication of discoveries at the Jin imperial tombs about 40 km southwest of the city (Fangshan County) has brought new attention to this long-neglected site. A survey and limited excavations exposed parts of the Spirit Path as well as several foundations and vaults holding sarcophagi with exceptional stone carving (fig. 1.7). Vandalized in the late Ming period in the face of the Manchu threat to "cut off the Ruzhen [Manchu] dragon veins," the tomb precinct served five generations of Jin emperors and imperial kin for the sixty years Zhongdu was the national capital. Only one-third of the site has been investigated to date. Added to the

1.7
Phoenix design on sarcophagus, Ruiling, Jin tombs, Fangshan, from *Jindai huang ling*, 78

national register in 2006, it should be open for visitors in the near future.

The Mongol destruction of Zhongdu was typical of extreme measures they employed elsewhere to exterminate hostile adversaries. After a lengthy campaign of attacks, siege, bribery, and renewed warfare, the city was overrun in 1215. The Muslim historian Juzjani described the devastation:

> When a few years later Baha ad-Din, leader of a mission from Sultan Muhammad of Khwarazm, approached the capital he saw a white hill and in answer to his query was told by the guide that it consisted of the bones of the massacred inhabitants. At another place the earth was, for a long stretch of the road, greasy from human fat and the air was so polluted that several members of the mission became ill and some died. This was the place, they were told, where on the day the city was stormed 60,000 virgins threw themselves to death from the fortifications in order to escape capture by the Mongols.
>
> RATCHNEVSKY, GENGHIS KHAN, 115

Even after the new Yuan capital was occupied, some parts of Zhongdu supported a population. Known as the Southern City (Nancheng), this area thrived as a commercial and residential zone in both the Ming and Qing periods. It was enclosed within the hastily built Outer Wall in the 1550s. Several temples survived the Mongol destruction, notably Minzhong Si, today called Fayuan Si [20 ▶], Tianwang Si (now Tianning Si [21 ▶], Baiyun Guan, and possibly the Mosque on Niu Jie [27 ▶]. Although, with the exception of the 58 m Tianning Si pagoda, no monuments from these early periods remain, a walk around Xuanwu District will introduce the visitor to the city's oldest lanes and precincts.

Beijing first entered the European imagination as the "Khan's Great City" (Khanbaliq, Cambaluc) courtesy of Marco Polo. Debate over the veracity of that account comes and goes, but some of Marco Polo's description bears a striking resemblance to the Yuan city and palace that modern scholars can recreate from both historical sources and archaeological research. Unlike the earlier cities, scholars have many documentary sources for the Yuan capital, including dated records of major events in its construction and the names of major figures. One text even provides a detailed description of all of the main halls and gates of the imperial palaces. Likewise, considerable archaeological work has taken place in Beijing, normally salvage digs spurred on by destruction and construction.

Cambaluc was known to its Chinese residents as Dadu (Great Capital), and was designed and constructed without the encumbrances of an earlier settlement, one of the few imperial capitals created from scratch. (Sui-Tang Chang'an was another example.) Although today little of the Yuan city can be seen or touched, the presence of Dadu is nonetheless felt on the ground. The plan of the Yuan capital determined the placement, size, and shape of the Ming-Qing city, the foundations of modern Beijing. Thus the story of historic Beijing properly begins with Khubilai Khan's city.

Genghis Khan, who conquered north China, died in 1227. The territories were occupied by Mongol princes who were granted fiefs there. One of these was Genghis' grandson, Khubilai (1215–94), who became the fifth Great Khan of Khans in 1260. While not literate in Chinese, as a prince Khubilai had acquired a coterie of Chinese advisors. These learned scholars determined the choice and design of a Mongol city in modern-day Inner Mongolia, known as the Upper

Khubilai Khan's City: Dadu (1267–1368)

Capital (Shangdu; Coleridge's Xanadu). In 1260, Khubilai's party encamped on the outskirts of the ruined Jin city at Jasper Flower Island in a lake that was ancestral to Bei Hai [30 ▶] and once part of a Jin palace. Rather than rebuild the devastated Jin capital, Khubilai and his advisors decided to create a new city with the lake as the centerpiece of its imperial precincts. Work began in 1267.

Many names are associated with the design and construction of Dadu, but none would fit modern definitions of city-planner or architect. Chief among Khubilai's advisors was one Liu Bingzhong (1216–74), Confucian scholar and Buddhist who had accompanied the Khan on his campaigns in the far southwest. Liu and several other officials are described as advisors who "assisted the Khan" in devising the overall scheme for the city. Their plan derived from the Confucian classics, specifically the ideals embodied in the "Royal City" (wang cheng), a late Bronze Age formulation. A capital constructed according to this idealized model was part of a broader effort establishing the legitimacy of the Mongol conquest regime. This program also included selection of a Chinese dynastic appellation, Yuan (meaning "primal"), in 1271.

Below the scholar advisors were supervisors of the Grand Capital Garrison and Branch Ministry of Works who shouldered the burden of assembling men and materiel. These men included Yegdir (an Arab?), and the Han-Chinese Zhang Rou and Duan Tianyou. Yegdir (Ye-hei-die-er in Chinese transcription) headed the "tent service" responsible for yurts and other furnishings required for the Mongol lifestyle. He also served as Supervisor in Chief of All Classes of Artisans, presumably the corps of skilled carpenters, masons, and brick makers who fabricated building materiel. Zhang Rou died early on, but his son, Zhang

Honglue, served as Supervisor for Building the Palace
Enceinte. Duan Tianyou in turn headed the Branch
Ministry of Works. More numerous but less well
known were skilled master artisans. One Yang Qiong
is named as a master stone artisan, for example. As in
the two alien regimes before them, the Mongols
depended on Han-Chinese artisans and laborers for
the construction of their cities and buildings. The
Grand Capital Garrison provided both unskilled labor
and artisan families enrolled in the military. Thus construction of the new city was a Chinese project at
every level.

The Great Capital (fig. 1.8) took shape around the
shores of the lake (now Bei Hai) where Khubilai had
camped. In making this area the heart of their new
city, the planners relied on the Gaoliang River, which
flowed from the Western Hills into what is now Zizhu
Park, as a water source. The Chinese scholar Guo
Shoujing (1231–1316) is credited with suggesting that
this river be enhanced by tapping the Jade Spring
(Yuquan, later itself a scenic attraction) in the area of
the present Summer Palace (Yihe Yuan). The lake we
call Bei Hai became known as Taiye Pond, and the
island as Longevity Mountain (Wansui Shan). The latter was flanked on the south by another smaller island
(now Tuancheng). Both were connected to the shore
by bridges. The imperial palaces rose on both sides of
the water: the Danei (Great Within) of the emperor to
the east and palaces for the Heir and Empress
Dowager on the west.

The layout of the Yuan city required surveys made
from a point north of the Khan's palace called the
Central Stele Pavilion (Zhongxin zhi Tai). Equal distances east, south, west, and north from this point fixed
the city walls. The ability to build on the south was
limited by the ruins of the old Jin capital, an area still

inhabited and at least partially walled. The four measurements were roughly equal, in spite of the difficul-
ties of surveying with ropes and the water obstacles
going west. However, the east wall was pulled slightly
inward (west) to avoid marshy ground. The south wall
stood on the south side of today's Chang'an Avenue,
while the east and west walls were identical with those
of the later Ming city which have since become the
Second Ring Road. The east–west and north–south
dimensions for the city, however, must have been
derived from the measurements of the Khan's palace

1.8
Map of Yuan Dadu, from
Kaogu 1972.1: 20. Numbers
refer to sites discussed in
this book.

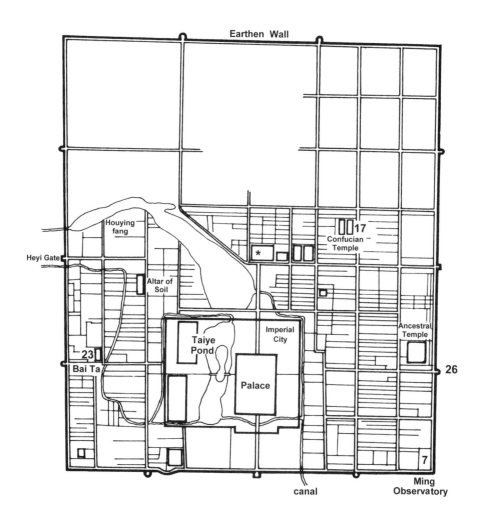

(fig. 1.9). Fu Xinian has pointed out that the Yuan city was nine palace-widths wide (A, east-west) by five palace-lengths long (B, north-south).

When the Institute of Archaeology performed its modern survey in the 1960s and 70s the outer walls of Dadu measured 28.6 km in length. The wall builders utilized the pounded earth (or rammed earth, *terre pisé*) technique. The city walls were found to average 24 m across; their lengths varied from 6690 m (the south wall) to 7600 m (west wall). The earth needed for this task was dug from the outside, creating a moat. Intact portions of the Yuan walls uncovered within the Ming brick walls suggest their original height was about 16 m, and the width at top about 8 m (compare fig. 2.6). This is higher than the wall around the Forbidden City or the Ming Inner City wall. Made of a combination of loess soil, lime, and broken shards of tile and brick with imbedded wooden stakes, the walls were very sturdy, but nonetheless easily degraded by the elements. Tiles protected the top surface, while reed matting was used to cover the sides. The four corners of the city had towers; their bases were identified during the 1960s survey. One of these survives as part of the foundations of the Ming–Qing Observatory [7 ▶]. Remarkably, portions of the original northern walls of Dadu survive as the so-called Earthen Wall (Tu Cheng; fig. 1.10) about half way between the Third and Fourth Ring Roads. These are now strip parks; a commemorative site is a part of the park on Xueyuan Road near Jimen Qiao.

Eleven gates governed access to the city, three across the east, south, and west, and two on the north. Timber-frame portals and guard houses fortified the points. Wooden bridges crossed the moat. In 1359, the city gates were improved by the construction of barbican gates (*weng cheng*), a lesser wall and second portal fronting the main entrances. One of these barbican gates was uncovered in the process of tearing down the Ming Xizhi Men in 1969 (figs. 1.11, 1.12). It stood 22 m tall, with a passage 9 m long and over 4 m wide. The

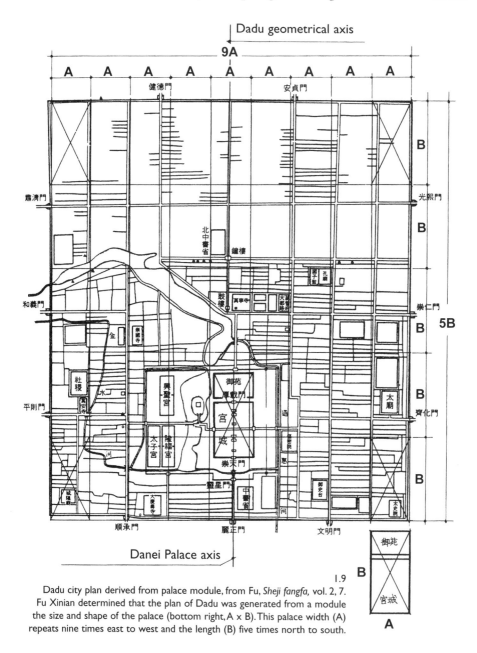

1.9

Dadu city plan derived from palace module, from Fu, *Sheji fangfa,* vol. 2, 7. Fu Xinian determined that the plan of Dadu was generated from a module the size and shape of the palace (bottom right, A x B). This palace width (A) repeats nine times east to west and the length (B) five times north to south.

floor of a three-room guard house was atop the portal; archaeologists also found stairs that permitted the guards to mount the gate. An artisan's inscription of 1358 confirmed the construction date. This portal was remade in the Ming in 1439 as a brick barrel vault.

1.10
"Remaining ancient wall of Kubli Khan, Peking," postcard by Chas. F. Gammon

1.11
Portal at Heyi Men (Xizhi Men), from *Kaogu* 1972, 1:VIII

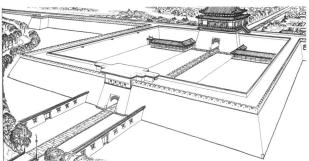

1.12
Heyi Men defensive walls, rendering by Fu Xinian, from *Lunwenji*, 381

The Yuan gates in turn determined the alignment of the main arteries of the capital, and it is this grid that underlies central Beijing today. The two northern gates in the east and west walls and the two gates of the north wall were abandoned when the city contracted after the Ming victory in 1368 (see fig. 2.7). The other four gates of the east and west walls continued in use through Ming, Qing, and modern times, albeit with changes in their names (see Box, p. 83). The main arteries of Dadu crisscrossed the city to create a chessboard grid, but only two extended from one wall all the way to the wall opposite. These primary roadways were about 37 m wide (24 paces, *bu* in the Chinese system). Secondary arteries were half as wide (18 m), and the ubiquitous alleys (*hutong*) half that (9 m). The areas contained within the main arteries were designated as fifty wards. These were simply areas crossed by alleys; they were not walled like those of Tang Chang'an. Probing in the 1960s north of the Ming north wall revealed twenty-two parallel alleys in the interval between adjacent city gates. The distance between alleys was 77 m (50 paces), more than ample for a large residence. Government establishments were built on plots several hutong long and several wide. The Ancestral Temple and Altar to Soil and Grain, for example, were assigned plots of five by four hutong. Lesser government sites were built in plots of four by three hutong. Many of the alleys north of Chang'an Avenue today were laid out for Dadu.

Circulation within Dadu cannot have been easy. The Imperial City walls and reservoirs to the north interrupted all the primary and secondary east-west arteries. By the 1290s the Grand (Tonghui) Canal connected the capital to the southeast. Channels allowed boats and barges carrying all manner of goods to sail directly into the city, north along the east side of the

Imperial City, and on to a great market just west of the Central Stele Pavilion (today's Hou Hai area). Other markets grew on both the east and west sides of the city near modern Xi Si and Dengshikou to serve those areas, as well as outside the gates of the new south wall. Unlike alien regimes before them, the Mongols did not segregate people by ethnic groups. A diverse international population lived throughout the city. Likewise, unlike the Tang capital, the main organs of state were dispersed.

The Khan's palace (Danei) was astride the city's central axis, but unlike the "Royal City" ideal it was not at the true center. Instead it was shifted to the south. A rectangle about 1000 m north-south by 740 m east-west, the Yuan palace was roughly the same size as the Ming Forbidden City. The Danei was divided in turn into a front component, the Daming Palace (fig. 1.13), and a rear one, the Yanchun Belvedere. The former had a three-tiered platform supporting its front hall, connecting corridor, and rear hall. Gates, bell and drum towers, and a rear hall were embedded in the perimeter galleries. A wide avenue separated this palace compound from the rear precinct, which centered on a two-story belvedere within even more spacious courtyards. Other compounds including storehouses and kitchens flanked the two main palaces. At the rear was an imperial park where tents were often pitched.

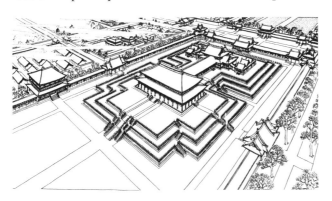

1.13
Daming Palace, Danei, rendering by Fu Xinian, from *Lunwenji*, 348

These Mongol palace halls lie under the present-day Forbidden City and Jing Shan (Ch. 3).

Palaces for the Heir and Empress Dowager were built to the west of Taiye Pond. Longfu Gong on the south was designed for the Heir; it was fronted by its own park but not surrounded by walls. The palace on the north for the Empress Dowager, the Xingsheng Gong, had its own walled compound equal in size to the Yanchun Belvedere as well as a park at the rear. The area of these palaces corresponds to the west side of today's Zhong-Nan Hai, home of the PRC leadership, and portions of Bei Hai Park. A red wall of modest dimensions demarcated the whole ensemble of palaces and parks, constituting the Imperial City. This wall had a base merely 3 m wide; the actual palace wall by contrast was 16 m wide! The palace enceinte was completed by 1274; the city's outer walls had been put up about ten years later.

The archaeology of the Yuan capital is inherently frustrating because Dadu literally became the foundation for the Ming and Qing capitals and has been occupied continuously since the fifteenth century. Stripping away the Ming city walls during the 1960s revealed the earthen cores of the original Yuan walls on the east and west (see fig. 2.6) as mentioned above. Stone water channels were revealed under the walls as were the footings of corner towers and gates. Tearing down the north wall of the Ming city, however, was rather more productive. It had been built when the Ming commander Xu Da decided to shrink the city in 1368. Put up in a month, this Ming wall covered the Yuan hutong and residential structures of wards along its path. Excavations yielded dozens of small finds and several large compounds (fig. 1.14). This strip follows the south side of the north Second Ring Road. Other Yuan discoveries have been fortuitous. For example, a marble bridge 38 m long with a stone channel below was uncovered north of Xi Dan. Open drainage ditches that ran at the sides of roads have also been identified south of Xi Si. In one a mason left an inscription dated 1328. Caches with porcelains, mirrors, and coins have been unearthed in and around Yuan Dadu as well.

For the modern visitor, only a few features of the Khan's capital can be experienced. Although much enhanced and expanded, Bei Hai is the descendant of both the Taiye Pond of the Yuan capital and before that the Da'ning Palace of Jin. The Bai Ta [23 ▶], or White Dagoba, is the only substantial monument of Yuan date (1271–79) standing in the city. Its precincts are much reduced compared to the Yuan period and the other buildings with one exception are Qing-era structures. The Confucian Temple [17 ▶], also an ensemble of Qing buildings, has a plan and ancient trees that date to the Yuan (1302–06). Finally, well north of the city on the way to the Great Wall at Badaling is the Cloud Terrace [3 ▶], the base of a pagoda erected in 1345 over the route from the Upper Capital to Dadu. This is the outstanding work of the Yuan period in the Beijing area, and well worth a special stop.

1.14
House foundations, Houyingfang, from *Kaogu* 1972, 6: IV. Compare with fig. 6.8.

3 ▶
Cloud Terrace
(Yun Tai),
Juyong Guan

YUAN PERIOD, 1343–45
NATIONAL
REGISTER, 1961
NANKOU, CHANGPING

The most impressive monument from the Yuan period in Beijing has been the object of scholarly study for more than a century. Unlike sites within the city, the Cloud Terrace (Yun Tai) at Juyong Guan (figs. 1.15, 1.16) offers a visual experience of the fourteenth-century world of the Mongol emperors and their Tibetan Imperial Instructors. Located 50 km northwest of the city on the highway to the Ming Great Wall at Badaling, this site is too often overlooked by visitors.

Juyong Guan has controlled traffic in and out of the Beijing plain since pre-Han times, when there was already a check-point (*guan*) located in this narrow defile. At an elevation of 500 m above sea level, this pass marks the transition to a winding valley that leads across the rugged northern mountains, a crucial passage when there were threats from the steppe. The landscape of the pass became one of the celebrated "Eight Views" of the capital region ("Layered Shades of Green at Juyong Pass") in both poetry and painting (see Box, p. 50). In the Mongol period, this route linked the winter capital, Dadu, to the summer capital, Shangdu (Upper Capital). As a rule, the Yuan emperors made their progression from one capital and palace to the other twice each year. The Cloud Terrace, built under the last emperor Shundi in 1343-45, brought protection to this key route by supporting a stupa over the roadway. Similar monuments were erected near the Marco Polo Bridge and old Jin capital, also key routes serving the capital.

The terrace (about 11 m in height, 28 m across at the base) probably served as the base for one or more Tibetan or Himalayan style stupas that have since disappeared. A sense of their appearance can be gained from the stupa held in the hand of the Guardian King of the North on the west wall inside the arch. This is the same kind of bulbous stupa (also known as a

1.15
"Chu-Yung kuan," postcard by S. Yamamoto, Peking

1.16
Portal of Cloud Terrace, Juyong Guan

chorten or dagoba) found at the Bai Ta [23 ▶] dedicated by Khubilai Khan in the 1270s under the direction of the Nepalese Anige (d. 1306). Whether the original monument had three identical stupas or a large central one flanked by smaller examples (fig. 1.17) is debated. Today all that can be seen on the terrace are stone plinths for a rectangular wooden hall that seems to have been built in the mid-fifteenth century and burned in 1706.

The magnificent decoration of the arch showcases inscriptions in six languages and outstanding reliefs. Inscriptions in Sanskrit (using Nepalese script), Tibetan, Mongolian, Uighur, Xixia (Tangut), and

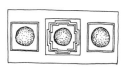

1.17
Three Stupas at Qiongzhu Si, Kunming, from Su, *Zangchuan Fojiao*, 363. Su Bai believes the Cloud Terrace originally supported stupas like this example in Kunming.

Chinese form the heart of the monument, occupying large panels of 6 m x 2.5 m on both sides. Two of these scripts are no longer in use: the old Uighur derived from Sogdian, now replaced by Arabic, and the Xixia Tangut, a derivative of Chinese graphs. Each text records two efficacious holy texts (*dharani*) that bring protection to the state as well as information about the construction and purpose of the Cloud Terrace:

"Dharani of the Victorious Diadem of Buddha"

Om, adoration to the blessed one. Adoration to you, the Buddha most excellent in all the three worlds. It is said: Purify, purify! Purify completely, purify completely! You, incomparable pure one, having the absolute nature of light ubiquitous in the sky and six existences of living beings, consecrate me with words of the great seals and mystic incantations, the anointment by means of nectar of the excellent instructions of all Tathagatas and Sugatas. Remove, remove calamities, oh, holder of my life! Purify . . .

TRANSLATION BY G. SARGENT
MURATA, *CHU YUNG GUAN*, 343

Tibetan Buddhist images protect these holy texts. On the reveals of the arches, about 7 m wide and high, are a complement of auspicious motifs often found as surrounds for holy icons (fig. 1.18): a Garuda bird at the top (the keystone), flanked by Naga kings and Makara (water creatures), with elephants carrying ram-like animals surmounted by small figures. This iconography will be found at Buddhist sites from the Yuan period onwards, for example the Ming sutra cabinet of the Zhihua Si in Beijing [22 ▶]. Some of this same iconography also entered later imperial architecture, for example, Makaras on the stone terraces of the Forbidden City (fig. 3.23).

1.18
Garuda and Naga kings,
south portal, Cloud Terrace

1.19
Guardian King of the
South, east wall

Reliefs of the Four Guardian Kings occupy the inside walls of the 15 m-deep portal: Vaisravana, Guardian of the North, Dhrtarastra, Guardian of the East (northeast), Virudhaka, Guardian of the South (southeast; fig. 1.19), and Virupaksa, Guardian of the West (southwest). These figures warrant close inspection. Powerful, animated warriors dressed in armor trample demons under foot, each wielding its own attribute (stupa, pipa, sword, serpent), and attended by two grotesque minions. The armor in particular is an exercise in fine carving. Look also for the rat demon in Mongol dress being trampled in the panel devoted to the Guardian of the North.

The iconography of the walls and ceiling is completed by reliefs of the Buddhas of the Ten Directions (north, east, south, west, northeast, southeast, southwest, northwest, upper, and lower) on the inclined panels of the ceiling. Each is accompanied by a Thousand Buddha pattern with 102 Buddhas, representing the myriad Buddhas of the *bhadra-kalpa* (present era). On the flat ceiling proper are five mandalas (cosmic diagrams) "cut with great precision," in the words of Murata Jiro, three facing north and two facing south. These are identified in the Uighur and Mongol texts as Aksobhya, Sarvavid, Vajrapani, Amitabha, and Sakyamuni Buddha, respectively.

SUGGESTED
READING

Nancy Steinhardt's *Chinese Imperial City Planning* (1990) introduces Chinese capital cities. Better maps and photographs will be found in Fu Xinian et al, *Chinese Architecture* (2002). Arthur F. Wright's "The Cosmology of the Chinese City," in G. W. Skinner, *The City in Late Imperial China* (1977) engages the ideas that shaped imperial capitals.

For the Mongol era, see Morris Rossabi, *Khubilai Khan: His Life and Times* (1988), and Ronald Latham's translation of *Marco Polo: the Travels* (1958). John Larner, *Marco Polo and the Discovery of the World* (1999), evaluates the book in its widest context. For the case against Polo's historicity; see Frances Wood, *Did Marco Polo Go to China?* (1996).

Walls and Gates

2

Towering forty feet above the Manchu-Tartar City, higher than a two-story building, broader than Fifth Avenue, these noble battlements encircle the city. The moral effect on those who dwell within them is curious. Strangers they impress painfully at first with a sense of imprisonment. But in time this feeling changes to one of soothing security—to the comfortable sensation that the massive grey arms can keep out the rush and worries of the restless world.

JULIET BREDON, *PEKING* (1931), 18

The construction of a new capital, the third project of its kind in the Ming, came after the death of the founding emperor Hongwu in 1398. It will forever be bound up with contested claims to the throne, the Mongols, and the pros and cons of south and north (Nanjing and Beijing). Many historians believe that late in his reign Hongwu himself was considering relocating the capital, both because of strategic concerns about the frontier and out of dissatisfaction with the Nanjing palaces (see Box, p. 70) built in the 1360s and 70s.

When the throne passed to a grandson of the founder, a minor known after the fact as the Jianwen emperor (r. 1399–1402), the stage was set for a contest involving Hongwu's fourth son, Zhu Di, who decades before was enfeoffed as the Prince of Yan. The details of this struggle were effaced from the historical record as if it had never occurred, and even the boy emperor's fate is unknown: Was he killed? Did he escape? Open

THE SOUTHERN CAPITAL, NANJING

In 1368, the Ming armies had achieved their final victories and Zhu Yuanzhang (known as Hongwu, r. 1368–98) proclaimed himself emperor. The new sovereign visited Kaifeng, the old Northern Song capital of Bianliang, and returned declaring that the city should be his "northern capital." With the fall of Dadu that same year, however, the question of capitals was re-examined. In 1369, construction began at another site, Fengyang (Linhao, Anhui), with the designation "middle capital" (zhong du). Linhao was chosen because it was the native place of the emperor and the site of his parents' tombs. By 1375, however, work stopped, and it was decided to make Nanjing the primary seat of imperial government. The Anhui site survives today as a ruin, its major gates and many large blocks of stone still in place. However, the details of its palaces and imperial city were copied at Nanjing, and eventually replicated at Beijing as well. Thus the obscure site in Anhui is one source of the Ming-Qing capital we call Beijing.

Zhu Yuanzhang had made Nanjing (which he named Yingtian, "responding to Heaven") his base as early as 1356 when he was the self-styled Duke of Wu. By 1366–67, now King of Wu, he had erected a new palace, altars, and an ancestral temple on the east side of the city. These were the minimal features for an imperial capital, with tombs added as necessary. Although divinations were performed to determine the location of the new palace, the construction occupied marshy ground. Over time the Ming palaces literally sank in spite of efforts to create adequate weight-bearing foundations. Today portions of the first Ming palace survive at Nanjing, notably the south, east, and west gates, the five bridges that approached the main courtyard, and the foundations of the great throne hall, the Fengtian Dian.

Over a span of two decades Nanjing was expanded repeatedly, creating the largest walled city in China (and in the world it is claimed) with 30.5 or 33.6 km of walls. The Ming walls enclosed the palace on the east, ran along Xuanwu Lake across the north, followed the heights above the Yangzi on the west, and then wrapped around such areas as Shitoucheng and the Qin-Huai River on the southwest. At Nanjing the walls varied considerably in construction and scale. Some were remade around earlier cores; others were newly built from pounded earth, rubble, or stone, with stone and brick for facing and top surfaces. Large gray bricks (40 cm x 20 cm x 10 cm) fired at kilns south of the city were the most common building material. Most of these bricks bear inscriptions giving their date and place of production (see Box, p. 79). Very detailed histories of each segment's construction can be documented as a result. Bricks came from as far away as Changsha, Nanchang, Wuchang, and Jiujiang, as well as from nearby Yangzhou, Changzhou, and Zhenjiang.

Defensive measures taken at Nanjing by the Ming engineers boggle the mind. Three of the gates on the south and west—Jubao Men (now known as Zhonghua Men), Tongji Men, and Sanshan Men—were outfitted with multiple defensive walls inside rather than outside the city wall perimeter. Each of these compounds in turn had tunnels built into their walls for stationing the guard. Tunnels at a single gate might shelter 3000 troops. The city was also surrounded by another, outer wall almost 60 km long. This was an earthen bulwark with eighteen reinforced gates; it is now in disrepair. The outer wall was designed to deny attackers the heights that overlooked the city. In Ming times the area between the outer and inner walls was rural.

By the end of the century Nanjing had a population nearing half a million (473,000 according to a record dated 1391), of which perhaps 200,000 were military forces, 45,000 were artisan families, and another 10,000 were local worthies.

conflict from mid-1399 through mid-1402 entailed several attacks on Zhu Di's base, the former Dadu, by loyalist troops, and ultimately the occupation of Nanjing by Zhu Di's own forces. By 1403 the Prince of Yan had become emperor, to be known by his reign name Yongle (r. 1403–24). One of the most dynamic figures in all of Chinese imperial history, Yongle on horseback led successful campaigns in the field against the Mongols and at the same time dispatched the admiral Zheng He on expeditions to the southern oceans.

Construction of Ming Beijing

Yongle's decision to make his fief the primary capital had several rationales. In Nanjing, he and his supporters were surrounded by a court and many high officials who were either openly hostile or secretly suspicious, while Yongle's own power base was far distant. Traditionally an emperor should honor his place of origin. Although Yongle could not claim to be either a founding emperor or a true son of the north, he was receptive to the idea of elevating the status of his former fief in honor of his accession. Thus in 1403, the first year of his reign, Beiping (Northern Peace, as Dadu was then known), became Beijing (Northern Capital). In accord with this new status as a secondary capital, the city acquired branch ministries and other governmental organs. Zhu Di's son was placed in charge.

Perhaps more significant, Yongle recognized the realities of the frontier and the dangers, real and potential, of Mongol forces across the Yanshan Mountains to the north. The Northern Capital would serve as a base to gather resources for campaigns on the steppe and from which to launch them. If the canal from the south could be revived and the economy improved more generally, its advantages would be even stronger. With these concerns in mind, new residents moved at government expense from Shanxi, and eventually also from Jiangsu, Zhejiang, Huguang, Fujian, Shaanxi, and Sichuan. The government exempted the new arrivals from tax levies for five years, and provided supplies and equipment to establish their farms. Meanwhile, guard forces established encampments in the suburbs.

In Yongle's fourth year (the intercalary seventh moon of 1406), the court announced preparations for a major reconstruction of the city. For most historians, this marks the beginning of the new capital. A cohort of able officials was charged with mustering the labor forces and materiel needed. For example, Song Li, the Minister of Works, traveled to the south to gather timber in the expectation that construction would begin the following year.

These preparations soon ground to a halt. In the seventh moon of 1407, the Empress Xu died after an illness. She was the daughter of the general Xu Da who had captured Dadu from the Mongols, and she had spent two decades in the city. The grief-stricken Yongle refused to appoint a new empress, and delayed attempts to inter the deceased Lady Xu in Nanjing near the tomb of Hongwu. At the same time, campaigns in the far south against Annam and Jiaozhi (northern Vietnam) strained manpower and resources. When Yongle returned to Beijing to select a suitable burial site for his empress and begin work (the fourth and fifth moons of 1409), he ordered the suspension of other preparations for reconstructing the capital city. The site selected for burial is now known as the Ming Valley, in Changping County. The tomb became the Changling [18 ▶], the emperor's own. Empress Xu was finally interred there in the second moon of 1413. Aboveground halls were not finished for another two years.

The city's construction restarted that same year (eighth moon, 1415) with renovations to the emperor's existing palace. Most scholars think this site, known as the Western Palace (Xi Gong), was on the shores of Bei Hai. It would therefore have been the palace intended for the Yuan heir (Longfu Gong) that became the Prince of Yan's residence when he assumed his fief decades before. But the fate of Dadu and its palaces in 1368 is not clear. Some writers argue that Xu Da leveled all the Mongol palaces when he occupied the city, including Longfu Gong. (How much destruction Xu Da wreaked also affects how much work the construction of a new palace entailed.) In any case, at the same time Zhu Di's palace was improved, the great canal linked to the south via Tongzhou was reopened, making it possible for the city to be supplied by water transport.

A court discussion was convened in the eleventh moon of Yongle 14 (1416) to discuss the designation of Beijing as the primary capital. The document approving the emperor's plan proclaimed:

> This northern capital is the holy place where the dragon emperor arose. To the north its pillow is Juyong Guan, to the west it nestles against the Taihang Mountains, to the east it connects to the Shanhai Guan, to the south it overlooks the Central Plains. Fertile and rich [lands extend] a thousand *li*; its mountains and streams are glorious. It is sufficient to control the four barbarian peoples and to govern all under Heaven. Truly this is a capital of emperors for ten thousand generations.

Thus 1416 is also cited as the beginning of construction of the new capital, a process that concluded five years later with its formal inauguration in 1421. Work on a new palace commenced in the sixth moon of 1417 (Yongle 15) and was substantially complete by the end of 1420 (Yongle 18). From the first day of the first moon of the next year, 1421 (Yongle 19), all official government organs and seals were renamed, dropping the prefixes that had designated them "secondary." By this date Yongle had been in continuous residence since 1417.

The capital derived its plan and major features from two sources. As an expedient matter, the city rose from the foundations of the Mongol capital, Dadu (fig. 1.8). Even if thorough destruction had been visited on the Yuan palaces (and this is debated), many parts of the city remained substantially intact. Yongle's capital thus retained the Yuan east and west city walls, and much of the Imperial City that surrounded the palaces and lakes on the west. It had the same central axis, as well as the main arteries issuing from city gates and the extensive network of residential lanes (hutong).

The other source for the city's design, especially the palaces and Imperial City, was the existing capital at Nanjing (see Box, p. 70), and indeed its prototype, the abandoned Middle Capital in Anhui. The layout of the Forbidden City and its supporting facilities, known collectively in Ming times as the "imperial palaces" (*huang gong*) followed Nanjing models closely in the names chosen for gates and halls, as well as such elements as the disposition of the Altar to Soil and Grain and the Ancestral Temple. The new site, unlike crowded, hemmed–in Nanjing, readily accommodated a balanced and regular plan, the better to manifest notions about the emperor as embodied in the classics.

Building continued intermittently for several decades after 1421. Just three months after its inauguration, on the eighth day of the fourth moon, catastrophic fires destroyed the Three Great Halls of the outer court (see Box, p. 118). Such a calamity was viewed as a sign or portent from Heaven. Yongle assembled a court conference to discuss the matter. The emperor asked for "straight words" from his high officials. Zou Ji spoke out about the suffering the ambitious project had created. "People's hearts" had been lost, and "Heaven's will offended." Some officials even suggested a return to Nanjing. For their temerity, the emperor punished his critics with imprisonment, exile in Annam, or even execution. The next year the Palace of Heavenly Purity (Qianqing Gong), residence of the emperor, also burned.

For two decades, the fate of the new capital hung in the balance. Yongle passed away while on campaign in 1424, his twenty-second year on the throne. His heir dutifully buried him at Changling with the Empress Xu. This new ruler, known as the Hongxi emperor (Zhu Gaozhi, r. 1425), lived only a year more himself. Early on he ordered new seals that would have made Nanjing once again the primary capital, and dispatched his heir to that city. This successor, the Xuande emperor (Zhu Zhanji, r. 1426–35), however, prolonged Beijing's primary status while his father's tomb at the Ming Valley was completed. Indeed, it was not until the following reign of the Zhengtong emperor (Zhu Qizhen, r. 1436–49 and 1457–63) that the question of Beijing was ultimately resolved. In 1441, Zhengtong proclaimed the northern capital primary once again. By this time, palace halls had been rebuilt. A major campaign to improve city gates and other fortifications went forward under the direction of an Annamese eunuch, Ruan An. Thus, the initial construction of Ming Beijing extends from 1403 to 1441, although many years in between saw no activity.

A coda to the city's construction history came in the next century, with the reign of the Jiajing emperor (Zhu Houcong, r. 1522–66). During forty-five years on the throne, he caused the altars, including the Altar to Heaven, the Ancestral Temple, and various other structures to be built or rebuilt after designs that more strictly followed what he and his advisors regarded as classical norms (see Ch. 4). Moreover, in the century and more since the capital had moved, the entire region experienced considerable economic development and population growth. This was especially true of areas outside the city walls on the east and south where traffic from the Central Plains and the south arrived. The population of Beijing consumed all things, if not itself producing most of them. Merchants from other provinces, markets, and craft production were concentrated in the area south of Zhengyang Men. The area of Chongwen Men also flourished; it was here that the government levied its lucrative tariffs on imported merchandise.

As early as 1542, a court official proposed erecting an outer wall to protect the southern suburbs. The proposal was renewed in 1553 (Jiajing 32) by Zhu Bochen. Zhu cited three rationales for his costly plan: (1) the founding emperor Hongwu had built an outer wall at Nanjing, a useful historical precedent; (2) the growth of markets and population around the city; and (3) the threat of Mongol attacks. Only a few years before, in 1550, Mongol raiding parties had come within shouting distance of Anding Men. Zhu's plan called for a new wall on all sides, about 17 *li* east and west by about 15 *li* north and south. The new wall would utilize the Yuan earthen walls on the north, have corner towers, eleven gates, and in general be comparable to the existing city ramparts. Work began in the third moon, but in less than a month the plan was recast with only the southern suburbs enclosed. When the palace halls burned in 1557—a major calamity in its history—plans to continue work on the remaining three sides of the city were abandoned. Instead, the new southern wall and its seven gates (fig. 2.1), named by the emperor himself, became permanent fixtures.

Improvements made in 1564 widened the moat and constructed defensive walls to front the seven gates.

From this time forward it became necessary to distinguish the main city, the northern walled area, as the Inner City (*nei cheng*), and the newly-enclosed southern tracts as the Outer City (*wai cheng*). After 1644, the Manchus imposed their own distinction. Manchu banners were settled in the Inner City, and its former Chinese residents were forced to relocate in the Outer City. This led foreigners in the nineteenth century to call the two the Tartar City and Chinese City, respectively. Unlike the original city grid for Dadu, areas now within the outer wall developed without any central planning. Only one main avenue ran east-west, while another emanated from Zhengyang Men and headed south. An irregular pattern of alleys fanned out from each of the Inner City's three southern gates. The Outer City also included the all important Altar to Heaven (Tian Tan) and the Altar to Agriculture (Xian Nong Tan). Some tracts were open fields dedicated to farming and fish ponds.

2.1
"Gate of Peking," postcard, anonymous. Compare Yongding Men and its defensive structures shown here with the Yuan gate at Heyi Men (Ming Xizhi Men, fig. 1.12).

Gate of Peking.

Beijing's Walls and Gates Today

Most contemporary visitors realize that Beijing's walls and gates have been torn down, stripping the city of its much admired historic character. Although the final destruction of the walls took place in the 1960s as part of a campaign to modernize roads and create the subway, wall demolition in Beijing has a longer history.

As early as 1900, after the occupation of the capital by the Allied Armies, a portion of the Outer Wall near Yongding Men was removed to allow the railroad to reach the Front Gate of the Inner City. The former Water Gate, between Zhengyang Men and Chongwen Men, was transformed into a roadway in 1905 for the convenience of the Legation Quarter. In the teens, still more of the walls and gates suffered when tracks for an urban railway running on the open area (glacis) between the moat and the Inner City walls were laid. The new rails severed the defensive walls (*weng cheng*) in front of five of the nine city gates or opened portals to allow the tracks to pass (see Box, p. 83). Wall sections adjoining the southeast and northeast corner towers also became disconnected. At about the same time (1914–15), openings flanking Zhengyang Men [4▶] (fig. 2.2) appeared in hopes of accommodating increased vehicular traffic. In 1926-27, another road-

2.2
Traffic at Zhengyang Men (after 1915), a postcard by Hartung's Photo Shop, Peking

CITY WALL BRICKS

The Ming built their city walls and many other large structures using specially produced bricks (fig. 2.3). During construction under the Yongle emperor, these bricks were produced in Linqing, Shandong province on the route of the Grand Canal. Canal boats, including those hauling grain to the capital, transported the bricks to Beijing without charge.

These bricks, each weighing about 60 kg, came in several sizes, the most common measuring either 48 x 24 x 12 cm, or 42 x 21 x 11 cm. The fuels used to fire them (coal and charcoal, respectively) determined their characteristic white and gray colors. Standards of workmanship were exacting: the clay was first screened several times, then washed, then allowed to settle. Using wooden draw molds lined with cloth, a skilled artisan could pull just enough raw clay to fill a mold without needing either to trim away excess or fill in around the edges. A brick formed in one gesture was inherently strongest. The goal was a brick that rang when struck and had no holes when cut open. If a single artisan could make 200 to 300 bricks a day, as suggested, then about ten man-days of work filled an average kiln (2500 bricks). Firing consumed a full month: half of that time for baking and the remainder for cooling. Twelve firings per year thus yielded 30,000 bricks. If, as one source claims, a million bricks were produced each year during Yongle's building campaign, over 300 kilns must have been in operation.

The bricks carry detailed inscriptions (fig. 2.4) documenting their place of production and in the fullest examples also the date and the names and titles of those responsible. Artisans (*jiang ren*) as well as supervisors (*zuo tou*) and managers (*yao hu*) are duly noted. The Ministry of Works operated many kilns; others were civilian or military. A study of bricks in the Ming Valley found that they originated in Hebei, Jiangsu, Shandong, Zhili, Anhui, and Henan provinces. On the other hand, almost all of the bricks associated with the Dingling were still derived from Linqing.

2.3
City wall bricks on stone base, Southeast Corner Tower

Square floor tiles associated with imperial construction were called "golden" or "metal" bricks (*jin zhuan*). These were installed as the floors of the Three Great Halls of the Forbidden City, as well as the Changling hall and the underground chambers of the Dingling. Originating in Suzhou, they measure 61.5 cm square after trimming during installation. Production standards in Suzhou were even more demanding than those for Linqing bricks. A batch required eighteen months: clay preparation and curing, and sixty days of air drying before firing which lasted 130 days. Only one hundred tiles were fired at a time. Finishing steps comprised polishing and application of *tong* oil. Like the lavish use of iron cramps in the Jin-period Water Gate [1 ▶] and Marco Polo Bridge [2 ▶], the care and expense required for these bricks demonstrate the high standards of imperial building.

2.4
Brick inscription, Dingling, reading: "Made for the kiln supervisor Wang Bao in spring of Jiajing 14 [1535]."

way connected to the Outer City by creating a new gate, Heping Men, midway between Zhengyang and Xuanwu Men. The Japanese occupation forces opened both the east and west walls (with Jianguo Men and Fuxing Men, respectively) in the early 1940s. Destruction gained momentum in the late 1950s under the banner of "modernizing the ancient capital" and culminated after 1969 with construction of the Second Ring Road. Thus many city administrations during the twentieth century participated in the destruction of Beijing's historic walls and gates.

Tearing down walls and gates has, however, yielded fresh information about their original construction. The four walls that comprised the Ming capital's defenses were built at three different periods (fig. 2.7). The Mongol rulers erected the east and west walls in the 1270s and they were retained by the Ming builders. During demolition in the 1960s, archaeologists examined the wall cores. They discovered that the Yuan-period west wall, for example, had a fill of pure loess, set in a trench 2 m deep and 25 m wide (fig. 2.6). Layers of pounded earth formed a base 15 cm thick versus 6 to 11 cm thick layers in the wall itself. The Ming renovation of the early fifteenth century added more pounded earth in thicker layers of 18 to 25 cm. Some layers held broken tile and brick. The outer face was given a brick skin during the initial Ming effort, but bricks were not added to the inside surface until the 1440s. Several layers of stone at the base carried these bricks (see fig. 2.3). The outer bricks could be as much as 2 m thick, the inner surface about a meter. Atop the wall core was a 20 cm layer of packed earth covered with brick. The west wall measured 4910 m in length, its average base dimension 15.6 m, height over 10 m, and width at top 12.75 m.

By contrast, removing the north wall showed that it had been thrown up in some haste after occupation of the city by Xu Da's army in 1368. It ran for 6790 m across the northern wards of Dadu (see figs. 1.14, 6.8) at a width of 24.5 m. The archaeologists commented on its irregular layers and poor quality pounding, as well as rounded profile. Many layers had extraneous materials mixed in.

2.5
"Scene of Place near Ping Tze Men Gate," postcard by L. Wannieck, Peking. Ping Tze Men was the Yuan name for Fucheng Men. Note inside the moat battlements (*duntai*) receding toward the horizon.

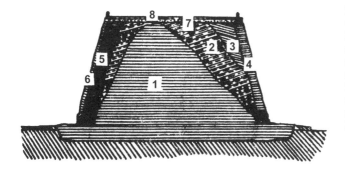

2.6
Cross-section of west Inner City wall, from *Beijing kaogu,* 192. Diagram shows: (1) Yuan earthen core; (2, 3) Ming earthen fill; (4) Ming inner surface; (5, 6) Ming outer surface; (7) packed earth; and (8) Ming brick top surface.

The Ming south city wall, finally, was built in 1419 as the new capital neared completion (fig. 2.7). Relocating this wall two *li* (0.8 km) south of its Yuan alignment on the south side of Chang'an Avenue created areas for the Altar to Soil and Grain (She Ji Tan) and Ancestral Temple (Tai Miao) in front of the palace [13, 14 ▶]. Today it is the only original wall standing, a segment 1245 m long designated the Ming Dynasty City Wall Relics Park. Eleven battlements (*duntai, mamian*) project along the exterior of the wall only some of which is at full height. (A much shorter segment of the east wall survives nearby, about 360 m with three battlements.) Railroad enthusiasts may enjoy visiting the signal house (1901) that served the Jing-Feng (Beijing to Shenyang) Railway preserved in the green strip that runs along the Ming wall park. A visit to the Southeast Corner Tower [5 ▶] should include this park.

4 ▶
Zhengyang Men
(Qian Men)

MING, 1436–39;
REBUILT 1902–07, 1915
NATIONAL REGISTER,
1988
SOUTH OF TIAN'AN
MEN SQUARE,
DONGCHENG

Zhengyang Men (Proper Yang Gate), more commonly called Front Gate (Qian Men) for its position astride the city's main axis (fig. 2.8), is the only Ming gate to survive into the twenty-first century. Before 1553, it was the principal entrance to the city as well as the Imperial City and palace. The comparable Yuan gate had been relocated in 1419; the Ming reconstruction in 1436–39 was part of the Zhengtong emperor's final push to complete the capital. The gate burned and was rebuilt in 1610, and later still destroyed in 1900 under a barrage of artillery from U.S. forces in the Altar to Heaven. After yet another rebuilding in 1902, the Beijing government commissioned a redesign of the Arrow Tower (Jian Lou) in 1915–16 by a German architect, Curt Rothkegel (1876–1946). This accounts for the baroque lintels of its arrow ports (obscured by the banner in fig. 2.9). During this improvement, the

NINE GATES OF MING BEIJING

The Ming city of 1421 had nine gates, two each on east, north, and west, and three across the south (fig. 2.7). Five were newly constructed, while the remaining four, two each on east and west, were Yuan-period structures. Stone bridges to cross the moat as well as defensive walls and gates improved all nine of the gates in 1437–43. The intact Heyi Men portal of the Yuan period (fig. 1.11) discovered within the barbican gate at Xizhi Men had been improved at this time.

    The city gates on the east served as the principal point of entry for many goods brought from the south. Dozens of rice warehouses, for example, stood inside Chaoyang Men, while a timber terminal lay inside Dongzhi Men. Factories for preparing building materiel remained outside the south gates. Taiji Chang ([stone] "terrace factory") and Liuli chang ("glazed [tile] factory") take their names from Ming imperial workshops. On the west, drinking water from the Western Hills entered the city by carts at Xizhi Men, while coal typically arrived at Fucheng Men. In 1900 the Boxers and Allied Armies badly damaged three gates—Zhengyang, Chongwen, and Chaoyang—as well as three corner towers (all but the southwest). At six gates (marked with asterisks below), the *weng cheng* walls were cut by the city railway ca. 1915.

Wall	Gate (Translation)	Year of demise of Arrow Tower / Gate House
North Wall		
(a) East	*Anding (Peacefully Settled)	1952 / 1969
(b) West	*Desheng (Virtue Victorious)	Intact / 1921
East Wall		
(c) North	*Dongzhi (East Direct)	1927 / 1965
(d) South	*Chaoyang (Facing Yang)	1958 / 1956
West Wall		
(e) North	Xizhi (West Direct)	1969 / 1969
(f) South	Fucheng (Mound Completed)	1935 / 1965
South Wall		
(g) East	*Chongwen (Exalted Civil)	1900 / 1966
Center	*Zhengyang (Proper Yang)	Intact / Intact
(h) West	Xuanwu (Proclaimed Martial)	1920 / 1965

Source: Wang Jun, *Cheng Ji* (Sanlian, 2003), 314–16

Letters a through h correspond to fig. 2.7.

gate lost its semicircular defensive walls. The "peaceful
liberation" of the city was celebrated here on February
3, 1949. Two small temples dedicated to Guan Di and
Guan Yin disappeared in the 1960s during construction of the subway. The *pailou* and stone bridges south
of the gate also vanished at this time. Both the
Zhengyang Men gate house and Arrow Tower have
been opened for visitors.

Zhengyang Men stands on a base (the original
Ming wall) almost 15 m high. The gate house stretches
41 m east to west, depth 21 m, and rises to 42 m in

2.7
Map of Ming and Qing
Beijing, from *Beijing gu
jianzhu* (1986), 6. Letters
and numbers refer to sites
discussed in this book.

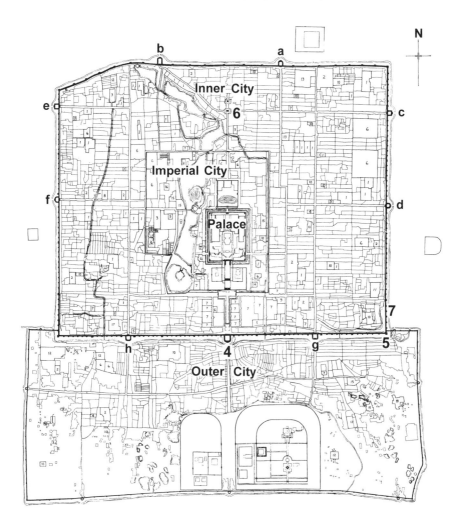

2.8
Gate house of Zhengyang
Men (Qian Men)

height. At 12 m the Arrow Tower's base (the remnant *weng cheng* defensive wall) is slightly lower, and it reaches a height of 38 m. Both structures are seven bays across, but the Arrow Tower (fig. 2.9) is significantly larger, at 62 m wide and 20 m deep. While the main gate house is timber frame with masonry walls and tile roofs, the defensive tower is built entirely of masonry. Ninety-four arrow ports pierce the three outward faces.

The only other gate structure that survives is the Arrow Tower of Desheng Men, once part of the western gate to the city on the north. Xu Da bestowed its name, signifying "victory through virtue," in 1368 after he conquered the Mongol capital. The structure again dates to 1436–39. The gate house disappeared in 1921. Since the city wall here was cleared away in 1955, the Arrow Tower has stood in isolation on the north side of the Second Ring Road. Like the Arrow Tower at Zhengyang Men this is a seven-bay wide masonry structure, but somewhat smaller at 34 m across and 20 m deep, total height 32 m.

The dispatch and return of military forces generally utilized Desheng Men and its twin on the east, Anding Men, the northern frontier being a constant concern during the Ming. The ill-fated Zhengtong emperor went on campaign through this gate in 1449; likewise Yu Qian took command of the city's defenses here after the emperor's unfortunate capture by the Mongols (see p. 96). Li Zicheng, the rebel who temporarily occupied the city before the Manchus arrived in 1644 entered through this gate. The Empress Dowager Cixi and the Guangxu emperor fled by this route in August 1900 as the Allied Armies attacked (see p. 298). Imperial funeral corteges exited the city from the north on their way to the Ming or Qing tombs. Both northern gates incorporated Zhenwu Miao, temples to the Daoist guardian of the north, inside their defensive walls.

2.9
Arrow Tower of Zhengyang Men, with banner reading: "Raise High the Great Red Flag of Mao Zedong Thought and Forge Ahead Courageously"

As part of his campaign to complete the capital, the Zhengtong emperor improved the watch towers on all four corners of the city wall in 1437-40. The Southeast Corner Tower, the sole survivor, rises above a base extending 20 m east and south outward from the line of the city walls (figs. 2.10-12). L-shaped in plan, the tower ascends 17 m above the wall to a total height of 29 m. Both arms are 35 m long by 16 m wide. This tower, like the Arrow Towers that once fronted every city gate, has ports for firing on attackers, in this case four tiers of 144. Decorative gables (*huashan*) sit on the roof slopes at the south and east, while proper hip-gable roof ends are seen at north and west. The circumferential railway built in 1915 separated the tower and its base from the city walls. Today the western portal used for the trains is the entrance to the site (see fig. 7.3).

◀ 5

Southeast Corner Tower (Dongnan Jiao Lou, Dong Bian Men)

MING, 1437–40;
REBUILT 1935
NATIONAL REGISTER, 1982
SECOND RING ROAD AT
DONG BIAN MEN

2.10
Southeast Corner Tower

Inside the tower extensive reconstruction in 1935 replaced the original "golden columns" with reinforced concrete pillars. Additional modifications took place in 1958 and 1981. During these efforts the contractors found various debris—cannon balls and shot—physical evidence for the assault mounted here in 1900 before the liberation of the foreign legations. The interior is used for a display about Chongwen District and its commercial history and by a gallery of contemporary art, Red Gate Gallery.

The other Ming corner towers did not fare well during the early twentieth century. The Northwest

2.11
Inside view,
Southeast Corner Tower

2.12
Arrow ports,
Southeast Corner Tower

Corner Tower was destroyed in 1900 by the allies and never rebuilt; the base was cleared away in 1969. The Northeast Tower was disassembled in 1920 and its base removed in 1953. The Southwest Tower was demolished in the 1930s and the base leveled in 1969.

Before the Mongols, Chinese cities did not have bell and drum towers. However, the custom of using these important musical instruments for timekeeping started at least by the Han, when the phrases "dawn drum" and "dusk bell" appear. In Tang dynasty Chang'an, drums at the main palace gate sounded to open the palace and city each morning at 5 a.m. Drums at each of the city's wards then echoed the palace drum. City timekeeping was first given monumental expression with the construction of Dadu. In 1272, a water clock (clepsydra) was set up in the Qizheng Lou, north of the Yuan palace and slightly west of the city axis. This drum tower was accompanied by a bell tower some distance further north; at the time this was the main market area of the city. The Ming perpetuated the

◀ 6

Bell and Drum Towers (Zhonglou and Gulou)

QING, 1745–47 AND MING, 1541

NATIONAL REGISTER, 1996

DI'AN MEN WAI, DONGCHENG

2.13
Drum Tower
(Gu Lou)

custom, but aligned the new towers further east on the city-palace axis. For the next five centuries the striking of drums and bell kept the city's residents on schedule. Both towers were first built ca. 1420, about 100 m apart, with the Drum Tower south. Each was built as a masonry podium surmounted by a wooden hall. Fires plagued them on several occasions. The present Drum Tower is a rebuilding of 1541. The Bell Tower was not so fortunate, and by 1745 (Qianlong 12) it was redesigned using stone and brick construction, the structure we see today.

The Drum Tower is a rectangular masonry pedestal 49 m wide and 29 m deep; it rises to 19 m (fig. 2.13). The red base could be entered either through three portals that face both south and north or by single portals at either end. A steep flight of sixty-nine high steps accessible from the north leads to the five-bay timber-frame hall above, 43 m wide and 23 m deep, its ridge reaching a height of 47 m. A complement of twenty-five drums, one large, is installed here. Only one badly damaged specimen is said to be original. It was the custom to strike the drums at the beginning and end of each night, at *qi geng* (corre-

2.14
Bell Tower (below, right)

2.15
Cross-section of Bell Tower, from Zhu and Zeng, *Beijing Zhong Gu lou,* 43. The air shaft (2) above and below the bell (1) and passages (3) extending in four directions top and bottom functioned as resonating chambers to amplify sound.

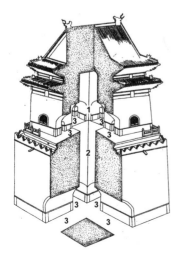

sponding to 7 p.m.) and *liang geng* (5 a.m.). Drums resounded eighteen times at a fast clip, eighteen times more slowly, and then the same was repeated five more times.

The masonry Bell Tower (fig. 2.14, 2.15), 48 m in height, stands immediately north of the Drum Tower, its 31 m-square base punctured by portals facing each direction. Here seventy-five difficult stairs ascend to the upper level which houses a huge bell cast in the Yongle era (1403–24). Heavy timbers of an eight-sided frame hold a bronze bell that is 7 m tall and estimated (by Beijing University of Science in 1990) to weigh 63 tons (fig. 2.16). It is the largest bell in Beijing, about 16 tons heavier than another great bell at the Bell Temple and Museum (Dazhong Si) also from the Yongle era.

Through the Qianlong era (1733–96), this bell reverberated at each double-hour of the night: 7 p.m., 9 p.m., 11 p.m., 1 a.m., 3 a.m., and 5 a.m. Recent studies suggest the bell was audible as much as 10 km distant, depending on the intensity with which it was struck. The sound of the bell at 3 a.m. roused capital officials to appear for a dawn court. In the nineteenth century the bell was struck only twice each night. The

2.16
Great Bell, height 5.6 m, weight 63 tons

practice stopped entirely in 1924 with the departure of Pu Yi, the last emperor, from the Forbidden City.

Both towers afford the visitor a 360-degree panorama of the northern city high above the axial roadway leading south to Jing Shan. Hou Hai and Bei Hai are visible on the west, and on a very clear day, the Western Hills. Hutong surrounding the towers are among the areas of the city identified as conservation districts (see p. 22). With the summit of Jing Shan (fig. 6.25) which overlooks the palaces, this view is essential to understanding the plan of Ming-Qing Beijing.

7 ▶
Ancient
Observatory
(Gu Guanxiang Tai)

—————————————

MING, 1442
NATIONAL REGISTER,
1982
JIANGUO MEN,
DONGCHENG

Specialized structures for observing the heavens and meteorological phenomena existed from ancient times. The Numinous Terrace (Ling Tai) south of the Han-Wei City of Luoyang provided court officials with an elevated platform from which to make observations which were transmitted to the emperor. Beijing has had an imperial observatory since 1127 when the Jin army brought back astronomical instruments from the fallen Northern Song capital. They were installed on the Hou Tai near Baiyun Guan close to the northern wall of Zhongdu. Under the Mongols the Chinese scholar Guo Shoujing, known for his important contributions to hydraulic engineering, created new instruments for Khubilai Khan in 1279. They were set up at the Si Tian Tai in the southeast corner of Dadu, the area now occupied by the Chinese Academy of Social Sciences on the north side of East Chang'an Avenue.

The Ming observatory was established in 1442 on the site of the Yuan southeast city corner tower (fig. 2.17). (It replaced an imperial observatory—called Lingtai—built near the western wall of the Imperial City.) When the east side of the observatory collapsed in August 1979, archaeologists found small Yuan-period bricks as well as larger Ming specimens. They also could document expansion of the tower during the Qianlong era (ca. 1744). In the Ming period, the terrace was about 18 m square at a height of 15 m above the ground, several meters higher than the city wall running north and south. Then as now visitors reached the terrace by climbing a 2 m–wide stairway on the west and north.

2.17
"Peking Observatory," postcard by Th. Culty, Peking

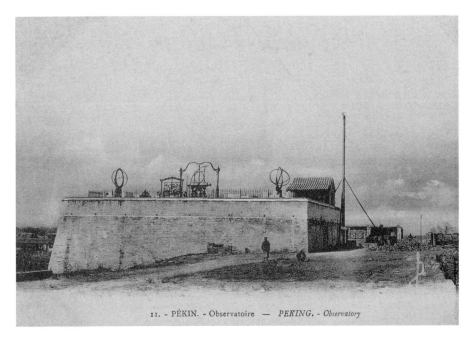

11. - PÉKIN. - Observatoire — PEKING. - Observatory

2.18
Observatory terrace with instruments

New instruments produced for the imperial court with the advice of Jesuit missionaries (fig. 2.18) necessitated the Qing expansion of the observation terrace. In 1669–73, the Belgian father Ferdinand Verbiest (in Chinese: Nan Huairen, 1623–88), an intimate of the Kangxi emperor, adopted designs of the great astronomer Tycho Brahe (1546–1601). These included a celestial globe (*tianti yi*), ecliptic (or zodiacal) and equatorial armillary spheres (*huangdao jingwei yi* and *chidao jingwei yi*), an azimuth horizon (or altazimuth, *diping jing yi*), an arc quadrant (*xiangxian yi*), and a sextant (*jixian yi*). In 1715, the German father Stumpf contributed a new instrument, a theodolite (*diping jingwei yi*). At this time some obsolete Ming-period instruments were apparently melted down for their alloy; two remain on display in the yard below. Thus the Manchu court was served by the best available European instruments from before the use of telescopes. The Observatory's mission also included meteorological observations. Weather records for the capital maintained from 1724 to 1902 are said to be the earliest compilation of such data in the world.

Eight instruments were still in place when Allied Armies arrived in 1900; some were removed to France and Germany at that time but later returned. In the 1930s, these instruments were taken to Nanjing for safekeeping, where some remain at the Nanjing Museum and the Purple Mountain Observatory. Today there are eight instruments in place on the observatory terrace, all handsome bronze castings with impressive dragon ornamentation. The Observatory courtyard west of the terrace, an island of solitude amid some of the most congested arteries of the city, has several display halls devoted to the history of Chinese astronomy and related topics.

Few topics in Chinese history have the name recognition of the Great Wall of China (fig. 2.19). Since Samuel Johnson famously lauded the virtues of being "a man who had gone to view" it, foreign visitors have flocked to the stone and brick battlements climbing the precipitous mountain slopes north of Beijing. The wall is commonly regarded as one of the wonders of the world. It generally tops any list of attractions for tourists both Chinese and foreign, and now has the distinction of being a UNESCO World Heritage Site as well. Searching the World Wide Web will yield a variety of opinions that either endorse or debunk the idea that the Great Wall is the only man-made feature on Earth visible (by the naked eye? with radar?) from orbit, the moon, or some other extra-terrestrial vantage point. It is also one of the few subjects with a considerable English-language reading list, although much of it is aimed at children.

Misconceptions about the Great Wall have proved remarkably robust. The fabric of the wall—its massive stone and brick parapets, watch towers, and signal towers—generally dates no earlier than the late fifteenth century. Most segments were built during the sixteenth-century heyday of this ambitious project. The sites open to visitors in the Beijing area cannot claim any greater antiquity. Certainly none date to the Qin (ca. 221–206 BCE) as is often implied. Nor is it likely that the Ming walls follow the path of earlier efforts (Han, Northern Qi, Sui, or Jin). Earlier walls differed completely in scale and construction. In their own time, these walls were known by various terms, most often generically as "long walls" (*chang cheng*) in distinction to city walls. They were not regarded as a colossal wall system (a Great Wall) perpetuated from antiquity. As Arthur Waldron has shown, there was no such

The Mongol Threat and the Great Wall

2.19
View of Great Wall at
Badaling

enduring edifice until the Ming went to the trouble of extending and connecting their walls in the sixteenth century. Portraits of the line of the Great Wall as a demarcation between the steppe world and the sedentary culture of China throughout history are also off target. The frontier changed constantly, and successive dynasties followed a variety of strategic and military policies toward nomadic peoples. In the Tang, Yuan, and Qing periods, walls were simply beside the point.

Moreover, the motivation to build this massive engineering feat resulted from a failure of military policy. Both the Hongwu and Yongle emperors achieved some success through forward engagements with the Mongols. All of that came to naught when the foolish emperor Yingzong (Zhu Qizhen, r. 1436–49 and 1457–1464) was captured by a Mongol force only sixty miles from the capital in 1449. This disastrous campaign was blamed on the eunuch Wang Zhen, patron of Zhihua Si [22 ▶]. Whatever the truth, a new emperor reigned for a time (1450–56) before the captive was released and partisans could replace Yingzong on the throne in 1457. For most of the next century danger on the frontier increased in response to the court's lackluster performance. Ultimately the Ming erected barriers to deter Mongol incursions into the capital region. When new wall building began, the Mongols simply extended their raiding around the segments then in place. Decades passed before enough connected and improved walls afforded a modicum of protection. As late as 1550 the Mongols brazenly rode up to the walls of Beijing.

Nor could the Great Wall succeed as a single line of defenses. Rather, it served a system controlled by nine military headquarters, reinforced by dozens of lesser forts, encampments, and checkpoints. Multiple wall lines and spurs branched out and ran parallel across the northeast, north, and northwest frontiers, from modern Liaoning to Gansu. If the forward watch towers and signal towers functioned properly, the frontier garrisons received early warnings of nomad movements. But, as with the French Maginot line, a mobile enemy found ways around walls and checkpoints or simply overwhelmed them. And any Ming commander who opened the gates instantly defeated the investment in bricks, mortar, and men at arms. This undermined the Ming in 1644 when General Wu Sangui allowed Manchu forces to enter via Shanhai Guan. Thus the much celebrated and indestructible Ming wall exemplified the worst of both worlds: it was extremely expensive to create and maintain and that investment could easily be rendered worthless.

For visitors to Beijing, several major points along the Ming wall are well developed for tourism. Certainly the most frequent spot for visitors is the checkpoint at Badaling about 70 km north of the city accessible by a freeway. The present structures are not earlier than 1505, but additions were made several times thereafter. The name, recorded as early as the Jin period, suggests that one can move in many directions (*ba da ling* means "eight points ridge"). The winding valley descending south from the checkpoint includes the Juyong Guan, one of the traditional historic and scenic sights of greater Beijing (see Box, p. 50). The wall at Badaling typifies construction in this part of North China, mixing stone and brick, about 7 m high and 4 m to 5 m wide at the top. Many block houses sit on the wall (fig. 2.20), and defensive towers and signal towers may be seen at a distance. The climbing here is moderately steep, but a cable car makes for a convenient ascent. Crowds and traffic can be extremely congested. If you want to have your picture taken where Richard Nixon set foot, however, this is the place.

The complex of walls, gates, and subsidiary structures around Juyong Guan, south of Badaling, is a recent improvement, but they capture the look and feel of a fortified strategic checkpoint. Climbing here

2.20
Block house, Badaling

is quite steep, and perhaps offers less expansive views than Badaling. However, crowds are usually thinner here, and there is the added benefit of the Cloud Terrace [3 ▶], an authentic Yuan portal. Both Badaling and Juyong Guan can be easily combined with a visit to the Ming Valley.

Other segments are more distant from the city. Simatai is another section of restored wall, 5.4 km in length with thirty-five block houses, northeast of the city (110 km) in Miyun County. The wall here was begun early, ca. 1465–87, and rebuilt several times. Mutianyu Guan, about 90 km east from the city, is another restored section known for being especially steep and scenic (fig. 2.21). The wall and checkpoint here also date to the fifteenth century with many later episodes of work under the supervision of Tan Lun and Qi Jiguang, the two great Ming proponents of the wall. Both of these sites see far fewer visitors than Badaling or Juyong Guan. They could also be part of a visit to the Qing Eastern Tombs (Ch. 4).

2.21
View of Great Wall at Mutianyu

These several checkpoints were built and maintained as part of the defense of the capital region. Other sections under the "nine garrisons" had similar construction, but the structures differ considerably depending on terrain and local conditions. While the walls near Beijing follow the ridges of moderately high mountain chains, further west the walls track across low land near the Yellow River and into the desert of the Gansu corridor. These wall segments were often built of pounded earth without any brick facing; blocks houses and other features are also less common. The many lines of walls built during the Ming make any statement about the total length of the project conjectural. Official sources claim a total length of from 6400 km to 14,700 km. Until a proper, accurate ground survey of all of the *bona fide* Ming walls is reported, the question must remain open. The State Administration of Cultural Heritage has announced plans for a survey.

SUGGESTED READING   On wall building in the Ming, see Sen-dou Chang, "The Morphology of Walled Capitals," in G.W. Skinner ed., *The City in Late Imperial China* (1977), 75–100. On Nanjing (Nanking), see the essay by F.W. Mote, "The Transformation of Nanking, 1350–1400," in the same volume.

For the creation of the Ming city, see Susan Naquin, *Peking: Temples and City Life*, 1400-1900 (2000), ch. 4. A more popular if somewhat dated exposition is Nigel Cameron and Brian Brake, *Peking: A Tale of Three Cities* (1965), esp. 95–120.

The best all-around treatment of the Ming Great Wall and its larger context remains Arthur Waldron, *The Great Wall of China: from History to Myth* (1990).

Emperors
and Palaces

3

A foreigner visiting the Forbidden City for the first time is surprised and overwhelmed. He can make nothing of it, cannot grasp it at all. With little knowledge of China's historical and ethical background to warn him of what to expect, he is prepared to see a palace in the western sense of the word—one large building with perhaps a few dependencies, like Fontainebleau or Windsor. But instead he enters the mazes of a city within a city . . .

JULIET BREDON, PEKING (1931), 82

Twice the size of the Kremlin, four times the size of the Louvre, and ten times larger than Buckingham Palace, the Forbidden City is overwhelming (fig. 3.1). On any day tens of thousands of visitors throng the portals of the Noon Gate (Wu Men) and pour into the huge yard before the Hall of Supreme Harmony (Taihe Dian). Local guides, often with megaphones, elevate the cacophony.

3.1
View of Forbidden City
from Jing Shan

As essential monuments both of the city and of later Chinese architecture, the Ming–Qing palaces should not to be missed. The largest ensemble of pre-modern buildings to survive, they offer unparalleled opportunities to experience the material culture of the imperial institution. No one should denigrate the importance of the Forbidden City for understanding pre-modern China.

The Imperial City

The Forbidden City in Beijing is the largest and most important of imperial palace complexes to survive. Also rewarding, the Shenyang (formerly Mukden) Palace in Liaoning (ca. 1625) served as the seat of the Manchus before their conquest of the Ming in 1644. Qing emperors maintained and improved it. The Imperial Summer Retreat (Bishu Shanzhuang) at Chengde (Rehe or Jehol in Hebei) beckoned Qing rulers from the reign of Kangxi onwards, and became the nucleus of a magnificent array of Buddhist temples. In Nanjing the remains of the first Ming palaces (see Box, p. 70) occupy a city park, while the ruins of the unfinished Ming Zhongdu (ca. 1369) in Fengyang, Anhui, can also be visited.

In Ming times, the emperor's residence and court fit within a larger construct called the Imperial Palaces (*huang gong*). These comprised both the Forbidden City and those surrounding institutions, warehouses, workshops, and parks now designated the Imperial City. At Nanjing, the Ming palace measured about 750 m east–west by 800 m north–south, almost 200 m less deep than the Forbidden City in Beijing. The palace lay within a walled area 2 km east–west by 2.5 km north–south. At Beijing (see fig 2.7), the palaces (at 760 by 960 m) and the surrounding Imperial City (at 2.5 km by 2.7 km) were both larger, and the level terrain favored a regular plan. Because the precincts of the

THE SON OF HEAVEN

A visit to the Forbidden City provides a chance to understand a unique social class of one: the emperor (*huang di*) or Son of Heaven (*tian zi*). Each of these English terms has its pitfalls. Some historians object to "emperor" on the grounds that the supreme rulers of China's imperial era (ca. 221 BCE–CE 1912) were not true emperors because they did not rule over an aggregation of diverse peoples as, for example, Roman emperors did. These writers prefer such locutions as "sovereign" or "thearch" to register specific nuances of the Chinese institution. Of course, any English translation necessitates a compromise. The term coined for the Qin First Emperor (ca. 221 BCE), *huang di*, combined two ancient names for deities in an effort to establish his new and unique status as ruler of "all under Heaven." He had to be distinguished from the *wang* (kings) of defeated states. After Qin, *wang* normally becomes "prince" in English translations.

Qin court officials also recognized the power of a more ancient concept. The "Son of Heaven" was the ruler who received a mandate (*tian ming*) from the all-powerful force that controlled the universe, the supreme power, Heaven. From Qin and Han times onward, the emperor as Son of Heaven signified that his rule was not merely a result of political maneuvers or military might or even birth. This status was conferred by Heaven and justified by the ruler's virtue. In spite of many changes in the imperial institution between Qin-Han and the last two dynasties, this term remained in play, the power of its underlying concepts unfaded. The role of Heaven appears also in the names for imperial gates and palace halls: the main gate to the imperial city is the Gate of Heavenly Peace (Tian'an Men) [8 ▶].

A Chinese emperor simultaneously ruled the earth and served Heaven. He was a lone figure atop society, a ruler-bureaucrat, the essential officiant in observances directed toward Heaven, and patron of the Three Teachings (Buddhism, Confucianism, and Daoism), as well as scholarship and the arts. His behavior and moral stature determined the fate not just of his reign but also of society as a whole. Imagine what he thought and believed: That Heaven would send down omens and portents if he neglected his moral duties. That the designs woven into his robes as elaborate symbols of cosmic roles were meaningful, not mere artistic motifs. That the seat he occupied, the Dragon Throne, the rites he performed at the Altar to Heaven (Tian Tan) [16 ▶], the court gatherings at which he presided, all encapsulated his unique status as intermediary between the human and natural worlds and as sovereign of All under Heaven. We should assume that most Chinese rulers after 221 BCE believed these propositions as surely as we subscribe to the law of gravity, as natural facts of our world and our lives. The Ming and Qing Sons of Heaven enacted their roles on the stage of the Forbidden City.

By custom emperors are known by several locutions. Formal, pre-modern sources may employ their posthumous title, often of considerable length and hence unwieldy. From the Tang through Yuan, the emperor's posthumous "temple name" was generally preferred; this title established the ruler's position in the dynastic descent group. From Ming times onward, however, a single auspicious-sounding phrase, an era name (*nian hao*) came to designate the reign of an emperor. This term applied to the ruler himself, the practice followed here. Thus "the Yongle emperor" presided over the era of that name (1403–24); likewise Wanli (1573–1620) and Qianlong (1736–95). Each of these individuals bore family and personal names. Yongle was Zhu Di; Qianlong was Aisin Gioro Hongli.

Imperial City shifted south compared to Dadu, they
extended almost to the city's south wall. Residential
wards housing the bulk of the capital population stood
in the shadow of the Son of Heaven. Anyone making
a trip across the city navigated around his palaces.
Only the two long avenues running north from
Chongwen Men and Xuanwu Men crossed the city in
uninterrupted straight lines. Most east–west travel, on
the other hand, involved detours, either on the south
inside the Front Gate (Zhengyang Men) or north of
the palaces using bridges over the lakes. This obstacle
at the city's center remains in place today.

When Yongle began construction in earnest in the
sixth moon of 1417, laborers (usually numbered at one
million), artisans (said to be 230,000), factories, and vast
supplies of materiel were all in place. The builders
retained the alignment of the east and west walls of the
Yuan palace, but shifted its north and south limits south-
ward about 400 m and 500 m, respectively. They positioned the new palace front hall (called Fengtian Dian,
the present Taihe Dian) approximately where the front
gate of the Yuan Imperial City had been. The palace's
north wall ran south of the former Yuan rear palaces
(specifically the Yanchun Ge; compare fig. 1.8).

Earth from the newly dug moat and debris from
the Yuan palaces piled up north of the Forbidden City
to become Wansui Shan (later Jing Shan, known to
foreigners as Coal Hill; see fig. 6.25). This man-made
mound provided a protective screen across the north,
as had been true of the natural terrain both at Ming
Zhongdu and Nanjing. The mound insured good
fengshui; it quite literally "suppressed" (zhen) the former seat of Mongol power. Deep underneath Jing
Shan (height 47 m) foundations and other relics of
Khubilai Khan's palace must slumber. The shift south-
ward required repositioning the new city south wall.

Whereas the wall of Dadu ran along the south side of Chang'an Avenue, the Ming city wall was built 0.8 km further south, creating space for the long approach to the Gate of Heavenly Peace, flanking ministries, and altars. Since Yongle retained the east and west city walls of Dadu (see Ch. 2), the layout of Ming Beijing replicated much of Yuan Dadu. Moreover, when the rectangular Ming palace is taken as a module, the Ming city as a whole constitutes nine modules east to west and 5.5 modules north to south.

Unlike the palace, the Ming Imperial City is not a symmetrical figure, nor is it evenly disposed across the city axis. Its walls ran around the lakes west of the Forbidden City To accommodate various functions, the Ming builders also pushed the Yuan Imperial City walls further east, north, and west. On the east, after 1432, the wall moved further east to enclose a north-south canal (the path of modern Bei and Nan Heyan streets) that connected the Grand Canal to the northern lakes. The north and south gates of the Imperial City—Di'an Men and Tian'an Men [8 ▶]—were aligned on the city-palace axis, but the east and west gates—Dong'an Men and Xi'an Men—were not paired. The former led directly to the Forbidden City east gate (Donghua Men), while the latter served the road south of Wansui (Jing) Shan crossing the bridge over Bei Hai and Zhong-Nan Hai.

The walls of the Imperial City, about 6 m in height, were torn down by the city government in 1927, with the exception of the south wall linked to Tian'an Men (fig. 3.2). In 2001 the original path of the east wall was reclaimed as a pleasant strip park, where several features of this historic wall can be enjoyed. At the intersection of Jinyu Hutong and Nan Heyan, two sunken plazas expose stone work from Dong'an Men several meters below street level. These are the footings for the bridge that spanned the imperial canal when the wall ran inside (west of) that channel. Further north, near Zhang Zizhong Road, is a reconstructed segment of the Imperial City wall (about 25 m long) with red bricks capped by yellow-glazed tiles.

Another improvement of recent years is the Changpu He strip park inside the Imperial City wall running for about 600 m between Nan Heyan and the east end of Tian'an Men. This channel drained water from the western lakes, palace, and the Ancestral Temple into the Imperial Canal (Yu He) that then exited through the Water Gate (now the path of Zhengyi Road.) The Art Galley of Imperial City (Huang cheng Yishuguan, Changpu Heyan No. 9) has been opened near the west end of this park. In addition to permanent displays and an excellent model of the Imperial City, the museum presents changing exhibitions.

Very few of the support buildings for facilities that were the raison d'être for the Ming Imperial City survive. The Qing reduced the number of imperial services and warehouses, and the area became a mix of temples,

3.2
Imperial City wall,
Chang'an Avenue

residences, and shops. The most important survivor is the Imperial Archives (Huangshi Cheng) [9▶] on Nanchizi Street, a short walk north of Chang'an Avenue. Since virtually the entire area of the Imperial City is designated for "conservation" (see p. 22), many lesser sites will no doubt be restored and opened in years to come. The national leadership occupies portions of the western half of the Imperial City surrounding the lakes as offices and residences. The Altar to Soil and Grain and Ancestral Temple [13, 14▶] are discussed in Ch. 4 and Bei Hai [30▶] in Ch. 6.

The Approach to the Palace

Visitors to the Forbidden City traversed a lengthy sequence of gates and yards while moving from south to north. The Great Ming Gate (Da Ming Men, later renamed the Da Qing Men or Zhonghua Men; fig. 3.3) immediately north of the Front Gate began the first stage, a transition from the city's most bustling east-west link to hushed imperial precincts. A solid masonry mass with three portals, a mate to this now-lost gate survives at the entrance to the Ming Valley (the Red Gate). Walls running north enclosed the Thousand Pace Corridor (Qianbu Lang) which consisted of 144 bays used to store archives for the Six Ministries in the Ming period. Near the north end of this constricted approach, the space widened into a large plaza before Tian'an Men, closed off at east and west by similar gates. These were the East and West (or Left and Right) Chang'an Men, torn down in 1952 and the source for the name of the city's main east-west avenue. This T-shaped zone funneled traffic to the north.

Fu Xinian demonstrated that the dimensions of the rear palaces determined placement of the several gates on this approach (fig. 3.4). The north-south length of the Three Rear Palaces (at 218 m) when doubled generated the distance between the Wu Men

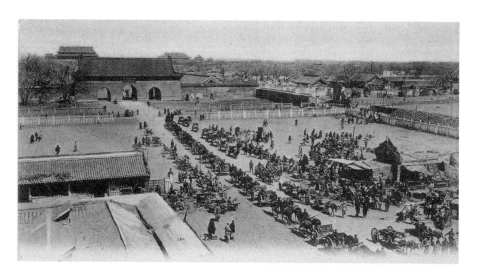

3.3
"Entrance Leading to the Forbidden-City," postcard by L. Wannieck, shows Peking carts lined up at the crossing known as "Chess-board Street" (Qipan Jie) north of Qian Men.

and Tian'an Men. When tripled it determined the interval between the latter and the Da Ming Men. Likewise the distance between the two Chang'an Gates equaled three times the width of the rear palace precinct. The overall distance from Da Ming Men to the rear wall of Wansui Shan (Jing Shan), moreover, came to thirteen times the length of the rear palaces. The inner court module, in turn, was laid out by using squares that were multiples of ten feet (one *zhang*). Thus the approach from the Gate of Heavenly Peace to the Three Great Halls can be scribed onto a grid of 10-zhang (100 foot) squares.

In the Ming, the areas flanking the long stem of this T-shaped approach were devoted to ministries of state and military commands. The expression "the east side manages life, the west side manages death" echoes this disposition. The five Chief Military Commissions occupied the west side with the Imperial Bodyguard and its prison, as well as the Court of Imperial Sacrifices and Office of Transmission. The Ministries— Personnel, Revenue, Rites, War, and Works—with the Imperial Clan Court, Court of State Ceremonial, Directorate of Astronomy, Imperial Academy of

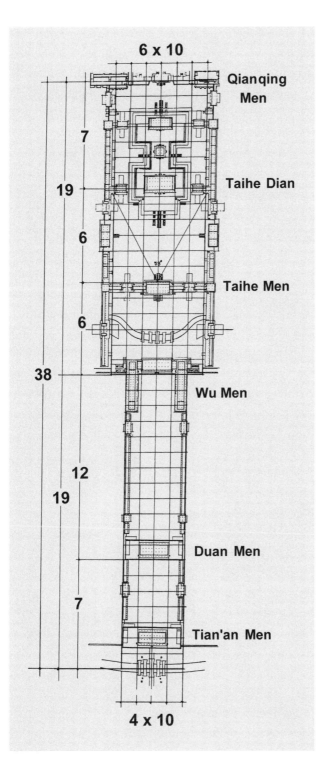

6 x 10

Qianqing
Men

7

19

Taihe Dian

6

Taihe Men

6

38

Wu Men

12

19

Duan Men

7

Tian'an Men

4 x 10

3.4
Palace approach and Outer Court, from Fu, *Sheji fangfa*, vol. 2, 26. Fu Xinian represents the approach from Tian'an Men to the Outer Court in ten *zhang* (100 feet) squares. By this measure the approach is four squares (400 feet) wide, while the outer court is six squares (600 feet) wide.

Medicine, Hanlin Academy, and Interpreters Institute filled an even larger area on the east. Thus all of the primary organs of state served at the beck and call of the emperor, but were excluded from the walled Imperial City. This concentration of state organs contrasts with the dispersed ministries of Yuan Dadu.

Many imperial ceremonies and government functions took place on this approach. The emperor's entourage proceeded down this path when he visited the Altar to Heaven (Tian Tan) for annual sacrifices. Imperial edicts were promulgated from the Gate of Heavenly Peace. An imperial marriage required processions up and down this approach, as did military expeditions going out on campaign or returning with their prisoners. The Ministries of Personnel and Justice also utilized the plaza. For example, civil service examination results were posted here (civil on the east, military on the west; see Box, p. 182). While the Allied Armies had transgressed this space and the palace in 1900, it remained off-limits to the civilian population until 1912, when the Chang'an gates first opened.

8 ▶
Gate of
Heavenly Peace
(Tian'an Men)

BUILT 1417; REBUILT
1465, 1651, 1970
NATIONAL REGISTER,
1961
CHANG'AN AVENUE,
TIAN'AN MEN SQUARE,
DONGCHENG

A silhouette of this gate (fig. 3.5) became the centerpiece for the national emblem of the People's Republic. Designed by a committee of eminent architects, the emblem memorializes the proclamation of the new regime by Mao Zedong on October 1, 1949, now celebrated as National Day. In the Ming capital this gate was named Chengtian Men to certify that the ruling dynasty had "received Heaven's Mandate." Mao's decision to announce the formal establishment of New China here thus co-opted longstanding imperial symbolism and charisma, implicitly claiming a mandate for the Communist state. The emblem is prominently displayed over the central portal with Mao's portrait. The formal abdication ceremony for

3.5
Gate of Heavenly Peace, with banners reading: "Long Live the People's Republic of China," (left) and "Long Live the Great Unity of the World's Peoples" (right)

the last emperor, Pu Yi, also took place here on the 25th day of the 12th lunar month of Xuantong 3 (1911). Thus this site witnessed both the demise of Imperial China and the inception of People's China.

The first Ming gate structure had a *paifang* on the podium (see Box, p. 186), but it burned in the Tianshun reign of Yingzong (1457). The new gate was five bays across by three in depth under a double eave. After another fire in 1644, the Qing rulers both redesigned the gate house and renamed it the Gate of Heavenly Peace. The Qing gate house was nine bays wide and five deep.

The underlying module for the podium and gate utilizes a square derived from the height and width of the eight bays that flank the center (fig. 3.6). Thus the podium is two squares tall and nineteen wide, an extra-wide central bay flanked by eighteen regular squares. The podium measures 119 m east-west and 40 m north-south. The walls are battered so that the dimensions at top are slightly smaller; the height

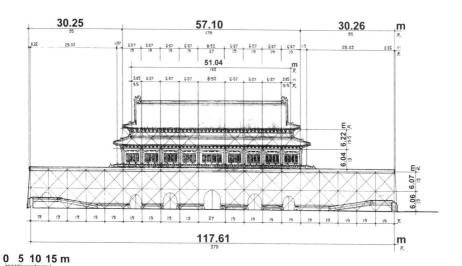

0   5   10   15 m

3.6
Elevation derived from
modules, from Fu, *Sheji
fangfa*, vol. 2, 193

reaches 12 m. This is a mass of city wall bricks punctured by five barrel-vault portals, the central one largest and those on both sides smaller in two steps. The lowest levels of the podium are courses of white marble shaped as a Mount Sumeru base (*Xumi zuo*) like the halls of state in the Outer Court. Twin stairways climb to the top level from the rear wrapping around both ends. The gate house stretches 57 m across the podium with a depth of 27 m. Thus it is eight squares with an extra-wide central bay. That central bay is 8.5 m across while the flanking ones are 6 m each. The lower eave is 8 m tall, the upper eave 14 m. The height of the gate is 34 m.

In front of the gate runs the Outer Golden Water (Jinshui) connected to Nan Hai on the west and to channels exiting the Imperial City at its southeast corner destined for the city moat. Seven white marble bridges built by Kangxi in 1690 cross this water course, five of them aligned with the portals of the podium. Pairs of monumental (9.6 m) stone columns (*huabiao*) erected in 1465 and carved with dragons spiraling up their shafts complement the gate both on the south and north (fig. 3.7). The crouching animals atop these columns face north inside the gate and south outside. They are said to "watch the lord exit" and "await the lord's return," respectively. A similar arrangement will be seen inside the Red Gate at the Ming Valley.

The gate, dating from 1970, is a near replica of the seventeenth-century design with modern structural elements and other modifications to accommodate state functions. A flag pole and viewing stands had been added as early as 1950, and there were further efforts at modernization in that decade with restrooms, an elevator, and viewing stands. The reconstruction of 1970 also addressed the danger of earthquakes by reconfiguring the framing.

Visitors can ascend the podium for a commanding view of Tian'an Men Square and central Beijing. The virtually identical Gate of Uprightness (Duan Men) directly north sits astride the axis but without any walls on each side.

3.7
Huabiao inside Tian'an Men

9 ▷
Imperial Archives
(Huangshi Cheng)

MING, 1534
NATIONAL REGISTER,
1982
NO. 16 NANCHIZI
STREET, DONGCHENG

The imperial state created voluminous documents. Written records were the life blood of the bureaucratic culture of the court and government, and of the officials, ministers, and emperors who generated them. Both provincial and court officials created documents for the ministries in the capital and for the emperor's eyes. When these were acted upon, multiple copies came down from the throne and its secretaries to be circulated. Originals and copies, drafts and finished work were filed away in the court archive. Yet relatively few of the hundreds of thousands of documents that once existed survive from before the Ming. It is not until the Qing that really large quantities of records from the imperial government make research productive.

In the Ming government the Grand Secretariat (Nei Ge) was the interface between the ministries and empire-wide officialdom and the court and emperor. Their archives were situated on the east side of the Forbidden City, south of the Hall of Literary Glory (Wenhua Dian; see fig. 3.16). Two buildings still stand: the Red Document Archive (Hongben Ku), named after memorials submitted to the throne, and the Veritable Record Archive (Shilu Ku), named after the chronicle of the court normally produced for each reign as a first draft of dynastic history. These are large masonry and wooden frame buildings parallel to the south palace wall with iron-clad windows. While they were very secure, they were not fireproof, nor did they address the problem of dampness. They have not been opened to the public.

In 1492 a Ming court official named Qiu Rui memorialized the throne on the importance of constructing a truly secure archive for the growing wealth of documents as well as imperial portraits and other valuables. Qiu wrote that "this age depends on them to know the past; later ages will depend on them to know the present." This is the classic rationale for keeping documents and indeed writing history in pre-modern China. Although the throne approved Qiu's advice, no action was taken until 1534–36. The site then selected was in the southeast corner of the Imperial City near several palaces known collectively as the Eastern Garden (Dong Yuan) or Southern Within (Nan Nei). The main hall (fig. 3.8) of nine bays runs east-west with a broad stone terrace in front. Two smaller halls facing inward flank the courtyard. Although the main gate was placed at the center of the south wall aligned with the main hall, the actual approach was from the west side (Nanchizi Street). These buildings were entirely of masonry construction without any flammable wood, either in the structural frame or in the decorative brackets and roof support (fig. 3.9). Hence they are called "beamless halls" (*wuliang dian*). The walls of the main hall are 6 m thick, so interior space is limited. Within the vaulted interior, stone platforms carry large, metal-covered coffers for document storage. The design was both secure and fireproof, and also resisted the damp. Today 152 coffers remain in place.

3.8
Main hall, Imperial Archives

3.9
Name placard of Huangshi
Cheng in Chinese (left) and
Manchu (right)

In the Ming the *Veritable Records,* imperial decrees, and the *Imperial Genealogy* were all stored here as well as a copy of the great *Encyclopedia of the Yongle Era (Yongle Dadian).* When the Qing occupied the capital, they removed the Ming records to the Grand Secretariat Archives inside the palace mentioned above, and deposited their own records in the Huangshi Cheng, along with the *Collected Statutes (Da Qing Huidian)* and seals of their generals. These Qing Archives were left in the hands of Pu Yi after 1912, but became the property of the Palace Museum after 1925. Many were destroyed or even sold as scrap, but others fortuitously were purchased by a scholar to become the core of collections now divided between Beijing and Taibei. In 1933, many Qing records were transferred to Nanjing (then the Nationalist capital), and later moved to Taiwan (see Box, p. 122). The documents left behind in Beijing became the property of the National Archives in 1955, and have been held in the No. 1 Historical Archives within the Forbidden City in buildings built into the wall north of Xi Hua Men. The official estimate of Qing archives is 14 million, a figure that must undercount the actual number of individual items. Chinese and foreign scholars with access to these primary sources have been writing new histories of all aspects of the Qing in recent decades. (Evelyn Rawski's work is often cited below.)

This site has been closed in recent years, with the exception of an art gallery in one side hall.

The Forbidden City

A visit to the Forbidden City is a trip through layers of history. The site was first developed under the Mongols in the 1270s as the Khan's Danei (Ch. 1). Traces of this compound must lie within the present-day palace, even if they are impossible now to recover. The building campaigns of 1417–20 (Ch. 2) excavated the area within the new moat and walls, and filled that great excavation with pounded earth and other fill, foundations, and paving. Hence most of what is now underfoot dates to the fifteenth century. In the case of courtyards and walkways used by visitors, however, the actual pavements were resurfaced in recent decades. The foundations and terraces that carry every architectural feature, from side galleries to main halls, also date to the fifteenth century, but they have been re-clad in later (Qing) white marble. The timber-frame halls with their lacquer-red columns, polychrome brackets and beams, and yellow-glazed roof tiles are with few exceptions buildings from Qing efforts between 1679 and 1888 (see Box, p. 118). Some of these halls and other features were redesigned in later centuries. Thus, the Hall of Supreme Harmony (Taihe Dian) grew in the Qing from nine bays to eleven, and the screen walls connecting it to each side replaced earlier covered galleries. But if the master plan of the Forbidden City retains a Ming design over a Yuan footprint, and the structures themselves are Qing reconstructions, the surfaces throughout are even more recent. Continual maintenance has been the norm for the palaces. The cycle of retiling and repainting is unending. The Palace Museum has a master plan for improvements which will play out until 2020. Thus we put our hands to twenty-first century paint as we step over an older if not original threshold. From this perspective, the Forbidden City is variously and simultaneously a thirteenth-century, fifteenth-century, Qing-period, and contemporary site.

MAJOR FIRES IN THE FORBIDDEN CITY

Dating any building within the Forbidden City is problematic because of its history of frequent fires. The table below lists many but not all of the fires that led to renewed construction. In most cases new structures replicated the old, but in some instances substantial revisions were effected.

Reign Period	Year	Structure
Yongle	1421	Three Great Halls
	1422	Qianqing Gong
Zhengtong	1449	Wenyuan Ge
Hongzhi	1498	Qingning Gong
Zhengde	1514	Qianqing and Kunning Gong
Jiajing	1557	Outer Court, Wu Men
Wanli	1596	Qianqing and Kunning Gong
	1597	Huangji Dian (Outer Court)
Kangxi	1679	Taihe Dian
Qianlong	1758	Galleries of Outer Court
Jiaqing	1797	Qianqing Gong and Jiaotai Dian
Guangxu	1888	Taihe Men
Republic	1923	Jianfu Gong

Source: Shan and Yu, *Zijincheng xuehui lunwenji* (1997), 343–44

Construction of the Forbidden City spanned four periods, as first pointed out by Shan Shiyuan, a senior scholar of the Palace Museum. The first episode was the period from 1417 to 1420, when most basic work was accomplished prior to the formal dedication of the new capital in February, 1421 (Ch. 2). Not all was complete by that date, and in any event a calamitous fire struck the Three Great Halls of State within three months. Yongle asked for criticism from his counselors at this time; some were subsequently punished for their responses. Thereafter yet another fire burned the emperor's residence, the Qianqing Gong (12th intercalary month of 1422).

Completion of the palaces was delayed until the reign of Zhu Qizhen (r. 1436–63, also known as Yingzong) whose rule spanned three eras: Zhengtong, Jingtai (when he was captured by the Mongols and effectively deposed), and Tianshun (when he returned to the throne). During the 1440s, after two decades of indecision, it was finally decided to make Beijing the permanent capital, and only then were efforts made to rebuild ruined throne halls and to complete unfinished tasks such as the city gates and altars. In this period the southeast quadrant of the Imperial City was developed as the Nan Nei; it was here that Yingzong was sequestered while his brother the Jingtai emperor ruled. The recently restored Pudu Si (Mahakala Temple, fig. p. 18) now stands on this site.

A third phase of construction took place during the lengthy reign of the Jiajing emperor (Zhu Houcong, r. 1522–66). Several major fires laid waste to the Outer Court (1522, 1525, 1531, and especially 1557). Rebuilding was accomplished by 1562. Jiajing himself preferred to reside around the lakes west of the

History of the Palace

Forbidden City, and was even blamed when one of his palaces there went up in flames. Rather than move back to the Qianqing Gong, he constructed a luxurious new palace west of Bei Hai (now the location of the Beijing National Library). Jiajing also patronized many city temples, and constructed the Dagao Xuandian west of Wansui Shan. (In 1542, one hundred of his palaces ladies were put to death after an attempted assassination.) The Ming construction history of the palace continued under the Wanli emperor (Zhu Yijun, r. 1573–1619) after yet another serious fire in 1597. Rebuilding was delayed until 1615, with completion in 1627. This was a period of decline (see the discussion of the Dingling below), and a number of Ming palaces surrounding the lakes and in the Nan Nei seem to have disappeared.

For their part, the Manchus pursued renovations of the palaces with some regularity after 1644, a fourth period. Thus Kangxi (Xuanye, r. 1662–1722) rebuilt the Taihe Dian in 1679; Qianlong refashioned the galleries of the Outer Court in 1758; Jiaqing (Yongyan, r. 1796–1820) rebuilt the Qianqing Gong and Jiaotai Dian in 1797, and so on. Less extensive re-workings of the Inner Court characterized the late nineteenth century [12 ▶]. The palaces were by no means frozen in time after 1421. Moreover, the actual look of the palaces changed. For the appearance of the Ming halls, the visitor must investigate elsewhere (see below).

Plan of the
Palace

An aerial image of the Forbidden City clearly displays its overall plan (fig. 3.10; compare fig. 3.16). A regular rectangle defined by smooth walls and a wide moat, the palace interior is organized as three axes (routes, *lu*) in parallel and two zones front and back. The central axis defined by the Noon Gate (Wu Men, south) and Gate of Martial Spirit (Shenwu Men, north) is dominated by the wide expanse of the several yards (*jin*) leading to and surrounding the Three Great Halls of State (San Da Dian), the Outer Court. The Noon Gate marks the transition from the palace approach to the first of these yards. The plaza within its arms was important for certain ceremonies in its own right [10 ▶], but is narrower than the yard inside sliced side

3.10
Aerial View of the Forbidden City Hou, *Beijing lishi ditu ji*, cover

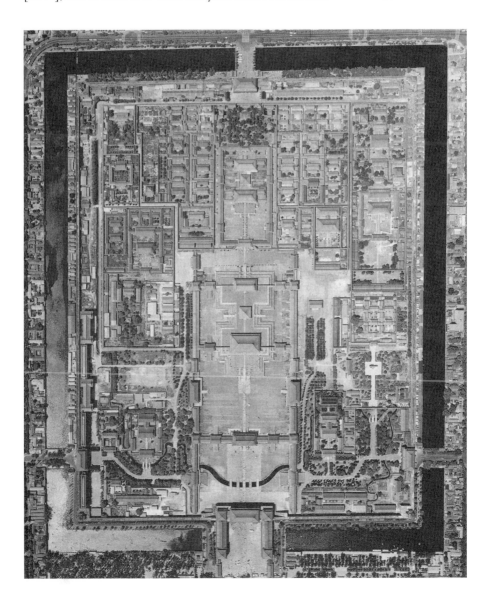

THE PALACE MUSEUM

With the Great Wall, the Palace Museum (Gu Gong Bowuyuan) is probably the site most often frequented by visitors. The Chinese name means "Museum of the Former Palace," a reference to the twenty-four emperors of the Ming and Qing who resided here from 1421 to 1924. It should not be confused with the Palace Museum in Taibei, known in Chinese as the National Palace Museum (Guoli Gu Gong Bowuyuan). This is the home of palace treasures removed to Taiwan in 1949 by the Nationalist government. Without denigrating that collection, it must be pointed out that most of the palace holdings—the works of art and archives as well as furnishings—remained in Beijing, ensconced in the largest complex of historic architecture in all of China. Thus the Taibei Palace Museum may be said to offer a splendid display of imperial treasures without, however, their larger contextual setting.

The Palace Museum has a complex history, tied at every stage with the turbulent times that accompanied its birth and first sixty years. The Museum officially opened on October 10, 1925, about a year after the last emperor, Pu Yi, was forced to remove himself and his modest court. Parts of the Forbidden City were co-opted for museum purposes as early as 1912, and by 1915 a Government Museum or Antiquities Museum (Gu Qiwu Chenlie Suo) was operating in the front part of the palace with the Outer Court serving as display halls. A storage facility in European style (Baoyun Lou) was built next to the Wuying Dian in this period. Many holdings of Shenyang and Chengde were transferred to the palace in this period.

Shortly after Pu Yi left, a committee was formed to take an inventory of the Forbidden City. They enumerated more than a million items in their investigation, which was not complete when the museum opened its doors. In its first year, only the central axis of the Inner Court was accessible to the public with entry through the north gate and a circuitous prescribed path that led through the Imperial Flower Garden and the Three Rear Palaces.

By the 1930s, Japanese militarism in the Northeast raised alarm in government circles. In January, 1933 the first of five shipments was sent from the palace to Shanghai. All were shifted to Nanjing (the Nationalist capital) by December, 1936. In this interval, a selection of treasures (93 cases holding 735 items) was carried by the Royal Navy to London for the great International Exhibition of Chinese Art at the Royal Academy from November, 1935 to March, 1936. (They were among 3300 exhibits viewed by 420,000 people, a true blockbuster.) The palace objects were displayed in Shanghai and Nanjing before and after exhibition abroad.

Increasing tensions with Japan led to a fateful decision by summer, 1937, the time of the Marco Polo Bridge incident. Three shipments (totaling 16,698 cases) were organized and transported from Nanjing to southwestern China by three different routes between August, 1937 and September, 1939. One batch went up the Yangzi River to Hankou, then south through Changsha and Guilin ending at Baxian, Sichuan. Another lot followed the same initial route and then moved up through the Gorges to Chongqing ending at Leshan, Sichuan. A final batch went north and west via train to Zhengzhou and Baoji before moving south to Chengdu ending at Emei, Sichuan. Warehouses and caves were used during the war years, and according to museum curators, none of the precious shipments were lost in transit or destroyed by military action. Indeed, during these years, a selection of objects was sent to Moscow, and several exhibitions were held in Sichuan.

After the Japanese surrender in 1945, which was re-enacted in front of the Taihe Dian on October 10 at 10:10 a.m., the next major event in the life of the palace collections was the removal of 2972 cases of treasures from the mainland to Taiwan between December, 1948 and February, 1949. Those objects were stored initially near Taizhong in a sugar warehouse, and after 1965 housed in a modern facility in the outskirts of Taibei. Thus a portion of the selection made in 1933 never returned to Beijing. Officially this collection numbers about 600,000 items, the majority archives and books. Its 50,000 objects include ancient bronzes and jades, ceramics, paintings, and calligraphy. Since 1945, the Beijing Palace Museum has regained many objects that left the palace in the early twentieth century (purloined by Pu Yi and others) through various arrangements including purchases and patriotic gifts. The collection has continued to grow by these means and by the addition of recently excavated objects as well. Today the Palace Museum probably has more holdings than when Pu Yi departed.

to side by the curve of the Golden Water (Jinshui). The next step and yard is larger still and overwhelmed by the looming triple terrace that carries the Three Great Halls. Walls flanking the Hall of Supreme Harmony (Taihe Dian) [11 ▶] delimit a final yard dominated by the throne halls. The Outer Court on axis is complemented by two lesser palace ensembles on the east and west secondary axes: the Hall of Literary Glory (Wenhua Dian) and Hall of Military Eminence (Wuying Dian), each in a park-like setting tied by the Jinshui to the central axis.

A wide alley fronts the Inner Court, location of the Three Rear Palaces (Hou San Gong). These halls occupy just one-fourth the area of the Outer Court, but replicate the dumbbell-shaped terraces that carry the rectangular front and rear halls and a square hall on the bridge between. Behind them, in an area about half as large is the Imperial Flower Garden (Yuhua Yuan; Ch. 6). At either side are the East and West Six Palaces [12 ▶]. With supporting buildings at rear, these two units occupy the same area as the Rear Three Palaces, but are set back (north). The rear palaces residential blocks still left considerable room for other palaces. Over time those areas were filled in, notably with the Hall of Imperial Supremacy (Huangji Dian) on the northeast (Qianlong's retirement palace), and several large palaces on the west for Ming and Qing empresses.

The relationship of the area of the rear palaces to the Outer Court is 1:4 as discussed above (see fig. p. 25). These areas were themselves laid out using squares of 5 or 10 *zhang* (ten-foot lengths, 1 zhang = 3.19 m). Thus the rear palaces are seven 5-zhang squares across (east–west) and thirteen 5-zhang squares deep (north–south). The Three Great Halls and their galleries were laid out by measuring six 10-zhang squares side to side and thirteen 10-zhang squares front to back (fig. 3.4). The 10-zhang squares were also used for the axial approach from Tian'an Men: twelve 10-zhang squares run from the Duan Men to Wu Men, another seven link the Outer Jinshui Bridges to the Duan Men. The width of this corridor is four 10-zhang squares.

The utility of these squares can also be read in the disposition of every component of the Outer Court yards. Consider the yard between Wu Men and Taihe Men. This space is a rectangle, six squares east–west and four squares north–south. The central axis, at the center of the Taihe Men gate house, is equidistant (three squares) from both sides. The five marble bridges spanning the Inner Jinshui occupy two squares across axis, set one square back from the south row. The gates that flank the yard have their mid-points aligned on the north limit of this two-square rectangle. Likewise the two small gates on the north flanking Taihe Men are precisely centered on a line one square from each side. This rigorous geometry is interrupted, of course, by the bending channel of the Jinshui. The water enters from the west in the third row of squares, swings down to the south to traverse squares in the middle of the second row, and then bends up north again symmetrically on the east side. Like the three gates that precede it (Tian'an Men, Duan Men, and the central portion of Wu Men), Taihe Men is two squares wide.

Walls and Moats

This carefully constructed ensemble of yards sits within a moat and walls that were the last lines of defense for the Son of Heaven (fig. 3.11). Dug 20 m from the base of the walls, the moat is 52 m wide with a depth of 5 m. A stone lining protects the sides, and a low wall of city wall bricks runs along the margins. The channel was known colloquially as the "tube river" (Tongzi He) because of this lining. Although Beijing is seemingly a flat plain, the elevation does incline generally from northwest to southeast. The Yuan engineers who designed Dadu took advantage of this slope when they dug the many channels that supply the city and palace. The Ming inherited this good

3.11
Palace moat

engineering. Since the north end of the palace is 1.2 m higher in elevation than the south, water from lakes on the north and west flows by gravity into the moat and then exits at the southeast near the Ancestral Temple. Secondary channels entered the palace at the north-west corner to supply the Inner Jinshui (see fig. 3.17). The Outer Jinshui draws its water from Nan Hai.

The water in the moat was both a defensive barrier and useful if fire broke out. It also enhances the scenery of the palace. Lotuses grown in the moats from the late Ming onward supplied the court kitchens and were also sold on the local market. Ice blocks were harvested in winter and stored underground within the palace for summer use. Several ice houses survive in the city.

The walls of the palace reach a height of 10 m; the base is 8.6 m and the width at top 6.7 m. Their entire circuit is crenellated with the same city wall bricks that cover their vertical surfaces in three layers (see Box, p. 79). An estimated twelve million bricks were required for the palace walls. The walls were reached

3.12
Ramps ascending wall at
Shenwu Men

by ramps at each gate (fig. 3.12). A visit to the refurbished gallery within Wu Men allows the visitor to experience this vantage point.

As the main gate for the Forbidden City (fig. 3.13), Wu Men outranks most structures within the palace. Looming on axis, it both controlled access to the court and Son of Heaven and was itself a major stage for the sovereign. The largest structure in the Forbidden City, the podium is aligned with the south wall of the palace and stretches east-west for 126 m (400 feet in Ming measure) with an augmented height of 13 m (40 Ming feet); the palace walls generally are 10 m. This podium contains five passages, three (each about 5 m wide) on or parallel to the central axis and two others at the corners (fig. 3.14) where the immense arms extend forward. Those arms are 25 m wide (80 Ming feet), and run south, across the line of the moat for another 79 m. Thus a square plaza measuring 240 Ming feet on each side fronts the gate house. The main difference between this gate and those from earlier periods is the solid mass of these arms rather than thin screen walls. On top of the podium are the main gate house, nine bays wide and five deep with a double eave, and four square pavilions: two forward and two flanking the gate house. They are three-bays square, or five bays counting porches. Wide, roofed corridors link the two rear pavilions (a drum pavilion and a bell pavilion, respectively) to the gate house, and again to the forward pavilions. This ensemble was sometimes called the Five Phoenix Towers (Wu Feng Lou).

Wu Men fulfilled multiple roles. For officials, it was the entrance to the Outer Court whenever a court assembly there was convened. At the first striking of the drum, they formed in ranks; on the second drum, they filed in following officials of the Ministry

◄ 10
Noon (Meridian)
Gate (Wu Men)

BUILT 1420; REBUILT
1558, 1647
NATIONAL REGISTER,
1961;
WORLD HERITAGE
SITE, 1987
FORBIDDEN CITY

of Rites. The central portal was reserved for the emperor, while that on the right (east) served nobility and that on the left (west) high-ranking officials. Most of those attending a large court event therefore used the two outside "arm pit gates." For the emperors the Wu Men had special functions. With a throne placed in the central bay (9 m wide), it became a venue for the Son of Heaven to hold court with a large audience. For example, on the fifteenth day of the first month of the New Year, the Ming emperors by custom celebrated the Lantern Festival by sharing *yuan shao* (sticky rice treats) with court officials. Similar holiday celebrations took place at the Duanwu (fifth of the fifth) and Mid-Autumn (fifteenth of the ninth) festivals. The Wu Men was also the site where a new calendar was presented each year, lowered in a special phoenix tray to expectant officials below. Military commanders returning with prisoners made their presentations here as well (fig. 3.15).

Punishing officials took place here in the Ming, a graphic demonstration of the autocratic style of the rulers of that dynasty. Ray Huang writes:

The first two memorialists were beaten sixty strokes in front of the Meridian Gate with whipping clubs. . . . The soldiers at the Silk Robe Guard always had a political sense of how exactly the beating should be administered, and in this case the wrath of the grand-secretary was carried out in full force. Thus the first dozen strokes had already ripped the skin of the victims; the successive blows simply kneaded human flesh with blood-soaked whipping clubs. One of the victims lost consciousness; it was a miracle that he survived. Another survivor, it was noticed, lost one buttock. After the beating the soldiers carried the offending memorialists away on canvas sheets and dumped them on the pavement outside the Imperial City.

1587: A YEAR OF NO SIGNIFICANCE (1981), 24

A traditional saying alludes to "execution at the Meridian Gate," but such punishments did not happen there. In the Ming, the city's West Market (at Xi Dan) was the venue for executions; in the Qing, the location was Caishikou in the Outer City.

The other three palace gates are also impressive. Their gate houses, five bays across but only a single bay deep, are skirted by porches under their lower eave.

3.14
Noon Gate officials' entrance

3.15
"The Emperor Daoguang reviewing his Guards, Palace of Peking," steel engraving by Thomas Allom, *China Illustrated*, ca. 1842; author's collection

Thus they are notionally seven bays by three with hipped roofs. Three square portals penetrate their massive podiums, which are several times thicker than the palace walls. Ramps on both sides allowed foot soldiers and horses to climb the walls.

The East and West Glorious (or Flowery) Gates (Dong Hua Men, Xi Hua Men) served court officials as they came and went, but also the Wenhua Dian and Wuying Dian, each a short distance within. The former was used by the heir in Ming times (note the nine rows of eight bosses each on the Dong Hua Men door panels, a step down from a nine by nine grid), while the Wuying Dian was intended for the Ming emperor's leisure. (This compound became famous for the palace editions produced here in the Qing period.) The West Flowery Gate also gave the palace access to the Western Gardens (Xi Yuan, the present Zhong-Nan Hai). The palace north gate was known first as Xuanwu Men (Gate of the Dark Warrior), an allusion to the ill-omened northern quadrant. It was renamed Shenwu Men (Gate of Martial Spirit) in the reign of Kangxi to avoid the character Xuan in his personal name (Xuanye). It became the front door to the Palace Museum when it first opened. The large characters over the portals are the calligraphy of Guo Moruo (1892–1978) added in 1971.

Three Great Halls

The two dozen Ming and Qing emperors acted out their roles as all-powerful rulers in several palace venues, but the grandest stage for their ceremonial duties was the Outer Court (*wai chao*), the large yards that hold the Three Great Halls of State (fig. 3.16). Court routines changed over the Ming and Qing, and Qing rituals in particular modified the usage of the palace. For much of the Ming, daily court was held at the Gate of Serving Heaven (Fengtian Men) just north of the

Jinshui (fig. 3.17). This gate was renamed Huangji Men or Imperial Ultimate Gate in 1562 and became Taihe Men after 1645 (fig. 3.18). By contrast, the usual daily court venue for many early Qing emperors was the Qianqing Men, south gate of the rear palaces (fig. 3.16-j). For much of Qing, however, the Hall of Mental Cultivation (Yangxin Dian) was favored (fig. 3.16-o).

Ceremonies that required the Three Halls were limited to accession of the new emperor, which happened irregularly, the annual celebration of the sovereign's birth date, the winter solstice, and the New Year. On these occasions in the Qing, as many as 20,000 persons might have participated. That number would encompass the emperor with his own attendants and guards, the highest court officials and members of the Manchu nobility, a complement of lesser officials of the

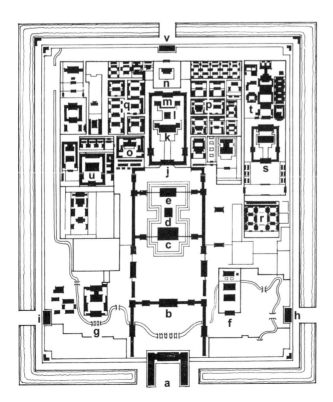

3.16
Plan of the Forbidden City, showing: (a) Wu Men, (b) Taihe Men, (c) Taihe Dian, (d) Zhonghe Dian, (e) Baohe Dian, (f) Wenhua Dian, (g) Wuying Dian, (h) Donghua Men, (i) Xihua Men, (j) Qianqing Men, (k) Qianqing Gong, (l) Jiaotai Dian, (m) Kunning Gong, (n) Yuhua Yuan, (o) Yangxin Dian, (p) East Six Palaces, (q) West Six Palaces, (r) Nan San Suo, (s) Ningshou Gong, (t) Qianlong garden, (u) Cining Gong, (v) Shenwu Men

court and capital, members of the imperial honor guard holding banners, parasols, and other paraphernalia, as well as musicians and attendants minding the incense burners. Without such a full house, the setting was wasted. Major events transpired before or near dawn, with the rising sun on the east gradually brightening the sky and illuminating the yards. The cracking of long bull whips to signal the actions of the officials, the music performed as they filed in, the rustling of stiff robes as those in attendance bowed and knelt to strike their

3.17
Marble bridges spanning
Inner Jinshui

3.18
Gate of Supreme Harmony

foreheads (kowtow) on the pavement, and the pungent aroma of burning pine needles must have created an unforgettable atmosphere. The paraphernalia employed for the imperial honor guard is now handsomely displayed in galleries on the west side of the yards before and after the Gate of Supreme Harmony. Readers are encouraged to view Bernardo Bertolucci's film *The Last Emperor* (1988) for an evocative recreation.

The architectural setting of the Three Great Halls expresses symbolism and aesthetic choices that characterize the Forbidden City as a whole. The yard is open to the blue sky, the round dome of Heaven, and strictly aligned with the cardinal directions. From the perspective of a Ming or Qing Son of Heaven, the squared shape of the Outer Court echoes the square shape of Earth, and the emperor is central (on axis), elevated (literally, both atop the terraces of the great halls and on his throne), and south-facing to receive the full power of the sun (*yang*). The open yard is paved but utterly bereft of plants or shade. The most important actors, immediately below the emperor, occupied the

3.19
Hall of Supreme Harmony

central, forward, and elevated stations on the moon terrace or at the front (north) of the yard, while lesser officials filled out peripheral positions. Surrounding gates, halls, and galleries accommodated support functions and lesser persons who served at court. Movement is directed by the many stone pathways, ramps, and gates. A brilliant, glistening white marble covers all surfaces of these various levels. The timber-frame structures by contrast are bright lacquer-red columns and dull blood-red plaster walls. The palette of decorative painting on beams, brackets, and ceilings incorporates costly gold, blue (lapis), and green (malachite). All roofs are yellow-glazed tile, a color reserved for the emperor.

Underlying codes distinguished the rank of buildings. Nine, the imperial number, was utilized as the underlying multiple for spaces occupied by the emperor. Lesser odd numbers (7, 5, and 3) were used for halls and gates of second-, third-, and fourth-rank.

3.20
Hall of Middle Harmony

Roofs were also graded: a double eave outranked a single one, and a gable roof was outranked by a hip-and-gable one and that in turn by a hipped roof. Thus the Ming Fengtian Dian (Qing Taihe Dian), the ultimate palace hall, was first nine (and then eleven) bays across by five in depth, under a double eave hipped roof (fig. 3.19). The Ming Huagai Dian (Qing Hall of Middle Harmony, Zhonghe Dian), which in the Ming served as a banqueting hall and in the Qing seems to have been a waiting area for the emperor before he went on stage, was the least important of the Three Halls (fig. 3.20). It is three bays square (or five with porch) under a pyramidal single-eave roof. Finally, the Ming Qinshen Dian (the Qing Hall of Preserving Harmony, Baohe Dian) was nine bays across and four deep under a double eave with a hip-and-gable roof (fig. 3.21). Flanking gates off axis naturally were single eave structures of five bays. The number of roof ornaments was also tied to rank (see Box, p. 140).

3.21
Hall of Preserving
Harmony

11▶
Hall of Supreme Harmony (Taihe Dian)

BUILT 1420; REBUILT
1441, 1562, 1615, 1627,
AND 1646; REMODELED
1669; REBUILT 1698
NATIONAL REGISTER,
1961; WORLD HERITAGE
SITE, 1987
FORBIDDEN CITY

3.22
Terraces of Outer Court

Standing on an immense three-tier terrace 9 m above the pavement, the Hall of Supreme Harmony (see fig. 3.19) commands the most prestigious position within the palace, the city, and indeed the realm. This area of the Outer Court, its domain, comprises one-sixth of the entire Forbidden City. To approach the throne here, one first transits the yard between the Noon Gate (Wu Men) and Gate of Supreme Harmony (Taihe Men). That gate (see fig. 3.18) is an impressive nine bays by four elevated 3.4 m above the paving, and flanked by two five-bay gates. Its yard is about 20,000 square meters. Passing through it, one then enters the even grander yard (about 36,000 square meters) of the Taihe Dian. Fronted by a large moon terrace, it looms over this segment of the Outer Court. Walls beside the hall screen our view northward and mask the area devoted to the Hall of Middle Harmony (Zhonghe Dian) and Hall of Preserving Harmony (Baohe Dian).

The terraces that carry the three halls are a debt to now-lost Song and Yuan imperial palaces (fig. 3.22).

Huge blocks of marble quarried in Fangshan District about 50 km southwest of the city were installed on axis for ramps over which the imperial palanquin was carried. The largest of these blocks is 16 by 3 by 1.7 m, and said to weight over 200 tons. Stonework facing the three terraces comprises a Mount Sumeru base with broad foot, recessed waist, and projecting cornice. Water spouts (fig. 3.23) at the corners and at intervals along the margins spew runoff in the rain; there are 1142 by official count. To promote runoff, there is more than a meter difference between the topmost terrace margins and the halls at center.

3.23
Rain spout

The hall itself is an eleven-bay-wide structure five bays in depth (figs. 3.24). This renovation from nine bays was carried out in the reign of Kangxi (1669) by one Liang Jiu, a master carpenter whose family had been in the employ of the palace for generations stretching back to Nanjing. The revised plan accommodated fifty-five bays with an area of 2377 sq m. This in turn required seventy-two huge columns; they

3.24
Plan of Hall of Supreme Harmony, from Shan and Yu, *Zijincheng xuehui*, 212

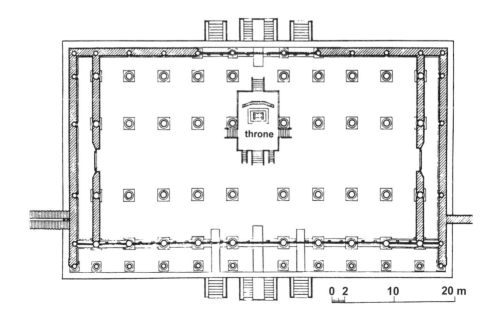

throne

0 2   10   20 m

stand almost 13 m tall with diameters of a meter. The
first bay under the lower eave serves as a shallow
porch. Door panels and windows separate the open
porch from the interior, which is otherwise undivided
except for masonry walls at each end enclosing the
outermost bays. Thus the real interior space is nine
bays across by four in depth. While the central bay of
the façade is 8.5 m wide, the eight flanking bays are
uniformly 5.5 m, and the terminal bays a mere 3.6 m.
In depth, the second- and fourth-row bays are 7.5 m,

while the middle or third row is slightly over 11 m. Rather than occupy the largest central bay (8.5 by 11 m), the throne is pushed back half a bay to straddle the seam between the third and fourth rows (fig. 3.25).

For an impression of the original appearance of this hall in the Ming, one should visit the Ling'en Dian of the Changling, Yongle's tomb (built 1416) [18 ▶], or the front hall of the Ancestral Temple (built 1545) [14 ▶]. In each case one sees highly polished tiles (*jin zhuan*) for the floor, unpainted dark brown Nanmu (a fine hardwood) columns atop plain round stone plinths, miniaturized brackets above the tie-beams, also unpainted, and subdued coffered ceilings in green and blue. This must have been the palette of the palace prior to Qing renovations of the seventeenth century and later. Since the Qing, however, the Taihe Dian décor has been as we see it: four gold columns flanking the throne platform, a field of red-lacquered columns, as well as red doors and windows across the front, and the gold-blue-green designs adorning beams, brackets, and coffers. This hall was restored in 2006–07.

Rear Three Palaces

In the canonical "Royal City" plan, the ruler and his councilors conducted the affairs of state in the forward portions of the palace (*qian chao*), while his private affairs were segregated in the rear quarters (*hou qin*). In late imperial times, this model was implicit even in commoner residences, where the women's "inner" quarters were ordinarily the rear of a household. Within the Ming and Qing Forbidden City, however, the situation was less rigid.

In the Ming, the rear halls on axis were built as residential palaces for the emperor and empress (fig. 3.28). The front hall, the Palace of Heavenly Purity (Qianqing Gong), was named to associate the emperor

RIDGE ORNAMENTS AND STATUS

Ming and Qing builders manipulated several features to distinguish the hierarchy of build-ings within the Forbidden City. Most important was position; high status was accorded any building on axis. Equally important was the numerology: nine bays in width was the maxi-mum in the Ming (eleven in the Qing), with odd-numbered alternatives (seven-five-three) designating lesser status. Roof structure also connoted rank: a hipped roof with two eaves was highest, while the hip-gable and gable types were less important. Not least, serving explicitly as status markers were the strange animals on the ridges.

The top-most roof ridge (*ji*) consisted of tiles above the ridge pole which was held down at each end by the ponderous mass of a pair of bizarre sea-creatures known as *chi wen* (or *zheng wen, da wen, long wen*; fig. 3.26). These were also called "swallowing ridge beasts" (*tun ji shou*). Some English writers apply the Greek term *acroterion* for this function. *Chi wen* could be made from as many as thirteen pieces. In the case of the largest exam-ples atop the Hall of Supreme Harmony, they reach a height of 3.4 m and weigh 4.3 tons. These creatures have large facial features with jaws that chomp down on the ridge; their tails curl above. The Indian Makara may lie behind this design. A sword hilt is often visible at the top, and a second, smaller dragon head may emerge from the back.

A sequence of creatures that fulfilled propitious and apotropaic roles runs down the four ridges from the ends of the ridge pole to the corner eaves. A smaller animal head, another variation on the dragon, precedes this sequence of one to ten creatures (fig. 3.27), in descending order: *xing shi* (also called *hou*, a monkey with a sword); *dou niu; xie zhi; suan ni* (a kind of lion); *ya yu* (note fish tail); *tian ma* (flying horse); *hai ma* (sea horse); *shi* (lion); *feng* (phoenix); and *long* (dragon). All are composite beasts merging disparate scales, hoofs, and tails. Each beast crouches alertly on its haunches. At the terminal position are *xian ren* (immortal), a relatively natural-look-ing bird with a plump figure on its back. This selection seems to have been established in the Ming; the terms used here are recorded in Qing documents. (Translations given are lit-eral and conventional.)

3.26 *Chi wen* (modern replica)

This sequence is disposed according to the rank of the building. Thus the Hall of Supreme Harmony (the grandest of all throne halls) has ten creatures after the dragon head and before the immortal and bird at the eave. The Hall of Preserving Harmony, Palace of Heavenly Purity (the Ming emperor's residence), and Hall of Imperial Supremacy (Qianlong's residence after retirement) all have nine creatures plus immortal. The Palace of Earthly Tranquility (the Ming empress's residence) as well as the Hall of Middle Harmony and Hall of Union have seven beasts, as do the four palace gates. The Hall of Mental Cultivation and the East and West Six Palaces (for consorts and princes) all have five creatures. The pavilions of the Imperial Flower Garden as well as the four corner towers of the palace, lastly, have only three creatures.

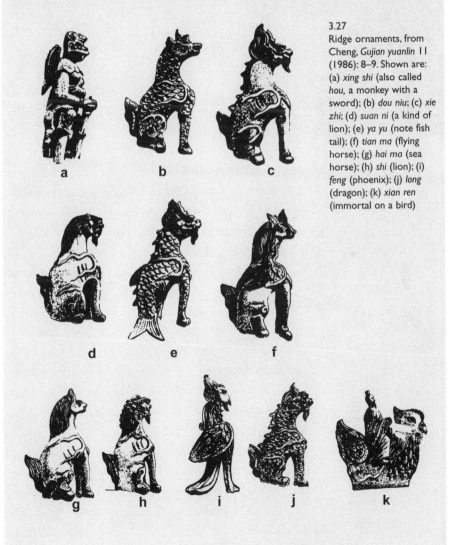

3.27
Ridge ornaments, from Cheng, *Gujian yuanlin* 11 (1986): 8–9. Shown are: (a) *xing shi* (also called *hou*, a monkey with a sword); (b) *dou niu*; (c) *xie zhi*; (d) *suan ni* (a kind of lion); (e) *ya yu* (note fish tail); (f) *tian ma* (flying horse); (g) *hai ma* (sea horse); (h) *shi* (lion); (i) *feng* (phoenix); (j) *long* (dragon); (k) *xian ren* (immortal on a bird)

3.28
Alley separating outer (left)
and inner (right) courts

with Heaven using the hexagram qian from the *Classic of Changes* (*Yi jing*). The rear hall, in turn, was the Palace of Earthly Tranquility (Kunning Gong), associating the empress with earth, again via a hexagram from the *Changes*. The names posit complementary roles: male and female; purity and tranquility; active and passive; *yang* and *yin*. But Ming emperors often favored other sites as their residence, notably palaces on the lakes west of the Forbidden City, as well as an area in the southeast corner of the Imperial City called variously the Nan Nei (Southern Within), or Dong Yuan (Eastern Garden). In general the lives of Ming emperors were lived out within the Imperial City, but were not confined to the moated palace.

By contrast, the Qing emperors created several residential alternatives. At the inception of Manchu rule, the Shunzhi emperor (Fulin, r. 1644–61) resided in the Hall of Preserving Harmony (Baohe Dian), the northernmost of the Three Great Halls of State. Thereafter throughout the Qing, the Gate of Heavenly

Purity (Qianqing Men) was a common venue for
court rather than the Fengtian Men (Taihe Men) used
in Ming. This shifted a court gathering to the front
door of the Inner Court, while still keeping it in the
Outer Court. After the extraordinarily long reign of
Kangxi (Xuanye, r. 1662–1722), who resided in the
Palace of Heavenly Purity (Qianqing Gong), his heir
Yongzheng (Yinzhen, r. 1722–1735) decided not to
inhabit his father's palace. Instead he moved west to a
compound off axis called the Hall of Mental

3.29
Hall of Mental Cultivation

3.30
Gate of Heavenly Purity

Cultivation (Yangxin Dian; fig. 3.29). This then became the primary residence for Qianlong (Hongli, r. 1736–95) as well, and was used by all later Qing emperors including Pu Yi (or Xuantong; 1909–11).

But most Manchu emperors divided their lives among several locations, reducing time in the

3.31
Palace of Heavenly Purity

3.32
Throne ensemble, Palace of Heavenly Purity. In the Qing, a second copy of the testamentary edict was kept behind the placard (reading "Upright and Pure") until the death of the emperor, who carried the original on his person.

Forbidden City. In an extreme example, Kangxi spent only eighteen days there in 1714, with 131 days at his garden-palace estate northwest of the capital (the Changchun Yuan; see Ch. 6), and 139 days at Chengde (Rawski, 35). In 1762, Qianlong spent one-third of his time in the Beijing palace, the remainder in travel or at Chengde. After creation of the garden-palace estates and Chengde, the Qing court established branch offices for the principal organs of state at these venues so that court affairs could be conducted on a regular basis away from the Forbidden City.

In its fifteenth-century plan, the Inner Court was to occupy less than half of the area within the walls of the Forbidden City, roughly north of the east-west line established by the Gate of Heavenly Purity (Qianqing Men; fig. 3.30). The rear residential palaces were modeled on the Three Great Halls, but at reduced scale. The Palace of Heavenly Purity (Qianqing Gong) was fronted by a moon terrace, and like the principal throne hall of the outer court was nine bays by five under a double-eave hipped roof (fig. 3.31). Here however, an elevated path led from the gate to the moon terrace, dividing the front courtyard into two sunken areas. The palace we visit is a rebuilding from 1797, one of the most recent compounds in the palace.

When Kangxi occupied the Qianqing Gong, the compound was a palace within the palace. The imperial wardrobe was installed in the east galleries, the imperial study was on the west side, Hanlin academicians were on duty in the southeast corner, and classes for the heir were conducted in the southwest corner. On the north were the court physician and head eunuch. After the Yongzheng emperor moved to the Yangxin Dian, the Qianqing Gong was used for receiving emissaries and for the lying in state of an emperor's coffin. After the Qing adopted the custom of a secret testamentary edict to name the heir, one copy was kept in a compartment behind the placard above the throne here (fig. 3.32).

The Palace of Earthly Tranquility (Kunning Gong) also is nine bays, but unlike the comparable Baohe Dian, it too had a double-eave hipped roof. The Manchus turned the Kunning Gong into the center of their in-palace shamanistic rites, with the east half used for the imperial nuptials. In the Ming this palace had direct access to the Imperial Flower Garden on the north, but by Qing times a gate was interposed to restrict traffic. With this hall taken over for other purposes, Qing empresses resided in smaller palace compounds on east and west [12 ▶]. The well-known Dowager Empress Cixi (1835-1908), for example, made her primary palace abodes in the Six West Palaces. She also favored the Summer Palace.

Situated between the two palaces was the Hall of Union (Jiaotai Dian). Many writers believe this was not a part of the original Ming plan, but there is evidence to the contrary. Like the Hall of Middle Harmony (Zhonghe Dian) of the Outer Court, this is a square three-bay building under a pyramidal roof. It was used by the Ming empresses to hold court. In the Qing it housed twenty-five imperial seals in coffers under slip covers of yellow silk, which are displayed there today.

Since the Ming and Qing imperial clans differed, the life of the rear palaces also changed. In the Ming, mature imperial princes except the designated heir (*tai zi*) were sent to fiefs scattered across the map. Only a single palace was required for the heir. This was situated on the east side of the Forbidden City at what are now offices used by the Palace Museum (Nan San Suo), on a line with the first of the Three Great Halls. Called

Duanjing Gong, this ensemble was north of the Hall of Literary Glory (Wenhua Dian), where the heir held court. In early Ming, the heir managed the affairs of the capital when his father, the ruling emperor, was away.

By contrast as minors Qing princes resided inside the palace but, after they married, lived in the capital. Since the heir was not made known until the demise of the reigning emperor, they had to be at hand. Their attendance in the palace allowed their father the emperor to judge their merits as he delegated various duties to them. Manchu princes were raised in several palace compounds both north and southeast of the Inner Court. Qianlong, for example, was raised in the Nan San Suo, former site of the Ming heir's palace, and later had a palace among the Xi Wu Suo. Upon marriage, ranking imperial sons were established in Princely Mansions (*wang fu*) in the Inner City (see Ch. 6.).

In the Ming palace, women attached to the imperial household as secondary consorts (*feipin*) occupied the Six East and Six West Palaces, two ensembles of compact courtyards flanking the imperial residences of the central axis. Long north-south corridors (*chang jie*) with high red walls divided the two files of three palaces, while east-west alleys connected them from side to side. The gates on these alleys we see today conform to a standard design with superb glazed tile decoration (fig. 3.33). These twelve palaces gave their residents convenient access to the Three Rear Palaces and the Imperial Flower Garden. Immature imperial sons were housed at the rear, adjacent to the garden. Their birth mothers were therefore not far away.

When first built, all twelve palaces had the same plan (fig. 3.34). Each compound was about 50 m square (an area of 2500 sq m) with two yards (*jin*) embracing a single main hall. The solitary gate opened

◀ 12

East and West Six Palaces (Dong Xi Liu Gong)

MING, 1419; MANY REBUILDINGS
NATIONAL REGISTER, 1961; WORLD HERITAGE SITE, 1987
FORBIDDEN CITY

3.33
Inner court gate

3.34
Courtyard plan, East Six
Palaces (Ming)

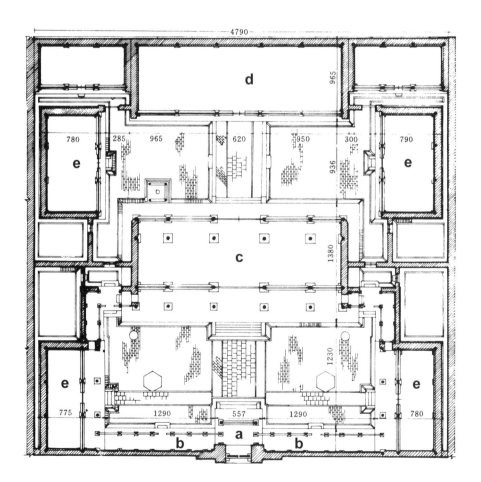

on the south, but a freestanding screen blocked direct access to the yard. Flanking covered galleries encouraged movement to both sides in order to reach the interior. One assumes that both the mistress of the household and her servants were intended to use this one gate. The sunny front yard complemented the main hall, which was connected to a rear hall by an elevated path. Four large chambers at both sides front and rear supported other needs, and still more chambers were tucked into the corners. These compounds compare well to the classic Beijing residential *sihe yuan* (see fig. 6.9). Today only one of the twelve compounds is said to preserve its fifteenth-century plan and palace architecture, the Palace of Gathering Essence (Zhongcui Gong; used for jade displays but closed to visitors in recent years).

Most of these palaces were refurbished in the early Qing, gaining a moon terrace before the main hall. More extensive renovations took place in the late nineteenth century. For example, on the west side, four palaces were made into two compounds of four

3.35
Palace of Eternal Spring,
West Six Palaces (Qing)

yards by eliminating the gate house of one and insert-
ing large halls open in both directions into that space.
Thus in 1859, the original gate of the Palace of Eternal
Spring (Changchun Gong; fig. 3.35) was replaced by a
new building (the Hall of Manifest Origins, Tiyuan
Dian). With the original alley and gate removed, the
northern yard was integrated with those of the Hall of
the Ultimate Principle (Taiji Dian) on the south. (That
compound had housed the Wanli emperor after the
Rear Palaces burned in 1596.) In honor of the
Empress Dowager Cixi's fortieth birthday in 1873, this
new palace was further enhanced with a large stage
facing north and galleries featuring *trompe l'oeil* murals
of the novel *Dream of the Red Chamber*.

Similarly, on Cixi's fiftieth birth anniversary in
1884, the Palace of Gathering Excellence (Chuxiu
Gong) was linked to the palace compound on its south
by replacing the gate with a hall. This had been the
palace where a younger Cixi gave birth to the Tongzhi
emperor in 1856. Other improvements to announce
its elevated status included large bronze animals (a pair
of dragons and a pair of deer) in the yard before the
main hall and extensive renovations to the interiors.
The Palace Museum now uses the Palace of Gathering
Excellence for displays about the life of the last
emperor, Pu Yi (with early twentieth century Western
furnishings), and the palace telephone system.

In the northwest corner of the west side, the
Palace of Complete Happiness (Xianfu Gong) remains
a self-contained unit of two yards. It has photographs
detailing the career of Cixi herself. A visitor can easily
progress from the rear of the Hall of Mental
Cultivation (Yangxin Dian) to the Changchun Gong,
then the Chuxiu Gong, and finally the Xianfu Gong
for an extended introduction to life in the late Qing
palace. Exiting the last palace toward the north leads to

a modern restroom, shop, and the restful Imperial Flower Garden.

Changes have been less pronounced on the east side of the Three Rear Palaces. Five of these yards remain self-contained units. All are devoted to exhibitions, including: jades at the Palace of Gathering Excellence (Zhongcui Gong); cloisonné at the Palace of Great Yang (Jingyang Gong); bronzes at the Palace of Inheriting Heaven (Chengqian Gong); the lives of palace women at the Palace of Eternal Harmony, (Yonghe Gong); and recent donations at the Palace of Great Benevolence (Jingren Gong). The Palace of Prolonged Happiness (Yanxi Gong) burned in 1845 after a fire in its kitchen. In 1900 a thorough redesign here yielded a three-story European-style house with a water feature surrounding its basement level (fig. 7.2). The bronze frame and stone cladding reminiscent of the Yuanming Yuan are intact, but the sense of decay is palpable. In 1931, the Palace Museum built halls on three sides of this architectural fantasy as storage facilities for museum collections. These have lately been reopened for the display of paintings and ceramics.

Much larger palace establishments were maintained for an empress dowager. These compounds took shape on the outer west and outer east sides of the Inner Court parallel to the main axis. The most important in the Ming period was the Palace of Compassion and Tranquility (Cining Gong) on the west side which, with its gardens, extended forward to the position of the Fengtian Dian (now Taihe Dian). This compound is now under restoration. The northeast corner of the Forbidden City was also developed. The Qing court modified the Ming palace, renaming it the Palace of Tranquility and Longevity (Ningshou Gong). Qianlong chose this same compound in 1771 to be his retirement palace;

today it had become galleries devoted to palace treasures (Zhenbao Guan). The Nine Dragon wall (Jiulong Bi) graces the forward yard of this compound. (Qianlong's garden is discussed in Ch. 6.) Still more palaces were built by the filial Qianlong for his mother on the far west side of the Inner Court.

Denizens of the Palace

In the Qing, internal operation of the palace was the responsibility of the Imperial Household Department (Neiwufu), with offices on the west side of the palace between the Wuying Dian and Cining Gong garden, areas not open to visitors today. The minister in charge (by custom a Manchu prince) held rank 3. As many as 1600 persons staffed this department, subdivided among fifty-six agencies. Major divisions of this department were the Eunuch Administration, the Bureau of Works, and the Six Vaults for warehousing such commodities as fur, silk, food, and silver.

Eunuchs (castrated males), bondservants, maids, slaves, servants, and artisans all served in the Qing palace. With the exception of eunuchs, who were Han-Chinese (to apply the contemporary term), palace personnel were Manchus drawn from the three Imperial Banners (Bordered Yellow, Plain Yellow, and Plain White). Bondservants were a hereditary servile class in Manchu society; many descended from early captives of the Manchus and hence they included some Han-Chinese. The largest group of bondservants was the "casual laborers" employed in such tasks as weeding the palace yards. Palace maids were also drawn from bondservant families, drafted annually from girls of twelve. They were presented at the north palace gate and selected for service in the Imperial Flower Garden. After five or ten years they left the palace. State slaves, Manchus serving a term of penal servitude, and wet nurses filled out the menial ranks.

As a group, eunuchs were denigrated under the Qing, ostensibly because of the notoriety they had attained in the Ming. In that period, the palace was very much their kingdom, and much abuse ensued. A decree of 1751 limited eunuchs to 3300, but this is probably more than normally served. Pu Yi still had 1137 eunuchs in 1927. Some eunuchs were ranked (but not higher than rank 4); their chief was a senior figure with decades of service. The palace gates were supervised by eunuchs of rank 7 or 8. Quarters for eunuchs and serving maids can be seen in the yard surrounding the terrace supporting the Three Rear Palaces. Ownership of eunuchs was a jealously guarded privilege of the imperial clan and some high-ranking officials.

The Manchus used marriage to advance political and social aims, but unions with Han-Chinese was prohibited. (On the other hand, there were Han banner units, and their daughters might enter the palace.) While the Ming emperors practiced what Rawski calls serial monogamy, the emperor moving from one consort to another, the Qing emperors had multiple consorts, in effect polygyny (Rawski, 128). Girls came into the palace every three years at ages 13 and 14 as "beautiful women" (*xiu nu*). Once inside the palace their identity was submerged and all family ties cut off. Some became wives, others ladies-in-waiting. In palace society, they entered a world with eight ranks: *daying, changzai, guiren, pin, fei, guifei, huangguifei,* and, at the pinnacle, empress (*huang hou*). The lower three ranks were often drawn from serving maids. Since in the entire Qing period only one emperor was born to an empress, these other women were crucial to dynastic fortunes. One can readily imagine the politics that swirled around them. The empress of a deceased emperor (the empress dowager) or birth mother of the emperor was even higher in status than an empress, and in effect these figures ran the inner court. Only twenty-four women attained this status in the Qing period.

SUGGESTED   For the Gate of Heavenly Peace, see Wu Hung,
READING   *Remaking Beijing: Tiananmen Square and the Creation of a Political Space* (2005), "Face of Authority: Tiananmen and Mao's Tiananmen Portrait," 51–84.

Many fine books discuss the palace, although none is truly comprehensive. Yu Zhuoyun and Graham Hutt's *Palaces of the Forbidden City* (1984) is the best pictorial overview of architecture. Also recommended is Wan Yi, et al, *Daily Life in the Forbidden City: The Qing Dynasty, 1644–1912* (1988), a companion volume. Among many exhibition catalogues presenting treasures from the palace, the most recent is far and away the most satisfying: *China: The Three Emperors, 1662–1795*, edited by Evelyn S. Rawski and Jessica Rawson (2006).

Ray Huang's *1587: A Year of No Significance, the Ming Dynasty in Decline* (1981) is a compelling narrative of the reign of Wanli derived from primary sources with many enlightening tales. Evelyn Rawski, *The Last Emperors: A Social History of Qing Imperial Institutions* (1998) presents the material culture, social world, and rituals of the Manchu rulers from research in primary sources.

Two first-hand narratives of life in the palace should also be mentioned: *From Emperor to Citizen* (the biography of Pu Yi), and Reginald F. Johnston's *Twilight in the Forbidden City* (the story of Pu Yi's tutor).

Altars and Tombs   4

*Without exaggeration we may say that no other sanctuary on
earth has a more profound or grandiose conception, or more
adequately expresses the instinctive desire of humanity to
show reverence for a Power above and beyond its puny self.*

*One man and only one, the Emperor, Son of Heaven, was
thought fit to ascend this worshipping place and, under the
dome of the sky which covers it like a hollow turquoise, to
make obeisance to the Supreme Being.*

JULIET BREDON, PEKING (1931), 157

The Son of Heaven (see Box, p. 103), the
emperor, was like no one else. He was committed for his mature life to a routine of ceremonial and sacrificial activities that were jealously
guarded imperial prerogatives. These activities dominated the emperor's schedule. They also assigned to
him a variety of roles that confound simple
dichotomies of private and public, family and state.
Although attendance at some rites and sacrifices could
be delegated to another person—an imperial prince, a
kinsman, or other noble—the ritual schedule was the
emperor's exclusive responsibility. An institutional
framework made them happen: principally the
Ministry or Board of Rites, the Court of Ceremony,
and the Imperial Household Department. Scholars
versed in the arcana of ritual and historical precedent
crafted the annual calendar for the emperor's approval.
They also wrote the scripts for each performance, be

they celebratory pronouncements to be declaimed by high-ranking officials in the emperor's presence or solemn utterances the Son of Heaven himself directed to Heaven or the ancestors. While the emperor was the human manifestation of power and authority in these solemn matters, he was also an actor, even a puppet, whose every action was directed by scholars serving him and the historical precedents of his ancestors.

Ritual (*li*) sums up these myriad activities and performances. The category was unusually broad, and any single equivalent can be misleading. *Li* encompassed the ordinary interactions of human beings in their home life and on the street, from greetings to the niceties of any transaction. In these contexts it was good manners, akin to etiquette. Deferring to an elder or showing respect for an equal manifested *li*. *Li* also governed the performance of family-based rituals for all levels within society—births, marriages, and deaths—as well as seasonal festivals of the community. Some of these actions today would be deemed religious, others merely social custom. At a more rarified level of society, *li* dictated the conduct and deportment of officials within the imperial government and their collective roles in any and all gatherings (protocol): a dawn court, a seasonal sacrifice, an imperial progress. It controlled the dispatch of an army or the reception of a victorious commander presenting prisoners. No one in pre-modern Chinese society was more a creature of *li* than the Son of Heaven.

State Rites

The ruler is the Son of Heaven; he should make reverence for Heaven and concern for the people his first task. Only thus will he obtain Heaven's favor.

QIANLONG; IN RAWSKI, *LAST EMPERORS*, 212

In most matters of state public ritual, the Qing emperors followed well-established practices of their Ming predecessors. These state rituals were classified into five groups:

(1) Auspicious rites (*ji li*) embraced the great sacrifices at the extramural altars (Heaven, Earth; fig. 4.2), visits to ancestral shrines including tombs, and the annual bestowal of the calendar;

(2) Joyous rites (*jia li*) centered on key events in an emperor's career: his accession, holding court, or reception of embassies;

(3) Military rites (*jun li*) regulated the dispatch of an army, its victorious return, submission of prisoners, as well as prudent responses to solar and lunar eclipses, which were regarded as portentous events;

(4) Guest rites (*bin li*) governed the formal reception of vassals, especially the Mongol princes allied to the Manchu court in Qing times;

(5) Rites of misfortune (*xiong li*), lastly, dictated the customs of mourning, funeral, and burial.

4.1
Hall of Prayer,
Altar to Heaven

All these rites were prioritized: some as first-rank, others as secondary or tertiary. The Son of Heaven was obligated to perform the higher ranking sacrifices and ceremonies. In the early Qing, an emperor had over fifty sacrifices to preside over each year. Over time this number grew: by 1786, there were sixty-two; by 1905, eighty-three (Rawski, 214).

Consider the year 1722, the last in the reign of Kangxi, by most accounts an exemplary Son of Heaven (Rawski, 211). On the winter solstice, the emperor sacrificed at the Altar to Heaven (Tian Tan) [16 ▶] in the Outer City. In the first lunar month, he

4.2
Map of Ming and Qing Beijing, from *Beijing gu jianzhu* (1986), 6. Numbers refer to sites discussed in this book.

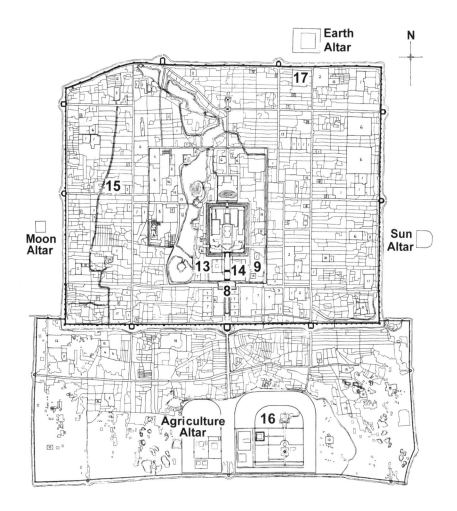

returned to pray there for a bounteous harvest. In the second month he performed rites at the Altar to Soil and Grain (She Ji Tan) [13 ▶] in the Imperial City. In the fourth month he prayed for rain, again at the Altar to Heaven, and at the summer solstice, sacrificed at the Altar to Earth (Di Tan) on the north side of the city. In the eighth month Kangxi revisited the Altar to Soil and Grain to offer thanksgiving for the harvest just gathered. These were all first-rank state rites. All manifested the unique status of the Son of Heaven as intermediary between Heaven and his people and his concern for their livelihood. Kangxi also appeared at the Ancestral Temple (Tai Miao) [14 ▶]. in the Imperial City every three months and at the end of the year. In addition, there were regular visits to the imperial tombs, although these were often delegated, as well as similar rituals at the Hall of the Ancestors (Fengxian Dian) within the Forbidden City. There were also rites for the rulers of earlier dynasties at a temple of this name (Lidai Diwang Miao) [15 ▶] west of the Imperial City. In practice, ancestor rites were also conducted within the inner court at various Buddha halls and shrines in the living quarters. These observances were private and familial, focused on near relatives, while public rites commemorated the distant dynastic founder and his mainline descendants. Last but not least, the emperor appeared at the several altars and the Ancestral Temple to make announcements (gao ji) of important events in the life of his family or affairs of state. The powers of the universe and the spirits of the ancestors were always present and must be kept informed.

The rituals discussed in this chapter might be termed state religion. This usage signifies their essential value to the ruler and his government: their claim to authority was legitimated by faithful performance.

The right to rule, the Mandate of Heaven, was reasserted by the annual round of ceremonies. The basic structure and functioning of the universe, as the imperial state understood these matters, was acted out. This term also serves the practical purpose of distinguishing other traditions of religious belief and practice with their own origins, such as Buddhism and Daoism (see Ch. 5). This does not mean, however, that a Ming or Qing emperor could not also and equally be a Buddhist or adherent of the Dao. This terminology also places Confucian rites within state religion, although many scholars would argue there was little or nothing religious about them. They are incorporated here because of the imperial role in the cult of the Sage for Ten Thousand Generations.

The outline for performance of state rites during the Qing was relatively consistent, whether the venue was in front of the Hall of Supreme Harmony in the Forbidden City or at the Altar to Heaven in the Outer City. In most cases, the preferred timing was dawn, although there were exceptions. The emperor was brought to the court or the altar by his attendants. Officials assembled at an appointed hour and filed in to take their positions. Ceremonies demanded both a chief celebrant and a human audience in addition to the unseen powers and spirits. Architectural settings were designed to position the actors in appropriate locations—central or peripheral, high or low—in keeping with their status and roles. Assuming their designated places was of supreme importance. The actors were directed and overseen by a staff of ushers from the Board of Rites and other agencies. For major sacrifices, the emperor went through a preliminary three-day fast. At the same time the staff and representatives of the emperor were busy preparing sacrificial offerings. A throne and screen were set up if needed, when the venue for court was a gate house, for example. Thrones were also present at sacrifices to hold the tablets of the power being honored as well as those for imperial ancestor spirits who "attended" the rite. Officials prepared and set out special documents, seals, and writing materials on tables. The event unfolded to the accompaniment of cracking bull whips in a court assembly, and to musical accompaniment (wind instruments, chimes, bells). Dress was specified for the occasion. For the emperor, assuming his seat and facing south were the irreducible actions of a court gathering. In a sacrifice, however, the Son of Heaven was required to kneel three times and prostrate himself nine times (*san gui jiu ke tou*) facing north, the direction of his usual position. Officials, for their part, performed their own kneeling and kowtow facing the emperor or altar. These rituals transpired under the dome of Heaven amid lanterns as the sun slowly illuminated the sky in a precinct cut off from the mundane world and suffused with incense, music, and the echo of commands and pronouncements.

Both this altar and the Ancestral Temple [14 ▶] have ancient pedigrees and long histories in earlier dynasties. Their position in front of the ruler's palace at right and left, respectively, was sanctioned by the "Royal City" plan of the *Rites of Zhou*. In traditional accounts, rites to the Soil Altar (She) and to Lord Millet (Ji) were essential elements of Bronze Age culture. Lord Millet was the mythical ancestor of the Zhou house. The Altar to Soil at the Zhou capital was the source of a lump of soil sent out each time a royal relation was enfeoffed at his new domain. Like the Shang before them, the Zhou also paid dutiful attention to their ancestors, and indeed some of the oldest architectural sites of the Bronze Age were quite likely ancestral

◀ 13
Altar to Soil and Grain (She Ji Tan)

MING, CA. 1420
NATIONAL REGISTER, 1988
ZHONGSHAN PARK, DONGCHENG

temples. If the culture of the Zhou was extolled by Confucius as a Golden Age, the perpetuation of these altars and temples was an attempt by imperial rulers to reaffirm ancient verities and implicitly sanction their position. From Qin and Han through Tang, imperial capitals had both types of sites, although details varied over time. In Western Han (ca. 202 BCE–CE 9), other cults had equal or greater status, for example the Nine Temples and Hall of Brightness. After Han, multiple altars to She and Ji often were maintained. In Tang and later eras, the cult of Heaven (see below) came to overshadow the twin ancient traditions, although ancestor veneration never flagged. In Tang Chang'an, we find the She and Ji altars within the Imperial City, as in Ming-Qing Beijing. The return to this siting amended the plan of Yuan Dadu, where the altar and ancestral temple were placed amid the residential wards of the city (see fig. 1.8) at some remove from the palace.

The She Ji Tan was built during the initial construction of Yongle's new capital, being as essential as his outer court throne hall or inner court residential palace. The site was refurbished during the Ming, and given a large-scale rebuilding under Qianlong (1756). Probably only the Offering Hall (fig. 4.3) north of the altar survives from Yongle's era. Because it served the emperor resident in his palace, the proper approach to this altar is from the north. The Lance Gate (Ji Men) and Offering Hall (Xiang Dian, now Zhongshan Tang) both stand between the Forbidden City and the altar. This hall—one of the oldest structures in the city—is five bays wide and three deep, carrying a hip-gable roof. The interior is one open space, and there is no ceiling, leaving the handsome roof frame in view.

The site is centered on the altar platform (fig. 4.4), which is 5-zhang (50 feet) square in Ming measure. (The earth was square, *fang,* in traditional Chinese cos-

4.3
Offering Hall,
Altar to Soil and Grain

mology.) It may have been two tiers when first built, but is now three, measuring about 18 m at the base and 15 m at top with a height of just 90 cm. The top surface is filled with five soils: yellow (center), green (east), red (south), white (west), and black (north), the canonical scheme of directional and color relationships subsumed under the rubric of "five agents" (or "five elements," *wu xing*). A square stone post (*she zhu*) once at the center has disappeared. The walls that enclose the altar, about 61 m long, are capped with glazed tiles of the same colors as the soils. Marble gate ways (*lingxing men*, a form of *pailou*) punctuate these walls. Taking the actual altar as the module for planning, Fu Xinian found the She Ji Tan's overall dimensions are thirteen squares east-west by seventeen squares north-south (206 by 267 m).

The emperor was expected to make two regular appearances at the She Ji Tan: in mid-spring, the second month, to pray for a good harvest in the coming growing season, and again in mid-autumn, the eighth

4.4
Altar to Soil and Grain

month, to offer thanksgiving for the completed harvest. Major events were also announced to the unseen spirits here, including drought or floods, military campaigns and victories.

After the creation of the Chinese Republic, the precinct became Central Park. In 1917, the Lanting Stele originally erected by the Qianlong emperor in Yuanming Yuan [31 ▶] was installed here. It is sheltered by an octagonal pavilion, and displays rubbings of famous renditions of the calligraphic masterpiece by Wang Xizhi. In 1918, the memorial arch built to honor the German minister von Ketteler, who had been killed on the eve of the Boxer siege, was re-erected here. The site was renamed Zhongshan Park in 1928 in honor of Sun Yatsen (1866–1925); the latter's honorific name is rendered Zhongshan in Mandarin. Sun, the father of the Republic, was laid in state for a time in the Offering Hall. Today this important early building is open as a memorial to the great man. Over the years a number of pavilions have been added to the park, making it an ideal resting place removed from the surging crowds of Tian'an Men Square and the palace.

On the east side of the long formal approach to the Noon Gate lies the precinct of the Ancestral Temple (Tai Miao), balancing the Altar to Soil and Grain on the west. Like the Altar, it was built by Yongle following the prototype established by the emperor's father in Nanjing. However, this site saw a major rebuilding in 1535 under the Jiajing emperor (r. 1522–66). Among his many reforms, he decreed that a complex of nine shrines be built for the imperial ancestors. Evidently eight small chambers were added, four on each side of the main hall. After a fire in 1541 destroyed all but one, however, these were torn down and the original scheme of three halls was reinstituted by 1545. The site changed again under Wanli and then under Qianlong (1736); the latter had the main hall expanded to eleven bays across rather than nine, as with the Hall of Supreme Harmony. Fu Xinian believes the Lance Gate here (Ji Men, fig. 4.5) is an early Ming structure. It follows early Ming values for a *chi-*

◄ 14

Ancestral Temple (Tai Miao)

MING, CA. 1420; REBUILT 1545 AND LATER
NATIONAL REGISTER, 1988
WORKING PEOPLE'S CULTURE PALACE, DONGCHENG

4.5
Lance Gate,
Ancestral Temple

4.6
Main Hall, Ancestral Temple

foot, while the three halls instead followed later Ming values. (See Box, p. 31 for other early buildings.)

The compound is defined by two walls. The outer one is 208 m wide and 272 m deep. Fu Xinian has shown this is a plot of 13 by 17 squares of 5-zhang each. The central area enclosed by the inner wall is much narrower, at 114 m, but as deep as the outer wall is wide, 208 m, a ratio of 5:9 like the terraces carrying the Three Great Halls of the Forbidden City. The Main Hall (fig. 4.6), built originally as nine bays by four, is at the geometrical center of this inner area. Marble terraces support both the main gate and the three halls on axis. The Middle Hall is significantly smaller than that in front and shares the terrace behind the former. The Rear Hall, however, is within a walled area on its own terrace. The approach to the Lance Gate has three marble bridges that cross the Outer Jinshui; four other bridges flank the central axis.

For most of the Ming and Qing, the emperor appeared in front of his own ancestors every three months, at the first and/or fifteenth days of the first, fourth, seventh, and tenth lunar months. He was also in attendance on the Qingming festival (fifth of the fifth month) and birth and death anniversaries. When the Manchu armies occupied the city in 1644, one of the first acts of the young Shunzhi emperor (Fulin, r. 1644–61) was to perform an ancestral sacrifice here. Subsequently the tablets of the Ming rulers were moved to the Temple for Past Emperors (Lidai Diwang Miao) west of the Imperial City [15▶]. Eventually the Qing installed their ancestral tablets, with Taizu (Nurgaci, r. 1616–26) at center, and subsequent generations placed alternately left and right. Shunzhi was the first on the west, Kangxi his successor was second on the east, and so on. Tablets of empresses were placed with their spouse. The many bays of the side chambers flanking the courtyard were reserved for imperial family members on the east and for worthy officials on the west. The Middle Hall (called *qin gong*, "retiring palace") had shrines for storing the tablets of the emperors and empresses. The Rear Hall (*zhao miao*) was dedicated to pre-conquest Manchu rulers.

Outside the outer wall is an expansive precinct with ancient cypress trees carefully numbered and registered with the city forestry bureau. The Ancestral Temple is accessible either from Chang'an Avenue at the east side of Tian'an Men or from the north by going east from the plaza in front of Wu Men. Separate admissions are charged for the park and temple. The latter is recommended both for a look at the somber Nanmu interior décor of the Main Hall and for its display of bells (fig. 4.7). The site was restored in 2006–2007.

4.7
Interior ceiling, Main Hall,
Ancestral Temple

15 ▶
Temple for Past
Rulers (Lidai
Diwang Miao)

MING, 1531
NATIONAL REGISTER,
1996
NO. 131 FUCHENG MEN
NEI, XICHENG

Among the obligations of a new dynasty was protection and maintenance of the tombs of its predecessors, as well as offerings to their spirits. Earlier sovereigns were conceived as political ancestors constituting an orthodox line of transmission for the Mandate of Heaven. The new emperor of a new dynasty proclaimed his legitimacy by honoring them. In the early Ming three dozen former rulers were accorded appropriate sacrifices, starting with the culture hero Fuxi and extending to the last Southern Song emperor, Lizong (d. 1265). There was even a shrine to Khubilai Khan under the auspices of the capital prefect (Naquin, 137).

Among the ritual reforms of the Jiajing emperor (r. 1522–66) was construction of a new consolidated site of worship called the Temple for Past (or Successive) Rulers (Lidai Diwang Miao). This became one of two dozen sites funded by the Ministry of Rites for regular sacrifices (in this case of the second rank). The Ming rites, however, excluded the rulers of the Liao and Jin "conquest" dynasties preferring to see the orthodox lineage as extending from the previous native dynasty, the Song through the (Mongol) Yuan. Former rulers were represented by name tablets, as was the custom at the Ancestral Temple and the Confucian Temple. The selection emphasized the founding emperors of each dynasty and their most illustrious ministers.

After the Manchu armies occupied Beijing, the new court placed the Ming emperors' tablets in the Lidai Diwang Miao, including that for Chongzhen (Zhu Youjian, r. 1628–44) who had "lost the Mandate of Heaven." The Qing also maintained tablets for the Liao, Jin, and Yuan rulers. The effect of these amendments was to raise the total number of past rulers from twenty-one under the Ming to one hundred sixty-seven. Likewise, the number of meritorious ministers rose from thirty-nine under the Ming to seventy-nine under the Qing.

The site is a large compound on the north side of Fucheng Men Nei Dajie. The main gate faces a large gray wall (*ying bi*) across the road. Inside, a five-bay gate house (Jingde Men) opens onto a large yard with side halls of seven bays and a main hall of nine bays on its own elevated moon terrace (fig. 4.8). Design and decoration are consistent with the main yards of the Forbidden City Outer Court. The main hall was subdivided into eleven niches for the shrines and tablets of past rulers, while the side halls were dedicated to their ministers. Today modernized displays occupy the side halls, but the orthodox lineage of rulers is clearly represented by an array of fresh tablets in the main hall. Large stele pavilions (figs. 4.9) erected by Yongzheng and Qianlong flank this hall; they commemorate the efforts of the emperors to honor their literal and fictive predecessors. A side hall on the east has been turned into a display about Chinese surnames.

The temple makes a good stop when visiting Bai Ta Si [23 ▶] further west on the same street. Guangji Si, also open to visitors, is located just east, as is the Geology Museum across the street.

4.8
Main Hall,
Temple for Past Rulers

4.9
Stele pavilion,
Temple for Past Rulers

The cult of Heaven (Tian) penetrated elite culture from early times to the late imperial era, beginning in the early Bronze Age. The first historic rulers, the kings of the Shang (ca. 1300–1046 BCE) revered a High God (Shang Di or Di) who was so remote that the king relied on the spirits of his deceased ancestors to communicate. Di controlled the operations of the natural world and fate of its human inhabitants. The Shang king, by proper divination and sacrifice, could insure the welfare of his people, at the same time reinforcing his position as the vital link between cosmic and human. The Zhou (ca. 1046–771) called their supreme deity Tian, and while in some respects comparable to Di, there were also differences. The Zhou ruler was styled Son of Heaven (Tian Zi), ruling by a Mandate of Heaven (*tian ming*) conferred by virtue of the king's moral and ritual rectitude. The Zhou king, unlike a Shang ruler, communicated directly with Heaven and Heaven responded directly to him. By proper ritual observances, the Zhou king justified his rule and attended to the welfare of his people. In spite of this traditional identification of supreme ruler and Heaven, the emperors of Qin and Han did not regard sacrifices to Heaven as their most solemn obligations. Instead a variety of natural powers (called *di*, using the same term as the Shang god) were honored within an elaborate scheme that required, in the Western Han, a suite of Nine Temples, a Hall of Brightness (Ming Tang), and a variety of other altars and shrines. Tian was but one of many objects of sacrifices and reverence for the first emperors. Only in the Tang did this change, with the institution of major sacrifices at an open-air altar just south of the city wall (the site survives). Later dynasties perpetuated this model.

The history of the Beijing Altar to Heaven is complex, responding to changing attitudes toward ritual and sacrifice. When Yongle built the new capital,

◀ 16

Altar to Heaven (Tian Tan)

MING AND QING, 15TH AND 18TH CENTURIES
NATIONAL REGISTER, 1961; WORLD HERITAGE SITE, 1998
YONGDING MEN NEI, CHONGWEN

the Altar was placed outside the walls southeast of the city center. (In 1553 this area became the Outer City; Ch. 2.) But this was an altar complex for sacrifices to both Heaven and Earth, following the Ming founder's decision to conduct joint sacrifices at Nanjing (fig. 4.10). Moreover, the altar platform was surmounted by a Hall of Sacrifice (Da Si Dian) in spite of the reservations of some ritualists who though an open-air setting *de rigueur*. The hall was flanked by other structures on elevated terraces within a single outer wall. This wall had rounded corners at the north and square ones at the south, echoing the classical injunction that "Heaven is round, Earth is square." It is likely that the main axis of the present complex is that established in 1420 and that the original sacrificial hall—Da Si Dian—occupied a position near the present Hall of Prayers for Bounteous Harvest (Qi Nian Dian). The Abstinence Palace (Zhai Gong) was also built at this time southwest of the altar-hall. The current east outer wall and west inner wall of the Altar to Heaven may also date to this phase.

In the 1530s the Jiajing emperor (Zhu Houcong, r. 1522–66) began a series of reforms that affected all of the sites used for state rites, including the Ancestral

4.10
Altars, early 15th century, from *Da Ming hui dian* from Fu, *Sheji fangfa*, vol. 2, 53. Diagram shows the Altar to Heaven as first constructed ca. 1420. A single sacrificial hall labeled Da Si Dian occupies the rear of a double-walled rectangular compound on axis at the north. The Abstinence Palace is in the lower left corner.

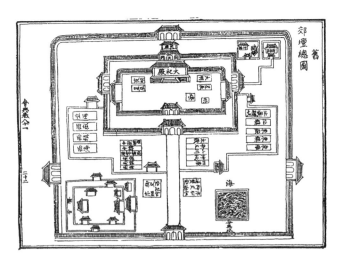

Temple and the Altar to Heaven. The decision was made to create a new separate altar for open-air rites, the Circular Mound (Huan Qiu; figs. 4.11, 12). This compound was located on the original site axis south of the original south wall, occupying a plot about 500 m deep and 1289 m wide. Three tiers of marble were erected in the center of this precinct, with diameters of 54, 38, and 23 m respectively. A round wall 104 m in diameter enclosed this mound, with gates on each side (fig. 4.13). A square wall 167 m on a side enclosed that, also with gates. The approach to this new altar was from the north. Thus the emperor left the Abstinence Palace, moved east and then south. Spirit tablets and other ritual gear were stored in a circular walled compound with its own small hall, the Imperial Vault of Heaven (Huang Qiong Dian; fig. 4.14).

Doubling the complex, however, did not satisfy the Jiajing emperor. Within a few years (ca. 1545), the northern altar-hall was itself redesigned with a new building (Qi Gu Tan, Da Xiang Dian) 24 m in diameter atop a circular, three-tier mound of 91 m diameter located where the sacrifice hall had been (fig. 4.15; see fig. 4.1). The original flanking halls and walls, however, were retained. This walled ensemble is 160 to 162

4.11
"Detail of Great Alter [sic] Temple of Heaven Peking," postcard by Chas. F. Gammon

4.12
Circular Mound

4.13
Gate at Circular Mound

4.14
Imperial Vault of Heaven

m on a side, an area ten squares by ten (using 5-zhang squares) according to Fu Xinian. However, the new round hall was not centered. Instead it was pushed back (north) by 24 m, the dimension of its own diameter. It may be that the main gate (Qi Nian Men) of this precinct dates from the original, early Ming construction. If so, it joins the Zhongshan Tang at the Altar to Soil and Grain, the Ji Men at the Ancestral Temple, and the Ling'en Men at Changling among early Ming survivors (see Box, p. 31).

The final phase in the evolution of the site took place after construction of the capital's Outer Wall in 1553. New walls erected on the south (tracking the Outer City wall) and west (flanking the axial road

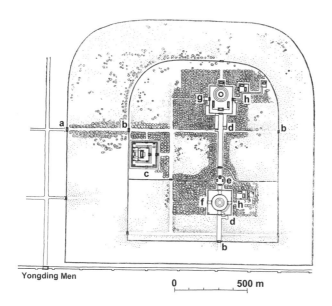

Yongding Men

0   500 m

4.15
Plan of Altar to Heaven, from *Beijing gu jianzhu* (1959), 13. Diagram shows: (a) entrance to the precinct, (b) inner gates (c) Abstinence Palace, (d) emperor's dressing ter- races, (e) Imperial Vault of Heaven, (f) the Circular Mound, (g) Hall of Prayer compound, (h) kitchens

from Yongding Men) were complemented by a new inner wall on the east (changing the original east wall into the outer boundary). Thus, the final plan of the complex has a main axis off-center! As might be expected the Qianlong emperor also had a hand in the history of this site, expanding the Circular Mound to its current dimensions in 1749–53 and reroofing the Hall of Prayers for Bounteous Harvest (Qi Nian Dian) with blue tiles in 1751.

The two principal altars are replete with elaborate numerical symbolism. Both sites are triple terraces, implicitly restating the triad of Heaven, Earth, and Humanity (Tian, Di, Ren). The three eaves of the round Qi Nian Dian echo this symbolism. When first built their tiles were different colors: blue at top, yel- low for the middle, and green for the lower eave. Now all are blue. The hall itself is a combination of four central ("dragon well," *long jing*) columns, a reference to the four seasons, a circuit of twelve columns, a ref- erence to the twelve months, and an eave perimeter of twelve more columns for the twelve double-hours of each day. The Circular Mound, for its part, uses odd numbers: the base is 21 zhang (7 x 3), the middle level is 15 zhang (5 x 3), and the top level is 9 zhang (3 x 3). Likewise the numbers of flag stones that cover the surface are multiples of nine. At top, a central circular stone is surrounded by eleven concentric rings (9 x 11 = 99), while at the middle tier are six more (12 x 9 through 18 x 9, total 90), and at the base nine more (19 x 9 through 27 x 9; grand total 243). The steps and railings also observe this numerology.

In the Qing calendar, sacrifices at the Altar to Heaven took place three times each year:

(1) At winter solstice (ca. December 21) at the Circular Mound, the essential rite necessary to restart a cycle of growing yang on that date, the shortest and coldest (most yin) day of the year;

(2) In the first month of the new calendar year (late January-February) at Qi Nian Dian to pray for the harvest;

(3) At the summer solstice (ca. June 21), the longest day of the year, to stop the yang and thus commence the re-growth of yin.

On each occasion the Son of Heaven fasted and readied himself mentally and spiritually for the great event within the confines of the inner court (the Zhai Gong, Abstinence Palace). Others designated to attend also prepared. On the day before the sacrifice, the imperial procession moved south from the inner court to the outer, out Wu Men and Tian'an Men, down the avenue leading toward Yongding Men, and entered the altar precinct. This was a grand procession with much imperial regalia (lu bu) on display. The city was quiet, streets empty of residents, their windows shuttered. After inspecting the offering preparations, the emperor retired to the Abstinence Palace.

The ritual began the next morning in the pre-dawn darkness. The emperor moved by palanquin to a tent on the elevated walkway that links the north and south precincts, and then to his appointed destination. At the Circular Mound, for example, he assumed his position on the middle terrace facing north and repeatedly ascended to the top level to make offerings and obeisance (kneeling and prostrations) to thrones with the tablets of High Heaven and former emperors. A staff of ritual specialists directed the emperor in his movements, when to kneel and bow. Incense burned, music played, offerings of jade and silk, and of meats, grain, and liquor proffered step by step.

Today a visitor can enter the Altar of Heaven site from any direction. This vast area, more than twice the size of the Forbidden City, was once a rarity among Beijing's public spaces featuring luxuriant grass with myriad trees, many quite old and picturesque. (Other parks now also have grassy lawns.) Both the side halls of the north precinct (Qi Nian Dian) and the Abstinence Palace (Zhai Gong) main hall have informative displays about history, ritual, and music (fig. 4.16). The site was restored in 2005–2006; the Abstinence Palace was not open at this writing.

Three other imperial altars were established on the other three sides of the city: the Altar to the Sun

4.16
Sacrificial offerings,
Abstinence Palace

4.17
"Temple de la Terre,"
postcard by Th. Culty,
Peking

(Ri Tan) on the east, the Altar to Earth (Di Tan) on the north, and the Altar to the Moon (Yue Tan) on the west. All three sites serve now as city parks. The Altar to the Earth (fig. 4.17), a short walk from Yonghe Gong and the Confucian Temple across the ring road, retains much of its original ambiance.

17 ▶
Confucian Temple
(Kong Miao)

YUAN, 1302–1306; 1411
AND LATER
NATIONAL REGISTER,
1988
No. 13 GUOZIJIAN
STREET, DONGCHENG

Several sites in Beijing claim a Yuan pedigree. The temple now popularly known as Bai Ta Si [23 ▶] and the Dong Yue Miao [26 ▶] are both introduced in Ch. 5. Here we discuss a third: the Confucian Temple (Kong Miao; fig. 4.18), built for the Mongols in 1302–06. The temple to Confucius was rebuilt by Yongle in 1411 and improved again by Xuande in 1429 and Jiajing in 1530. Qianlong also did his duty. At his initiative from 1737 the temple bore yellow roof tiles, normally an imperial prerogative. A final restoration of the temple began in 1906, six hundred years after founding, and continued until 1916. The last rites sponsored by the government took place here in 1928.

The compound is a rectangle running north-south; only the impressive ancient trees surely date

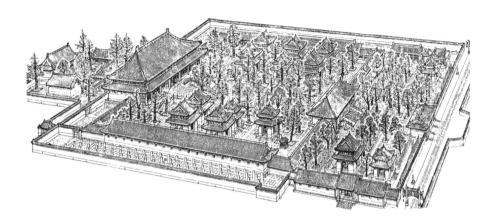

from the Mongol era. An exception may be the front gate (Foremost Teacher Gate, Xianshi Men) on Guozijian Street, which retains large bracket clusters typical of the pre-Ming eras. The rear portion of the site has been lost. Devoted to a Kong family ancestral hall, it is unlikely that the present small rear yard follows the original plan.

The approach to the main hall (fig. 4.19) is nonetheless magnificent: a shallow yard with its imposing array of steles, the Great Achievement Gate (Da Cheng Men), the principal yard with its many trees and eleven oversized stele pavilions, and the Great Achievement Hall (Da Cheng Dian; fig. 4.20)

4.18
Bird's eye view, Confucian Temple, from *Beijing Kong Miao*, inside cover

4.19
Yard before the Main Hall

looming on a raised platform. All of this is Qing building and decoration, including the stone ramps and
balustrades, the stele pavilions, and the main hall,
expanded to nine bays by five in 1906–16, under a yellow, double eave, hipped roof. (The hall had been
seven bays.) The steles in pavilions testify to the great
interest and generous patronage of the Qing emperors,
especially Kangxi, Yongzheng, and Qianlong.

Confucius (551–479 BCE) came to epitomize
classical learning, the virtues of a good ruler and his
wise ministers, and indeed the family values of
respectable society. By the Western Han period, scholars of wide learning had been appointed by the imperial court to expound texts associated with Master
Kong (as their redactor or author). These works
became known eventually as the Confucian Classics.
Imperial academies were founded in most periods
from Eastern Han onward, and authorized editions of
the classics cut in stone were produced repeatedly,
most famously in Eastern Han Luoyang (the Xiping
Era Classics of 175 CE) and Tang Chang'an (the
Kaicheng Era Classics of 837). The latter can still be
seen in the Forest of Steles in Xi'an. Veneration of
Confucius led to a profusion of honorific titles: First
Teacher (Xian Shi), First Worthy (Xian Xian), and

Model Teacher for Ten Thousand Generations (Wan Shi Shi Biao). A stele commemorating the sage, a bestowal by the Mongol emperor in 1307, stands on the east side of the forward yard here within a protective wooden box (fig. 4.21). Confucian Temples became known as Wen Miao (Temple of Culture). They are found in all major cities and often house the local museum.

Sacrifices to the Sage were scheduled twice a year in the Qing, mid-spring and mid-autumn, as well as on his birthday, the 27th of the 8th lunar month. These were second-rank rites, and were often delegated by the emperors. In the Ming, Confucius was the only cult figure accorded such honors. By the Qing several legendary figures (Guan Yu and Wenchang, for example) were given similar rites. A sacrifice was much like a court gathering, with music, officials in attendance, and sometimes the emperor kneeling before the tablet of the Sage.

The temple houses a number of interesting artifacts in addition to the 1307 Yuan stele mentioned above:

(a) On the street east and west of the gate are two large steles (4 m in height) ordering officials to dismount. These employ six different scripts: Chinese, Manchu, Mongol, Uighur, Tuote (Tuotui), and Tibetan.

(b) The forward yard is lined across the rear with 198 steles (fig. 4.22) recording the names of Yuan, Ming, and Qing *jinshi* ("presented scholars;" see Box, p. 182). Only three Yuan steles are to be seen, having been dug up and replaced in the Kangxi era; most had been effaced. The seventy-seven Ming steles date from 1416–1643; the 118 Qing steles cover the Shunzhi through Guangxu reigns (1644–1904). Altogether 51,624 names are recorded. (Early Ming *jinshi* are recorded in Nanjing.)

4.21
Stele Honoring the Sage, 1307

THE EXAMINATION HELL

The nearly two hundred steles (fig. 4.22) arrayed in the courtyard of the Confucian Temple document the importance of the civil examination system in late Imperial China. This route to social status and official position had its roots in the early and middle empires, but truly came into its own in the Song (960–1279). While appointments based on recommendation (by social elites or officials) and privilege (typically being the son of an official) were the norm in early dynasties, written and oral examinations had begun as early as Han. By Tang times, specialized examinations were created to test mastery of the classics, such topics as military affairs, and skill at poetry and calligraphy. In Song times, access to education and to the examinations was sufficiently wide that a meritocracy came to dominate much of imperial officialdom.

Examinations on a three-year schedule characterized late Imperial times. The practice was interrupted in the early Yuan (but restored from 1315) and again in early Ming (after a false start in 1370, they resumed in 1384). In the Ming there were state-supported schools in county and prefectural cities; some students attended on government scholarships. Graduates (called gong sheng, "tribute students") could attend the imperial academy in the capital (Guozijian) and then assume minor posts. But the more significant entrée was via examinations in the provinces administered by local officials. Successful candidates became sheng yuan (rendered as "licentiates"), a privileged status marked by special attire and exemption from public works labor. Benjamin Elman estimates that only 30,000 (1.5 percent) of the two million examination candidates achieved this status in the Qing (143). These students then formed the pool for triennial provincial examinations that tested classical learning, literary skills, and application of both to policy making. Success here led to status as ju ren ("raised candidates"). Such men assumed positions in the bureaucracy, for example as county magistrates. The ju ren, in turn, attempted the metropolitan (or national examinations) held in Beijing to gain the top degree of jin shi ("presented scholar," or doctor). Success rates were modest, starting at 10 percent and then declining. Over Ming-Qing times smaller and smaller real numbers attained this lofty status as compared to the huge total number of men in all levels of the system.

To skim the cream from the top, a final oral examination was conducted in the palace by the emperor to rank jin shi. Success here led to extraordinary privileges: the number one examinee (optimus or zhuang yuan) was allowed to exit the Forbidden City through the central portal of the Noon Gate normally reserved for the Son of Heaven. More important, these scholars could be sent to the Hanlin Academy to be groomed for service in the Grand Secretariat, the highest level of policy making in Ming times.

Examination candidates came to the capital on a regular schedule, and found temporary lodgings in hostels (huiguan), temples, and with families. The yard of 8,000 individual cells where the testing took place (Gong Yuan) was located near the present Academy of Social Sciences, north of Chang'an Avenue and Jianguo Men. It was demolished by 1913; the examinations had been abolished in 1905.

(c) Replicas of the Stone Drums (*shi gu*), boulders in the shape of drums with early inscriptions, are installed in the Da Cheng Men. The replicas were produced by Qianlong in 1790. The originals from Shaanxi had been held in the Northern Song capital, were taken by the Jin, like the Tai Hu rocks at Bei Hai, when they overran Kaifeng, and later became fixtures of the Yuan temple. The original Stone Drums are now in the Palace Museum.

(d) A set of Stone Classics endowed by Qianlong can be viewed under a roof in the corridor between

4.22
Stele listing *jinshi*, successful examination candidates

the Kong Miao and the Guozijian to the west. This set comprises 190 steles with a grand total of 630,000 characters for the Thirteen Classics.

The site was under restoration in 2007. Visitors should be alert for new historical displays in the galleries and halls flanking the court yards that were once used by the Capital Museum. The street in front leads eastward to Yonghe Gong [25 ▶], while a stroll to the west will bring one first to the Guozijian and eventually to the Bell and Drum Towers [6 ▶].

The Ming Valley

Like all imperial capitals, Beijing required imperial tombs. For this purpose, Yongle's advisors selected a scenic valley 40 km to the north in the foothills of the Tianshou Mountains (fig. 4.23). The Ming founder, Zhu Yuanzhang (Hongwu, r. 1368–98), by contrast, had sited his tomb, the Xiaoling, a short distance east of the Nanjing palaces in nearby suburbs. Following the Xiaoling as his model, Yongle began work on his tomb, named Changling, upon the death of his empress née Xu in 1409. As the first emperor to utilize the valley, Yongle chose a prime location near the center of the valley floor nestled against the eastern hills. Over the next two hundred years, twelve more Ming emperors were to be buried here. None of their tombs, however, can match the scale of Changling. (The last Ming emperor, a suicide, was buried ignominiously in a tomb already prepared for one of his consorts.)

With the fall of the Ming in 1644, the Manchu armies vandalized some of the tombs as pay back for the desecration by the Ming of the Jin tombs in the Western Hills (see p. 51). (The Ruzhen Jin dynasty was regarded as ancestral to the Manchus, who as they were in the ascent even styled themselves Jin.) Over the long term, however, the Qing court protected the Ming Valley, and even restored some tombs, including the Dingling (see below). The valley was under guard until the early twentieth century. Today most of the compounds in the valley are in ruinous condition, and only at Changling do an original gate and sacrificial hall survive. The "thirteen tombs of the Ming valley" (Ming Shisan Ling) were placed on the National Register in 1961. The valley has become one of the most visited locales in Beijing and is now enrolled as a World Heritage site with the Eastern and Western Qing imperial tombs in neighboring Hebei (see below).

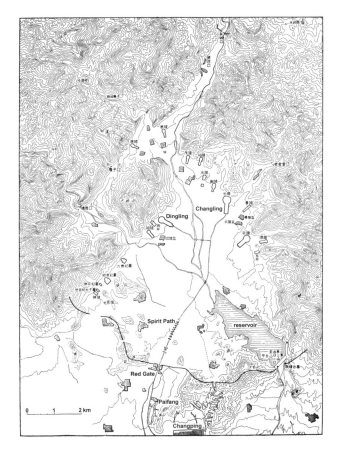

4.23
Map of Ming Valley, from *Dingling*, 3

PAILOU AND PAIFANG

One encounters a characteristic monument of the pre-modern city while visiting the Confucian Temple: *pailou* and *paifang*. The street leading to the temple is Guozijian Jie, National Academy Street, and is marked at each end by a well-maintained *pailou* (fig. 4.24). The custom of signaling important locales (palaces, gardens, temples, and tombs) and streets or intersections with a gateway was widespread in Ming and Qing times, with a hundred or more major examples in the capital as well as the less imposing gates associated with neighborhoods. The latter were called *shalan* (pronounced *shala'r* in Beijing speech). In 1794, some 1200 neighborhood gateways were refurbished upon imperial command.

Gateways of this general type started in the Han, if not earlier. They were customary in the early imperial era when neighborhoods (*fang*) were walled and sealed by gates that opened and closed at dawn and dusk each day. From Song times onward city wards were not enclosed, but the use of gateways without doors to name neighborhoods continued. *Pailou* also gave their names to several of the most important intersections in old Beijing, for example Dong Dan and Xi Dan (east and west single *pailou*) and Dong Si and Xi Si (east and west four *pailou*). These four spots are prominent on Zhang Jue's map of 1560 (see p. 11). Beginning in the early twentieth century, many Beijing *pailou* were torn down to make more room for vehicular traffic.

The simplest *pailou* consist of a pair of wooden columns anchored by stone bases with a lintel connecting them. They

4.24 *Pailou*, Guozijian Jie

PORCELAIN PAILOW BEFORE THE HALL OF CLASSICS.

4.25 "Porcelain Pailou before the Hall of Classics," from Eliza Ruhamah Scidmore, "The Streets of Peking," *Century Magazine*, 58.6 (1899), 869

may or may not be capped by a miniature tile eave running across the lintel. Variations on this structural type range up to five bays (six columns) at the largest sites. Some timber *pailou* have eaves over each bay (fig. 4.26) and sometimes in lower flanking positions as well. Thus a three-bay *pailou* could have nine miniaturized arrays of brackets supporting eaves. An example can be seen fronting Baiyun Guan, with three bays and seven eaves (see fig. 5.32).

Stone *pailou* (also called *paifang*) survive in greater numbers at many protected sites. Stone examples have been seen already at the precincts of the Altar to Heaven (see fig. 4.13) and other altars around the capital, and will be seen on the approach to the Ming Valley (fig. 4.27) as well. Inherently more massive, stone gateways do not require the bracing struts placed against the columns or the iron straps that were used to hold lintels and brackets in place often found on their wooden analogues. A late example of a stone *pailou* is the so-called Ketteler Memorial erected after the Boxer Uprising to memorialize the German minister killed at the beginning of hostilities. After World War I, it was relocated to Zhongshan Park, the former She Ji Tan [13 ▶]. It has been rededicated as a peace memorial.

4.27 *Paifang*, approach to Ming Valley

A final category, also called *paifang*, is the glazed tile masonry gateway found at several large temple sites, such as Dong Yue Miao. Within the Guozijian is a fine example from the Qianlong era (fig. 4.25), with brilliant yellow and green tiles comparable to the best work in the Inner Court. These masonry examples have thick barrel vault portals. Carved tile is used to imitate all parts of the timber prototype.

4.26
Dong Si *Pailou* looking to Chaoyang Men, postcard, anonymous

The Approach:
Great Archway
to Spirit Path

On the way into the Ming Valley just north of Changping, one encounters a massive marble ceremonial archway (*paifang*) built in 1540 and now on the east side of the road (figs. 4.27 and 4.28). This structure mimics the timber-frame gateways that once adorned major crossroads in the capital, here at grand scale (see Box, p. 186). The archway designates the approach to the imperial tombs. This function is documented at least from the Han period when gate towers (*que*) were erected to announce the "spirit path" (*shen dao*) at tomb sites. The archway was not a part of Yongle's original design, however. But by the time it was erected the valley had become the necropolis for all the Ming sovereigns and surely required such a statement. With five bays, the *paifang* is 29 m across, the six square pillars rising from large blocks surmounted by crouching magical animals. Three tiers of lintels cross overhead; the top tier carries miniaturized brackets and roof tiles. The carving of this structure is some of the finest work from this period.

The 40 sq km of valley floor and surrounding hills was encircled by a red brick wall manned by a garrison from Changping. The main entrance, called the Great Red Gate (Da Hong Men), closely resembled the Great Ming Gate that commanded the approach to the Imperial City in the capital (see fig. 3.3). This gate has a yellow-tile roof over three vaulted portals. Note the use of plain cornices to carry the eaves, rather than miniature brackets. Walls flanking the gate long ago disappeared.

Behind this gate and aligned with the central opening stands a stele pavilion, a double eave of yellow tile over red masonry, with vaulted passages on all four faces. This structure houses a stone slab almost 8 m in height that proclaims itself the memorial stele of Changling. This text was written by the emperor's son

Zhu Gaozhi (the Hongxi emperor, r. 1425), but was
not erected until 1435 by his grandson, Zhu Zhanji
(the Xuande emperor, r. 1426–35). On its back face
are poems commemorating the Ming tombs written
by Qianlong as well as a record of expenses incurred
restoring the site. A walled compound where the
emperors changed their attire during the labors of visiting the valley once stood on the east.

Four marble columns (*huabiao*) flank Yongle's stele
pavilion, comparable to those at the Gate of Heavenly
Peace (see fig. 3.7). Dragons spiral up their shafts,
which are supported by round Mount Sumeru bases.
Clouds spew forth on two sides; the caps are carved
with lotus petal borders and topped by kneeling animals. Thus the entrance of the Ming Valley makes
explicit its equivalence with the Imperial City as residences of the Son of Heaven in life and death respectively. This equivalence between capital and suburban
tombs was current at least by the Tang.

The ceremonial approach or Spirit Path built for
Yongle's own tomb by default came to serve all thir-

4.28
Recumbent lion above
playing lions

teen burials. The approach was probably completed ca. 1435 when the grand stele above was erected by Xuande. The oldest spirit paths with arrays of stone sculpture are found at the imperial and princely tombs of the Southern Dynasties near Nanjing, but the custom has roots in the Han. Now free of traffic, the Spirit Path is a secluded area shaded in season by luxuriant willows. The sequence of carvings starts with a pair of simple pillars, and then continues over 1060 m with twenty-four stone animals in standing and kneeling pairs and twelve officials (fig. 4.29). The selection of animals and figures is indebted to the Tang and Song necropolises. Some of the animals are imaginary, auspicious or apotropaic creatures (*qilin, xiezhi*), while others could have been part of the imperial entourage and menagerie (camels, horses, lions, and elephants). The larger-that-life human figures represent both military and civil officials including censors (fig. 4.30). A Spirit Gate (Lingxing Men) with three stone lintels separated by short walls ends this pathway. Similar gates can also be found at the Altar to Heaven and other ritual sites around the capital (see fig. 4.13).

Moving farther north into the valley, the first left turn on the highway leads to the Dingling, while proceeding straight takes one to the Changling.

4.29
"Minggraber,"
postcard by Hans Bahlke,
Peking

4.30
Head of official

Yongle's determination to bury his empress, daughter of general Xu Da, outside Beijing preceded his efforts to make the city into a new capital. The proximate model for Changling, which became their joint burial, was the tomb of his father, Hongwu, at Nanjing. In general style, the buildings follow the official architecture created in the first decades of the new regime by designers and builders (themselves southerners) charged with constructing palaces and altars around Nanjing. Although the mausoleum is no longer complete, Changling offers glimpses of this early Ming building idiom. Little as early survives today in the Forbidden City or capital (see Box, p. 31).

Aboveground, the Changling comprises three courtyards appended to a huge walled burial mound (fig. 4.31). The first yard is entered through a masonry gate with three portals fronted by a broad paved terrace. A red wall capped with yellow tile extends to both sides, enclosing a compound 141 m wide. This first yard is shallow, only 60 m deep, and bisected by the 5 m-wide imperial way (*yu dao*). On the east side is a stele pavilion. The face of this slab, however, bears

◀ 18
Changling

MING, CA. 1409–27
NATIONAL REGISTER,
1961; WORLD HERITAGE
SITE, 2003
MING VALLEY,
CHANGPING

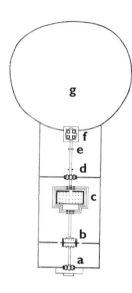

4.31
Plan of Changling, from
Beijing gu jianzhu (1986), 52.
Diagram shows: (a) front
gate, (b) Gate of Sacrificial
Offerings, (c) Hall of
Sacrificial Offerings, (d)
Lingxing Men, (e) Altar, (f)
Spirit Tower, (g) mound

no text, although the Qing emperors Shunzhi, Qianlong, and Jiaqing added short inscriptions. Galleries of five bays that were used for storage and as kitchens once faced onto this yard.

The second, main yard is entered through the Gate of Sacrificial Offerings (Ling'en Men), a five-bay structure 31 m wide on a low marble terrace. The gate house supports a single eave, hip-gable roof. Walls with secondary gates extend on each side to the perimeter. This yard is considerably deeper at 152 m, with the Hall of Sacrificial Offerings (Ling'en Dian) occupying the rear. There were once fifteen bays of galleries on both sides. The hall stands on a triple terrace mounted by ramps and steps on axis (fig. 4.32). It is nine bays by five, 66 m wide and 29 m deep, a double eave with hipped roof. Both main hall and yard are comparable to the buildings of the Outer Court of the Forbidden City or the Ancestral Temple. The hall is almost as large as the remodeled Taihe Dian, making it one of the largest wooden structures in China or the world. Fu Xinian's plan shows that the geometrical center of all three yards is at the center of this structure. Fu also determined that the entire compound, from front gate to the wall against the mound at rear is based on 5-*zhang* (50 foot) squares like the Inner Court of the Forbidden City.

As at the Ancestral Temple [14▶] main hall, the interior of the Ling'en Dian presents a forest of mammoth Nanmu columns aligned in parallel rows and files (fig. 4.33). The main columns are 6.68 m tall; the width of the hall is ten times their height. Eave columns are smallest in diameter at 79 cm; interior columns are 107 cm, while the central bay was given even larger specimens of 117 cm. This bay is more than 10 m square. All the columns are linked at the top by a heavy frame of tie beams running front to back and side to side. The huge lintels support a coffered ceiling. Miniature bracket sets are arrayed around the perimeter atop the exterior walls.

These timbers were harvested in the far southwest, floated down the Yangzi River and eventually up the Grand Canal in great rafts. They were prepared at the Shenmu Chang outside Chongwen Men at the capital. Their rich brown hues may not be their intended original appearance. Textual references suggest they were lacquered and some given a gold sur-

4.32
Hall of Sacrifices

4.33
"Ming Tombs," (Hall of Sacrifices), postcard by S. Yamamoto, Peking

face. They are probably irreplaceable today. The columns in all of the large halls of the Forbidden City today are composite construction instead. They were assembled from smaller timbers joined together, then wrapped in cloth and plaster and lacquer painted. Today this hall is used to display treasures removed from the Dingling (see below). The larger-than-life bronze image of Yongle is a recent addition, inspired by imperial portraits. In its day the center bay would have had a throne and altar table for venerating the spirit tablet of the deceased.

A third yard adjoins the mound (*bao cheng*) and is intermediate in scale when compared to the first two at 112 m deep. A square tower (*fang cheng*) on the south edge of the mound carries a Spirit Tower (*ming lou*), 18 m square, for the emperor's stele. The stele text reads: "the imperial tomb of Cheng zu, Wen huang di of the Great Ming." The stele itself is colored red, and does not rise from the customary tortoise. The mound is about 300 m in diameter. A 15 m-tall brick wall with parapets comparable to the walls of the capital encircles the earthen fill, which is overgrown with conifers. The prospect from the stele pavilion provides appealing glimpses of the valley.

19 ▶
Dingling

MING, CA. 1584–90,
1620
NATIONAL REGISTER,
1961; WORLD HERITAGE
SITE, 2003
MING VALLEY,
CHANGPING

The Wanli emperor, Zhu Yijun (r. 1572–1620), built his tomb over a period of six years beginning in 1584. He visited the site several times during his reign, and lived for some thirty years after its completion. One conservative estimate suggests the cost of this tomb over that period was equivalent to the total revenue of the imperial court for two years. Named Dingling, it became the resting place for the emperor and two of his consorts.

In 1955, the vice mayor of Beijing—a student of Ming history—proposed opening the Changling, tomb of Zhu Di (Yongle, r. 1403–24), the man who built Beijing. The State Council gave its approval and a working group was established. According to later accounts, this group decided to excavate a less challenging tomb first in preparation for the main event. So work began instead on the Dingling in June of 1956. Opening this tomb and clearing its chambers posed problems, but conserving the grave goods was even more difficult. Two years later, as the Great Leap began and with the experience of Dingling behind them, the advocates of excavating Changling decided not to proceed. Reading between the lines, it appears there was considerable opposition from the outset to excavating. Chinese archaeologists were not prepared, said critics like Xia Nai, to take responsibility for preserving what they might find. The resulting losses would be irretrievable. The deterioration and loss of imperial robes and silk textiles taken from the Dingling after excavation confirmed the reservations expressed by critics.

Like all of the Ming tombs, the Dingling is a walled precinct, rectangular in overall plan with a mound at the north (see the discussion of Changling above). The front portions of this precinct are courtyards divided by gates and walls akin to the Forbidden City in plan, architectural vocabulary, and style. However at Dingling only the stone platforms of the main gate and main hall survive. Behind the foundation of the sacrificial hall in the third yard is a stone altar table (*gong an*) with its standard complement of ritual gear: a tripod incense burner, two vases, and two candle sticks, all rendered in stone. The altar is situated under the open sky before the burial mound (*bao cheng*). Faced with the brick like the capital's walls and the Forbidden City, this mound is fronted by a masonry tower (*fang cheng*) topped by a pavilion (*ming lou*) that holds the stele commemorating Wanli. The view of the valley from the parapet is well worth the climb (fig. 4.34). The entrance to the underground burial chambers lies ahead.

In 1956 no other imperial tomb had been excavated, and no one could be certain what might lie within. In the event, the excavators enjoyed remarkable luck. While appraising the site, they noticed that bricks in the wall surrounding the mound west of the main axis had subsided. Opening a trench against this wall, they found themselves on a stone and brick ramp helpfully labeled by inscription "gate to the entrance ramp" (*sui dao men*). This access ramp wound east toward the central axis. To save time and avoid disturbing ancient pines growing on the mound, the archaeologists then opened another trench on axis midway between the stele tower and the crown of the mound. Their good fortune continued. Here a stone block left by the builders bore an inscription (fig. 4.35) detailing the distance to the underground chamber. These

4.34
View from mound
parapet, Dingling

explicit directions had been left by the tomb's builders, in the knowledge they would need to re-open the chambers for later interments of the imperial ménage.

Gaining entry, however, posed a further challenge. Inside the entry chamber, the excavators found a door locked from within that barred their way (fig. 4.36).

4.35
Inscription on stone block found during excavation *Dingling*, 13, reading: "From this stone to the chamber wall surface is 16 *zhang* [160 feet] at a depth of 3 *zhang* 5 *chi* [35 feet]."

0   5 cm

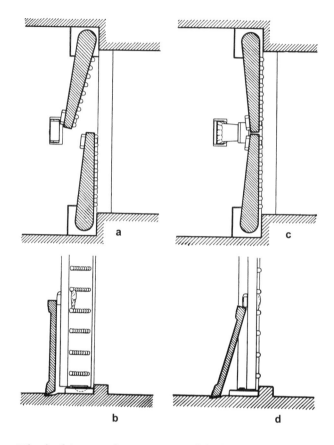

4.36
Self-locking door mecha-
nism, from *Dingling*, 20.
Above are plan views
showing door panels open
(a) and closed (c). Below
are side views showing
doors open (b) and closed
(d). Resting in a slot in the
floor, the strut falls into
place as the doors are
closed from the outside.

The locking mechanism was a slab that had fallen into place after the door panels were closed from the outside. This slab was anchored by slots in the floor and the back of the door panels. An ingenious laborer working with a length of wire inserted between the panels was able to yank this slab out of position. A film of the excavation in the Ling'en Dian of Changling features the opening of the door or a reenactment of it.

The chambers of the Dingling (fig. 4.37) that awaited the excavators are gigantic. The front chamber is a space 20 m long and 6 m wide with an interior height of 7.2 m. The central chamber behind it on axis is even longer at 32 m, similar in width and height. Across the axis a rear chamber measures 30 m wide and 9 m deep. These axial chambers are flanked by two parallel rooms of equivalent scale. All five chambers are stone, highly polished marble blocks that show no trace of deterioration, and vaulted construction. Large ceramic tiles (*jin zhuan*; Box, p. 79) were used for flooring, the same kind that glistens in the halls of the Forbidden City. Visitors enter the tomb today from the northeast corner by descending several flights of stairs and then proceed through the chambers toward the front, exiting at the south by climbing more stairs and ascending a ramp.

Today the tomb chambers are almost empty. At the time they were opened, however, decayed timbers were found covering the floor from the front door to the rear as protection for the surface when the huge coffins were hauled in on a sledge. Three stone thrones were placed at the rear of the central chamber, thus blocking the door to the coffin chamber. Each throne is accompanied by a small altar set like that above ground and large blue-and-white porcelain crocks

4.37
Plan of Dingling chambers, from *Dingling*, 14

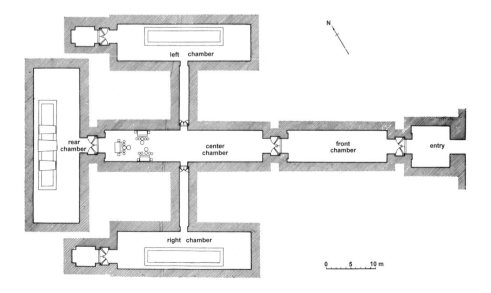

that held oil. In the rear chamber were three wooden double coffins on a low platform. All had decayed and collapsed, but their contents had never been disturbed. Replicas have been installed in their places. (The side chambers were never used for the consort burials.) From these coffins and additional chests placed at either side, the excavators retrieved large quantities of imperial robes and silks, plus many objects of gold, silver, and jade, 2600 items by official count. Many of these valuables are now displayed at Changling within its imposing sacrificial hall (the Ling'en Dian). A visit to Dingling logically should be followed by a viewing at the latter site.

The Eastern and Western Qing Tombs

The imperial tombs of the Qing emperors are located at considerable distances from Beijing. One group, the Dongling (eastern tombs), lies about 125 km northeast of the city in Zunhua County, Hebei, and accommodates five rulers. The other site, the Xiling (western tombs) located 110 km southwest of the city in Yixian, Hebei is the resting place of another four Manchu sovereigns. Pu Yi, the last emperor, was cremated; his ashes were placed initially at the Babaoshan cemetery west of the city. In 1995, however, they were removed to Xiling. With the thirteen mausolea of the Ming Valley, the Ming founder's burial at Nanjing and yet another Ming tomb in Hubei, the Qing tombs are now enrolled as World Heritage sites.

The first two rulers after 1644—Shunzhi and Kangxi—chose to locate their burials east of the capital amid terrain reminiscent of the Ming Valley (fig. 4.38). Indeed, most features of the Qing tombs closely follow the Ming: clusters of tombs in a natural bowl, arches, steles, and spirit path figures for the approach, and individual tomb precincts integrating aboveground yards with underground chambers. It is said

that during construction of a third tomb for the
Yongzheng emperor at Dongling the conditions were
found unacceptable, and the response was to choose
an entirely new siting for his tomb southwest of the
capital. While this may be true, the next emperor,
Qianlong, had no difficulty building his tomb in prox-
imity to his grandfather at the eastern site. The expla-
nation for two clusters is undoubtedly more complex.
In part it may involve the ancient system of alternate
left and right (*zhao* and *mu*) positions for different
generations found in the Confucian classics. The final
disposition of all nine tombs is shown in the table
below.

While the Ming model determined the design of
the Qing tombs, Manchu customs for interring
spouses led to a significantly greater number of imperial tombs (*ling*) at these sites than at the Ming Valley.
If an empress died before her spouse, the emperor was
expected to be interred upon his demise in the same
tomb. If, however, an emperor died before his empress,

4.38
View of Qing Dongling

it was not acceptable to reopen the imperial burial for her interment. Hence, tombs for empresses proliferated, generally at the east side of the emperor. The Dongling is home to five emperor's burials, but altogether has fourteen *ling* for a total of 156 (or 161) individuals. The situation at the Xiling is similar, with four emperor's tombs, and a total of 72 (or 80) individuals. (If Pu Yi is counted, there are five emperors.)

Other features distinguish the Qing burial precincts. The Qing placed great emphasis on an auspicious geomantic siting, carefully aligning each of the five Dongling with an individual peak to the north for example. However, the overall effect is quite different from the Ming Valley, where individual tombs are nestled into vales running into the foothills. At Dongling, the precincts are on the level plain. Moreover, the plan of each tomb was altered from the Ming model as seen at Changling, for example. The stele pavilion was placed on axis at the approach to the walled yards, rather than at one side in the first courtyard. Second, burial mounds and their walls at rear are downsized, and hence better integrated within a continuous perimeter. Third, at Dongling three additional spirit

Reign	Name, Death Year	Tomb Name	Relative Position
Dongling (Zunhua County, Hebei)			
1	Shunzhi, 1661	Xiaoling	center
2	Kangxi, 1722	Jingling	E
4	Qianlong, 1796	Yuling	W
7	Xianfeng, 1861	Dingling	2nd W
8	Tongzhi, 1874	Huiling	2nd E
Xiling (Yixian, Hebei)			
3	Yongzheng, 1735	Tailing	center
5	Jiaqing, 1820	Changling	SW
6	Daoguang, 1850	Muling	2nd SW
9	Guangxu, 1908	Chongling	NE

paths were constructed after that for Shunzhi, the founder. At Xiling, on the other hand, several tombs lack spirit path sculptures or have incomplete arrays.

At Dongling it is possible to enter the underground chamber of Qianlong (the Yuling), which is distinguished by extensive and unique relief carving on the doorways and walls. The reliefs embrace Tibetan Buddhist subject matter with inscriptions, like the Huang Si or Biyun Si in Beijing. The Ding Dong ling, the tomb for Cixi the famed late Qing Empress Dowager (d. 1908), is notable for the construction of its halls using rich hard woods adorned with gilt bronze fittings (fig. 4.39).

4.39
Sacrificial Hall, Dong Dingling (tomb of Cixi)

For an emperor's own view of his roles cosmic and mundane, see Jonathan Spence, *Emperor of China: Self-Portrait of K'ang-hsi* (1974). Evelyn S. Rawski's *The Last Emperors* (1998) presents the public and private rituals of the Manchu rulers in detail.

For the imperial altars, see Jeffrey F. Meyer, *The Dragons of Tiananmen: Beijing as a Sacred City* (1991), ch. 3, "'Heaven Is Round, Earth Is Square': the

SUGGESTED READING

Suburban Altars of Beijing." James L. Hevia considers one great ceremonial event in all of its intriguing detail: *Cherishing Men from Afar: Qing Guest Ritual and the Macartney Embassy of 1793* (1995).

Benjamin Elman had written the ultimate account of the examinations in *A Cultural History of Civil Examinations in Late Imperial China* (2000).

On the Ming tombs, see Ann Paludan, *The Imperial Ming Tombs* (1981); also Evelyn S. Rawski, "The Imperial Way of Death: Ming and Ch'ing Emperors and Death Ritual," in *Death Ritual in Late Imperial and Modern China*, eds. James L. Watson and Evelyn S. Rawski (1988), 228–53.

Temples for Gods and Buddhas

5

Apart from the worship of Heaven and of Earth—official rather than popular rites—there were many religious cults in China and many temples to different faiths in Peking. That these existed so peaceably side by side was due to the innate toleration of a people not given by nature to strong religious convictions or antipathies and willing to let each man seek truth in his own way.

JULIET BREDON, *PEKING* (1931), 174

It might be supposed that most of the great old temples of Beijing have disappeared. To be sure there have been numerous losses in the last century. Yet in Ming and Qing times the city supported no more than two or three dozen very large establishments; the great majority of temples were quite small.

Susan Naquin compiled detailed data on the number of temples of all kinds in Peking. She came to a total of 2564 establishments mentioned between 1403 and 1911, and concluded that even this large figure represents an undercount (Naquin, 710). The number of temples fluctuated over time, of course. From 1400, about forty temples are known; by the late Ming (ca. 1590) the number rises to 480. By 1800 the total is over 600, and by the 1880s, 700 (Naquin, 19–20). Nonetheless, fewer than 10 percent were larger than a single hall and yard (24). And of that small fraction, fully 90 percent were medium-sized establishments, defined as between two and five halls (26). No more than two or three dozen temples were larger. Naquin can be certain of twenty-seven sites with more than five halls during the five centuries she studied. The temples treated below are almost all in this latter, quite exceptional, category. Thus the great loss of temples has not affected grand halls and images, but rather modest temples that served a hutong or market.

Naquin also developed estimates for the clerical population of Beijing temples. A proper census attempted in 1908, the best source, found about 2000 professional religious: monks and nuns, Daoists, and lamas, about a third of them resident in temple precincts (Naquin, 49). Such small numbers of professionals, however, misrepresent the importance of temples for the life of the capital.

In pre-modern times, temples served a variety of purposes for a broad segment of the population. Temples were the recipients of imperial patronage, as they had been under the Liao, Jin, and Yuan rulers as well. Of some 1091 temples known during the Ming, forty-four had been founded by emperors (149). The mother of the Wanli emperor, Empress Li, herself established thirteen temples, restored a dozen more, and certainly made gifts to many others (156). Temple names were "imperially-bestowed" (*chi cì*) in 185 cases which usually signals imperial family and eunuch patronage (164). The Manchu rulers were no less invested in sponsoring religious devotions, dedicating steles and images, gifting canons of Buddhism and Daoism, and otherwise fulfilling their roles as benefactors of virtue and moral conduct. Indeed, every temple that can be visited in Beijing today is essentially a Qing site, its size, layout, halls, images, and other assets evidence of pious support from Kangxi, and/or Qianlong, and their descendants.

Temples also served residents of the capital, both local and temporary, the latter a large proportion given the constant comings and goings of examination can-

didates and officials. For these ordinary residents, temples were public spaces, a rare thing in pre-modern
China. With the exception of markets and theaters,
there were few venues where people could gather,
engage in formal and informal group activity, perhaps
find an identity outside their family, or trade news and
gossip. Temples were the sites of mixing genders, ages,
and economic and social status. The great temple fairs
(Box, p. 209) that developed on a regular schedule
were the closest approximation in pre-modern times
to civic events (except perhaps that rare imperial occasion visible to the general population). Several of the
temples that thrive today (fig. 5.1) were known for
their periodic fairs, and some have been revived, such
as New Year visits to Dong Yue Miao [26 ▶].

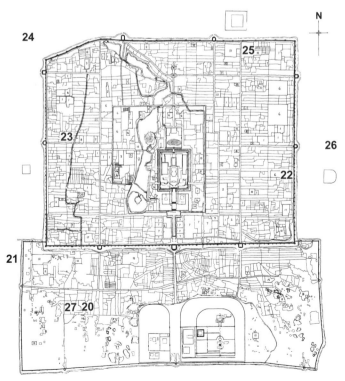

5.1
Map of Ming and Qing
Beijing, from *Beijing gu
jianzhu* (1986), 6.
Numbers refer to sites
discussed in this chapter.

In spite of their Qing-era guises, many Beijing temples claim ancient pedigrees. Naquin's pre-modern sources cite about two dozen temples in the capital region with origins in the Tang or earlier (117), and another twenty from the Liao. Records also mention seventeen temples of Jin date. The oldest temples to survive are found in the Outer City, the southwest quadrant of old Beijing (see Ch. 1). Other ancient establishments are nestled in the Western Hills and elsewhere amid the mountains (see Box. p. 247).

Buddhist Temples

A recent volume illustrates ten Buddhist temples in the city today, a small fraction compared to the numbers that flourished in any earlier period. Several of these sites have assumed new primary identities as museums (Wanshou Si as an art gallery; Juesheng Si as the Bell Museum), while others are historic sites, fragmentary compounds without halls (Tianning Si, Cishou Si). Another eight or ten temples can be found on any good city map showing the area within the Third Ring Road, but these are not open and are in various states of repair. Another five temples dedicated to Tibetan (and Mongolian) Buddhism are considered separately below.

5.2
"Feather Dusters for Sale—Entrance gate of Lung-fu-ssu," from Eliza Ruhamah Scidmore, "The Streets of Peking," *Century Magazine*, vol. 58.6 (1899), 872

HALF-TONE PLATE ENGRAVED BY C. SCHWARZBURGER.

FEATHER DUSTERS FOR SALE.—ENTRANCE GATE OF LUNG-FU-SSU.

TEMPLE FAIRS

Temple markets (*miao shi*) and fairs (*miao hui*) were a characteristic feature of Beijing in late imperial times. The markets were largely a Qing development. After the Manchu banners occupied the Inner City, the one periodic market at the City God Temple was moved to Baoguo Si in the Outer City (Naquin, 441). Gradually a schedule for these markets developed so that by the late eighteenth century every day of the month had a market operating in one area or another (see Table). Markets usually convened at ten-day intervals so that one might say this or that market was on the "fives" or the "nines." Thus the largest market at Longfu Si, northeast of the Imperial City, opened on days with a 9 or 10: the 9th, 10th, 19th, 20th, 29th and 30th. The temples earned fees ("incense money") for renting out space; the merchants gained a venue and ready-made neighborhood clientele. Shoppers not only found merchandise (fig. 5.2), but also food, entertainment, and a variety of services.

Qing-era Temple Markets	
Days of Month	Temple (District)
11, 21	Tian Qiao District
1 & 15	Dong Yue Miao [26 ▶]
	Yao Wang Miao
1, 15, 25	Baoguo Si
1–15	Chongyuan Guan
1–10	Dazhong Si
3, 13, 23	Tu Di Miao
	(Xuanwu Men Wai)
4, 14, 24	Hua Shi District
5s–6s	Bai Ta [23 ▶]
7s–8s	Huguo Si
9s–10s	Longfu Si

Sources: Naquin, 442–43 and 629; Gamble, Survey (1921), 475

By contrast, temple fairs were annual celebrations linked to the temple's god or founder. For example, on the 19th day of the first moon, the Immortal Qiu was said to reappear at Baiyun Guan. On the 23rd day of the third moon, the Daoists of Dong Yue Miao celebrated the birth anniversary of the Lord of Mount Tai. Such fairs combined the commerce of a market with religious activities: a procession, special offerings, or theatrical performances. In the *Adventures of Wu*, the author describes such an event:

> Almost quite as important in the schedules of the Peking-ren as making new year calls is visiting the Buddhist and Daoist temples during the festivities. Of these temples the most outstanding ones are the Dong Yue Miao or "Temple of the Eastern Sacred Mountain" ... people come from different parts of the city to worship there on new year's day ... Here then, before the images of the gods and goddesses of Buddhistic and Daoistic Pantheon, the Peking-ren kowtow and pray for the realization of their fond desires, for health, wealth, marriage and so on as new year's day is an important day to begin a new page of life ... In the spacious temple courtyards a big fair is held where there are found all kinds of small merchants with their special stalls selling different varieties of seasonal toys and souvenirs and which activity overshadows all the rest of the business life in the temple premises except perhaps the collection of donations from pilgrims.

H. Y. Lowe, *The Adventures of Wu* (1940), 2.162–63

20 ▶
Fayuan Si

TANG THROUGH QING,
CA. 645–1733
NATIONAL REGISTER,
2001
NO. 7 FAYUAN SI QIAN
JIE, XUANWU

Fayuan Si (Temple of the Origin of the Dharma) traces its history from the Tang invasions of the Korean peninsula. It can claim not only the patronage of emperor Taizong, but also that of An Lushan and Shi Siming, the generals who nearly overthrew the Tang house in the mid-eighth century. Located near the east wall of the Tang and Liao cities, it was established in 645 (Zhenguan 19) as Minzhong Si by a vow of the emperor (Li Shimin) in memory of fallen soldiers of the Korean campaigns. Twin pagodas that graced the compound were erected in 755 and 757 by the two generals (see fig. 1.1), and indeed the oldest stele at the temple records the second. Other Tang-era inscriptions claim this temple was the only Buddhist establishment to survive the great proscription of Buddhism in the mid-ninth century. However, a fire in 882 destroyed the whole compound, and the subsequent history of the temple through the Liao, Jin, and Yuan eras is one fire after another with much rebuilding. The revival of the temple by a Ming eunuch, Song Wenyi, in 1438 insured its survival. Renamed Chongfu Si, the present temple plan originated with this fifteenth-century resurrection. But, as so often happens in Beijing, it was reconstruction in 1733 by the Yongzheng emperor that erected the present buildings and determined the current name.

Today Fayuan Si is one of the largest temple precincts in the city, measuring 220 m north-south and 76 to 103 m east-west. Even so this is only a fraction of the Tang foundation. Six yards are disposed along the central axis from south to north, with other compounds arrayed in parallel on east and west, a layout typical for Beijing's Buddhist temples (fig. 5.3). Indeed, the components listed below are found at most city temples.

The Front Gate (Shan Men) comprises three masonry entrances covered by gray tile with a pair of white marble lions at the central door. The Chinese term means "mountain gate," a reference to Buddhist establishments sited in the mountains away from population centers. A screen wall (*yingbi*) opposite shares the red and gray colors of the gates.

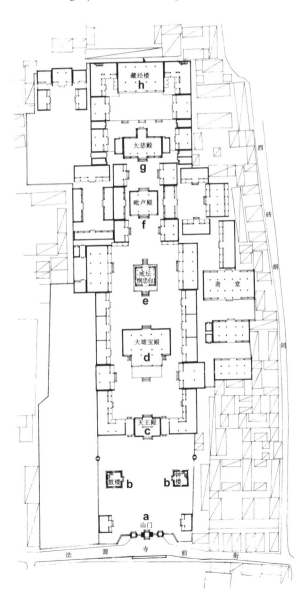

5.3
Plan of Fayuan Si, from Wang, *Xuan Nan,* 112. Diagram shows: (a) Front Gate, (b) Bell and Drum Towers, (c) Heavenly Kings Hall, (d) Buddha Hall, (e) Ordination Platform, (f) Vairocana Hall, (g) Dabei Hall, (h) Sutra Repository

The entrances open onto a shaded yard with Bell and Drum Towers (Zhonglou, Gulou) disposed on the east and west sides, respectively. These are simple two-story buildings of square plan with masonry lower floors and timbered upper ones. At some temples, such as Zhihua Si [22 ▶], it is possible to enter and, for a modest fee, strike the bell. On the paved path leading north is a large iron censer; two bronze lions of imperial manufacture front the steps to the next hall. All date from the eighteenth century.

The Heavenly Kings Hall (Tianwang Dian) serves, in turn, as the gate house for the second yard (fig. 5.4). Its arched doorway and matching stone window frames are a design common among Ming and Qing temples. Galleries connect the gate to the compound behind. Inside the gate house facing the visitor is Maitreya, the Future Buddha, in a form known as Da Du ("big stomach"), the prototype for the "happy Buddhas" found in Chinese restaurants around the world. Maitreya's smiling face and rotund physique contrast with the four stern guardian kings (*tian wang, lokapala*) in the end bays and the armored guardian Weituo behind, all protectors of the Buddhist law (*fa, dharma*). The bronze images seem to be a set, probably Ming. All Buddhist precincts are given protection, although today many gate house images are recent replace-

5.4
Heavenly Kings Hall,
Fayuan Si

ments. These images were vulnerable, and easily fell prey to Red Guards during the Cultural Revolution.

Six steles arrayed before the terrace ahead (fig. 5.5) document imperial patronage of the temple, as do inscriptions on the iron censer, a bell and drum in the porch, and the placard over the door written by Qianlong. The Buddha Hall (Da Xiong Bao Dian) sits across the axis on an elevated foundation with a moon terrace in front. The Chinese phrase used to name this hall refers to Sakyamuni Buddha from the Indian term Mahavira, rendered as "Great Heroic One." The term *bao* ("treasure") refers both to the Buddha and to his precepts, two of the canonical "Three Treasures" (Buddha, *dharma,* and *sangha,* the last being the monastic community). Inside the five-bay hall a seated image of Vairocana (Pilushana, the Cosmic Buddha) is attended by standing Great Bodhisattvas, Manjusri (Wenshu) and Samantabhadra (Puxian), principals of the *Avatamsaka Sutra.* All are Ming wood-core lacquered sculptures. They in turn are attended by eighteen *lohan* (*arhat*) of later date. Look in the central bay here for two stone column bases with lotus petals; they are thought to be traces of a Tang hall.

Another step north is the Ordination Terrace (Jie Tai, Minzhong Tai) with a high foundation and square, three-bay plan. By temple tradition this was

5.5
Buddha Hall,
Fayuan Si

the location of the Tang-era principal hall. This hall now displays Buddhist images and inscriptions linked to the history of the *dharma* in the capital region. Ordination platforms are not found in most temples, although Beijing has several others including Jietai Si and Yonghe Gong [25 ▶].

The third major hall on axis is the Rushana Hall (Pilu Dian, Vairocana Hall). The hall's main image is an enormous cast bronze representation of Vairocana above Buddhas of the Four Quadrants with myriad Buddhas of the universe on a lotus petal globe.

Yet another worship hall (the Dabei Dian dedicated to Avalokitesvara) stands another step north; it is now used to house gifts from Buddhists around the world.

The main axis concludes at the two-story Sutra Repository (Zangjing Ge) within its own shaded yard (fig. 5.6). Multi-story buildings of this kind are common at the rear of temple precincts. Three images are in worship on the upper level, while sutras are displayed below. Four more stone plinths here have attracted scholarly attention; they may date to the late ninth-century rebuilding of the temple.

5.6
Sutra Repository,
Fayuan Si

Residential yards and gardens fill the temple's east and west secondary routes, the abbot's quarters (*fang zhang*) and refectory both on the east. Fayuan Si is the seat of the Chinese Academy of Buddhism (Zhongguo Foxue Yuan), which trains monks, and also houses a Buddhist Library. Its facilities are now next door on the west.

Most of the larger Buddhist and Daoist temples of Beijing have comparable plans. Temples vary in the number of yards and halls on the primary axis and the presence of parallel, secondary ones. Because of Qing patronage, the architectural idiom of most temples is akin to the imperial palaces and altars described in Ch. 3 and Ch. 4 above. The primary distinction among these sites is the use of glazed roof tiles (yellow or green) in some instances, and gray, unglazed tiles in most cases. Most of the temples that are open today have been among the sights of the capital since the Ming period. Then as now they attracted both the faithful (local residents and pilgrims) and the merely curious. Offerings of incense and other items are common at most, posing a perpetual challenge to the preservation of these sites.

Within modern Beijing, the only monument to survive from the cities that predate the Mongol capital is the pagoda at Tianning Si (Temple of Heavenly Tranquility; fig. 5.7). Like many other capital temples, Tianning Si was founded in the medieval era and experienced repeated transformations that have left little from former incarnations. Known as Guanglin Si in the Northern Wei and as Hongye Si in Sui, the temple was renamed Tianwang Si (Heavenly Kings Temple) in the Tang, a name it retained under the Liao. In the Jin period, the temple was again renamed (as Dawan Si), but in the Xuande era of Ming (1426–35), gained its present appellation.

◄21
Tianning Si
Pagoda

LIAO, 1119–1120
NATIONAL REGISTER,
1988
TIANNING SI QIAN JIE,
XUANWU

In the Ming and Qing periods, temple traditions recorded in steles at the site attributed this brick pagoda to the Sui (ca. 581–617). Its true date became a matter of debate in the 1930s when the architectural historian Liang Sicheng (1901–72) first investigated. Lacking specific documentary evidence, Liang carefully analyzed the design and structure. From comparisons with other, firmly dated pagodas, he suggested the early twelfth century (Liao). This dating was confirmed in 1992 when a stele was recovered during restoration. This handsome structure can now be dated with assurance to 1119–1120 (Tianqing 9–10), the reign of Yelu Chun, a Qidan imperial uncle and the only ruler of an upstart regime known to history as Northern Liao. Yelu was served by a pair of brother masons, Kou Shiying and Kou Shixing named in the stele text, who managed construction. Building required a mere ten months.

Halls surrounding the pagoda have come and gone; today only the front gate and a single worship hall remain, both from the Qing (Qianlong reign?). In recent times, the site has been overshadowed by the smokestack of a nearby power plant on one side and crowded by a record factory on the other. In 1976, the Tangshan earthquake caused the brick spire to fall; the spire itself was a restoration from the eighteenth century. Today the site is well protected, but not at this writing open to the public. Refurbished gate and placards suggest it may soon be possible to visit.

The pagoda (fig. 5.8) is solid masonry, and surely was intended to hold precious relics (*sheli, sarira*). In recent years, Liao pagodas with imperial connections have yielded copious relics during restorations. Deposits could be placed in an underground chamber, near the top of the structure, or in wall niches. For example, a pagoda of mid-eleventh century date

5.7
Tianning Si pagoda

(1051) that collapsed in suburban Fangshan County in 1977 held a stone sutra pillar in its base and five ceramic miniature pagodas in chambers within the main story containing Tang relics and fragmentary images recovered after the ninth-century persecution of Buddhism. The Tianning Si pagoda may well encapsulate relics, perhaps dating as early as its pre-Tang founding.

Liao temple plans often place pagodas (*ta*) or multi-story belvederes (*ge*) in a central position on axis (unlike Minzhong Si above; see fig. 1.1). Tianning Si pagoda is eight-sided, rising from a broad terrace on a high pedestal, with a full-scale main story and thirteen closely set eaves capped by a tile roof and elaborate spire (height 55 m). The proportions are pleasing: the height of the pedestal and main story is about half that of the upper eaves. The original iron spire would probably have been about the same height as both the pedestal and main story. Elaborate brick bracket clusters carry the eaves, and like doorways, windows, and corner columns mimic timber-frame construction (fig. 5.9). According to the dedication of 1119–1120, the reliefs applied to the main story represent an assembly of deities and their attendants derived from the *Yuanjue* and *Huayan* (*Avatamsaka*) sutras, two important texts of Esoteric Buddhism.

5.8
Elevation of Tianning Si, from Wang, *Xuan Nan*, 226

5.9
Doorway and guardians, Tianning Si

The Cishou Si Pagoda (dated 1576–78) in Linglong Park, Balizhuang, west of the old city and endowed by the late Ming Empress Dowager Li (d. 1614), is an imitation of the Tianning Si pagoda with brackets and details that conform to its own period.

22 ▶

Zhihua Si

MING, 1443–46
NATIONAL REGISTER,
1961
NO. 5 LUMICANG
HUTONG, DONGCHENG

Hundreds of temples of all persuasions flourished during the Ming period. Today only one relatively complete ensemble of structures from this era survives, on a narrow hutong on the city's east side. Zhihua Si (Temple of the Realization of Wisdom) was enrolled on the National Register in 1961 in recognition of its several assets: buildings from the fifteenth century associated with the imperial court, a rare sutra cabinet and imperial edition of the Chinese-language Tripitaka (Buddhist Canon), and a tradition of palace music.

Zhihua Si was constructed as a family temple by the notorious Ming eunuch Wang Zhen (d. 1449), intimate of the Ming emperor Zhu Qizhen (r. 1436–49 and 1457–64, known as Yingzong). It was this emperor's sad fate to be captured by the Mongol leader Esen in 1449 while on a campaign that had been advocated by Wang. The catastrophe led to the installation of the hostage emperor's brother, Zhu Qiyu, as sovereign (r. 1450–56), known to history as the Jingtai emperor. Even after the captive Son of Heaven's release, the Jingtai emperor remained on the throne. The former sovereign was incarcerated in the southeast corner of the Imperial City at a site now known as Pudu Si (the Qing-era Mahakala Temple; see p. 18). Zhu Qizhen was eventually restored as the Tianshun emperor (1457–64, his second reign). By then Wang Zhen has been forced to commit suicide. The temple was given imperially patronage thereafter.

Wang's temple was imposing (an area 279 m by 44 m is still intact) and, more important, was erected by artisans who utilized building materials from imperial construction depots.

Four courtyards are open. In a forecourt accessible by the Front Gate on Lumicang hutong stand two steles (fig. 5.10) that document the "imperially bestowed name" and mention Wang Zhen. (Note, however, that Wang's name has been effaced with a few chisel strokes.) The forecourt also contains Drum and Bell Towers (fig. 5.11); both can be entered, and for a modest sum the bell can be struck. A central yard can be entered via the Tianwang Dian (or Zhihua Men). Several ancient fruit trees between the two small-scale side halls (the Zang Dian and Dazhi Dian) and the main image hall (Zhihua Dian) shade this yard. A third yard fronts the two-story Rulai Dian, while a fourth, rear yard contains the Dabei Tang, now used for a display about palace music. All of these halls have black-glazed roof tiles, a sign of status below the yellow and green tiles available to the emperor and imperial princes, respectively.

The image hall (Zhihua Dian; fig. 5.12) on the north of the main yard is three bays across (18 m by 14.5 m) with a single-eave, hip-gable roof. On the altar sit images of Sakyamuni (Shijia Fo), the Historical Buddha, Amitabha (Emituo Fo), the Buddha of the Western Pure Land, and Bhaisajyaguru (Yaoshi Fo),

5.10
Below left: Gate and steles, Zhihua Si

5.11
Below: Bell Tower in front courtyard

5.12
Above: Image Hall,
(Zhihua Dian)

5.13
Above right: Tathagata Hall
(Rulai Dian)

the Healing Buddha. Behind the altar ensemble in a porch is another temple treasure: a fifteenth-century mural depicting the bodhisattva Ksitigarbha (Dizang) on a plastered wall (3 m by 4.6 m). This is one of few Ming Buddhist wall paintings extant in the city today, and likely the work of palace painters. (The Dahui Si, ca. 1513, in Haidian District, preserves Ming murals and a spectacular sculptural ensemble of the Twenty-eight Protectors of the Law at larger-than-life scale; the suburban Fahai Si, ca. 1439, in Shijingshan District, is renowned for its murals.) The caisson ceiling (*cao jing*) of this hall was sold in the 1930s by penurious monks to the Philadelphia Museum of Art.

The Sutra Hall (Zang Dian) on the west side of the main yard, unassuming on the exterior, has an extraordinary hexagonal sutra cabinet on a stone Mount Sumeru base (height 4 m). The design imitates rotating sutra library cases; this one is fixed. Guardians of the law are carved on the stone base, while the wooden frames for each face carry an array of motifs like the arches of the Cloud Terrace at Juyong Guan: Garuda, Makara, Naga kings (see fig. 1.18). Above a Buddha seated atop the cabinet is a circular caisson ceiling, superlative carpentry from a Ming palace workshop.

The temple's third yard is overshadowed by the two-story Tathagata Hall (Rulai Dian; fig. 5.13), named for the Sakyamuni image on the lower level. It is fronted by a low moon terrace (8 x 8 m) and a pair of blank steles. This is a five-by-three bay structure measuring 18 by 11.6 m, with a single-eave, hipped roof. Masonry walls fill three sides; a balcony at the second level is mounted over skirting eaves below. On the ground level is an octagonal Mount Sumeru base with an image of Sakyamuni 4 m tall, and two standing attendants. Sutra cabinets fill both sides. Stairs at the back right corner allow the pious and curious to climb to the second level, called the Ten Thousand Buddha Pavilion (Wan Fo Ge) for the miniature niches filled with Buddha images against the walls. Here another octagonal base supports an image of Vairocana, height 3.5 m. Strong men (*dvarapala*) and armored guardians (*lokapala*) perching on this base like marionettes are among the visual delights of this temple.

The caisson ceiling once over Vairocana—about 4 m on a side with a gilded dragon coiled at center—has also been removed. It now adorns the Nelson-Atkins Museum in Kansas City, Missouri. Since most of the early Ming halls within the Forbidden City have burned and been rebuilt, usually more than once (see Box, p. 118), the ceilings of Zhihua Si—including that still above the Sutra cabinet today—are rare evidence for Ming-period palace carpentry. Another benefit of climbing to the second level is the opportunity to view at close range unrestored gold, green, and blue designs painted on the beams and brackets.

Zhihua Si is famed for a living tradition of palace music (*gong yue*) with a history of five hundred years. The monks of the temple have preserved musical texts, instruments, and the performance practices of their predecessors through over twenty-eight generations. A troupe of musicians makes the temple its home; they can often be heard practicing. In recent years, performances have been scheduled daily both mornings and afternoons.

Tibetan Buddhist Temples

Confucian teachings to rule the nation,
Buddhist teachings to rule the heart-mind

ATTRIBUTED TO KHUBILAI KHAN

Tibetan Buddhism came to the Beijing region with the Mongol occupation of the thirteenth century. Sometimes inappropriately called Lamaism, our term emphasizes instead the importance of those developments in Buddhist thought and practice that originated on the Qinghai-Tibet plateau, rather than foregrounding the role of great monks, lamas. Those developments built on the medieval esoteric Buddhism that flourished across the Himalayas in modern-day India, Bhutan, and Nepal, as well as on indigenous religious practices. Tibetan practices incorporate competing traditions grounded in holy texts and secret teachings associated with particular masters and lineages. This form of Buddhism spread to populations in modern-day Qinghai, Sichuan, Gansu, Ningxia, and Inner Mongolia. Upon their rise to power, the Mongol confederation patronized these lineages.

In Beijing five Tibetan Buddhist temples are open, all cloaked in Chinese architectural garb. From the street, therefore, they are indistinguishable from the Buddhist sites introduced above. The pious devotee enters the expected sequence of Front Gate, Bell and Drum Towers, Heavenly Kings Hall, and Buddha Hall within Chinese-style courtyards.

23 ▶
Bai Ta Si (Miaoying Si)

YUAN, 1271–79
NATIONAL REGISTER, 1961
FUCHENG MEN NEI DAJIE, XICHENG

The common name for this temple describes it great stupa, the White Dagoba, the largest structure of its kind in modern-day China, and the only Yuan architectural monument within the city (fig. 5.14). It is associated with the founder of the Yuan capital, Khubilai Khan (r. 1260–94) whose vow initiated its creation while Dadu was under construction. After the stupa was completed, a large temple precinct was laid out by the Mongol custom of shooting arrows in the four

directions. This was the Great Holy Longevity Myriad
Peace Temple (Da Shengshou Wan'an Si) completed
1288. The temple grew even more over the next several decades, and was used for rehearsing grand court
ceremonies. Upon Khubilai's death in 1294, a memorial hall was built here in his honor. A major fire in
1368 shortly before the Mongols fled Dadu leveled
the compounds. Rebuilding took place ca. 1457, at
which time the temple was renamed Temple of
Miraculous Response (Miaoying Si). In the Qing
period a large temple fair was held at Bai Ta Si on the
fives and sixes of each lunar month.

After several renovations, the first courtyard
extends from the Front Gate (now below street level
on Fucheng Men Nei Dajie) to the Heavenly Kings
Hall with the Bell and Drum Towers in a paved plaza.

5.14
Bai Ta dagoba

The plaza is also used for parking. The present compound, much reduced from its original plan, contains four halls: Heavenly Kings Hall (Tian Wang Dian); Hall of the Three Buddhas (Sanshi Fo Dian); Hall of Seven Buddhas (Qi Fo Dian, dated 1505); and Three Jewels Hall (Sanbao Dian). The great stupa rises behind the latter.

The Hall of the Three Buddhas (with five bays and hip roof; fig. 5.15) fronted by a moon terrace occupies a wider area between north-south galleries. The hall is now used for a display of Tibetan bronze images gathered from various Beijing temples and collections. The pair of marble lions placed before this hall, much the worse for wear, are attributed to the Yuan (fig. 5.16). The west galleries here have displays that narrate the history of the temple and a fine model of Dadu.

The yard flows around this hall to the second major building, the Hall of Seven Buddhas, also five bays with hip roof. An elevated terrace connects this hall to that in front, an echo of its Yuan origins (cf. the Yuan palaces). The Three Buddhas from the first hall are installed here: Sakyamuni (Shijia Fo) attended by his disciples Kasyapa and Ananda at the center, Bhaisajyaguru (Yaoshi Fo, the Healing Buddha of the East) to the right, and Amitabha (Emituo Fo, the Buddha of Long Life) to the left. Each is carved from Nanmu covered by recent gilding. The rear yard is an elevated terrace supporting both a small three-bay hall and the massive stupa.

When Khubilai Khan vowed to build the great stupa, he was following the counsel of his state teacher (di shi), the Tibetan Ye-ses rin-chen (Yilinzhen in Chinese; 1248–94), a disciple of the great prelate Phagspa. The site had been a temple under the Liao, and its tenth-century relics were re-interred in the new edifice along with other valuables:

First, a stone chest carved with the Buddhas of the Five Directions was placed at the bottom of the stupa, and images of white jade stone were then set up and distributed in order. Nearby was put a wheel of the Eight Great Demon Kings and the Eight Demon Mothers...Below these were placed on stone Sumeru thrones sculptures of the gods who protect the dharma, the Lord of Riches, the Eight Great Gods, the Eight Great Brahma Kings, the Four Kings, the Nine Luminaries, and the Heavenly Nagas Guarding the Ten Directions.

H. Franke, "Consecration of the 'White Stupa,'" 174

The design of this structure is credited to Anige (1245–1306), an artisan from Nepal who came to the Mongol realm in 1261. A fictive portrait sculpture in national costume now stands before the stairs leading to the stupa (fig. 5.17). Anige supervised creation of a massive Himalayan stupa known as a dagoba (or

5.15
Three Buddha Hall,
Bai Ta Si

5.16
Yuan lion

5.17
Portrait of Anige

chorten). The stupa has a square base 9 m in height whose four sides extend outward surmounted by two Mount Sumeru registers of the same plan (fig. 5.18). Above is a ring of twenty-four large, down-turned lotus petals carrying the bottle-shaped dome (diameter 20 m), which bulges slightly as it rises. The flat top carries a smaller Mount Sumeru base from which rises a thirteen-layer conical spire, capped by a round iron canopy (9.7 m in diameter) and a bulbous finial (5 m tall, weight 4 tons). The 51 m high stupa is a cosmic diagram evoking the shape of the earth and the heavens and the layered structure of the universe. It is also the center of a sacred precinct for the ritual of circumambulation (*pradakshina*), moving clockwise (the direction of the sun) around holy relics.

This Bai Ta is not to be confused with the Bai Ta of Bei Hai (the Yong'an Si, built in 1651 on Qionghua Island; see fig. 6.28), visible throughout the western and northern portions of the Imperial City. A similar form of stupa surmounted the portal at Juyong Guan (see fig. 1.17), and small versions will also be found at Huguo Si and Biyun Si.

24 ▶
Wu Ta Si
(Zhenjue Si) and
Beijing Stone
Carving Art
Museum

MING, 1403–24 AND 1473
NATIONAL REGISTER,
1961
NO. 24 WUTA SI,
BAISHI QIAO,
HAIDIAN

Although the Mongol khans were evicted from China after 1368, large Mongol populations remained within Ming territory. The first emperors of the new dynasty promoted harmonious relations with Tibetan and Mongol prelates. At least nine Tibetan Buddhist temples are documented in the Ming capital, including two chapels in the Forbidden City according to Naquin (208), all recipients of imperial patronage. The Yongle emperor promoted Tibetan Buddhism, and commissioned the Temple of True Awakening (Zhenjue, Zhengjue Si) in the northern outskirts of his new capital. The gift of five Buddha images by an Indian pandit spurred the construction there of a massive stone stupa called in Chinese a *jingang baozuo ta*, "vajra jewel throne stupa" (*vajrasana*; fig. 5.19). It was completed in 1474 under the Chenghua emperor (Zhu Jianshen, r. 1465–1487). The temple became an attraction for capital scholars, recommended as a place to take in the view by early guide books. The Zhenjue Si compound was among the many casualties of the 1900 suppression of the Boxer Uprising by the Eight Allied Armies. Nonetheless, many of its halls remained intact until they were sold off by the Beiyang government in 1927, when they were disassembled. Today the stupa stands within empty grounds (fig. 5.20).

The Vajrasana Stupa can be understood from historical, iconographical, and architectural angles. Within the historical traditions of pan-Asian Buddhism, this stupa refers to Bodhgaya, site of the Buddha's enlightenment or awakening, the revelatory experience when the prince Siddhartha became a buddha. Thus the monument exemplifies the fundamental truth of all Buddhist teachings while also acknowledging the distant, non-Chinese origins of the *dharma*.

5.18
Elevation (height 51 m), Bai Ta Si, from *Miaoying Si Bai Ta*, 7

5.19
"Ou-T'a-Seu – A Buddhist pagoda, near Peking," postcard, anonymous

31. - Ou-T'a-Seu - Pagode Boudhique, près de Pékin
Ou-T'a-Seu, A Buddhist pagoda, near Peking

5.20
Wu Ta Si foundations,
view to south

The *vajrasana* is the point of origin of the Three Jewels (Buddha, *dharma*, *sangha*). Iconographically, plan and decoration manifest the *vajradhatu* or "diamond realm" of esoteric Tibetan Buddhist teaching: the Cosmic Buddha (Vairocana) and four emanations occupy the heart of a great cosmic schema (a mandala). The five images presented by the Indian prelate should be invested in chambers within this stupa. The central pagoda with thirteen eaves must stand for Vairocana, while the four lesser spires of eleven eaves represent other powerful deities (hence the popular Chinese name, Wu Ta Si, Five Pagoda Temple). In architectural style, finally, the 7.7 m-tall base and pagodas document a conflation of Tibetan or Himalayan Buddhist decoration with Chinese architectural idioms, a trend previewed in the Cloud Terrace at Juyong Guan [3 ▶].

The modern visitor approaches the stupa as a devotee would. After entering the precinct, circumambulate the stupa at ground level moving from south to west to north to east. The Mount Sumeru base (19 x 16 m; fig. 5.21) is carved with moldings akin to the terraces of the

Forbidden City (see fig. 3.22). Here the waist register is divided by *vajras* into panels filled with vases, lotuses, lions, and elephants (fig. 5.22). The five tiers of Buddha niches stacked above are divided by mock tile eaves; the many Buddhas here display a variety of *mudras* (hand gestures). Entering through the portal on the south, one can circumambulate the interior. Its core has niches with directional Buddhas on all four faces, stone Sumeru base below, and carved eave above. The passage is used for a display on the history of stupas and the temple.

To ascend, the visitor climbs a stairway at front left or right: forty-four winding, ill-lit, and uneven steps. A single-story pavilion over the top of this stairway has a conical green-glazed tile roof. The central pagoda (8 m in height), like the four that surround it (at 7 m), is square in plan (fig. 5.23), and features a Buddha niche on each face above a Mount Sumeru base The arch reveals repeat the decoration of the ground-level portal, while standing bodhisattvas and trees fill out the registers (fig. 5.24).

Other examples of this stupa type are found at Biyun Si (Temple of Azure Clouds) northwest of the

5.23
Pagoda on roof terrace

5.21
Below left: *Vajrasana* platform

5.22
Below: Reliefs, including *vajras* and elephants

city in Xiang Shan Park, and at Xi Huang Si (Western Yellow [Sect] Temple), northwest of Anding Men (fig. 5.25). Both were created under the diligent patronage of the Qianlong emperor, in 1748 and 1782, respectively. The Biyun Si stupa is significantly larger in scale than the Wu Ta Si monument, but clearly indebted to it. The stupa at Xi Huang Si was erected in honor of two great lamas of the Yellow Hat sect: the Fifth Dalai Lama (when he visited the capital) and the Sixth Panchen Lama (whose ashes were interred here). A popular tourist site in the early twentieth century, today this is a Tibetan Academy.

5.24
Pagoda base,
Wu Ta Si

5.25
"Peking, Lama Tempel,"
postcard, anonymous

The Beijing Stone Carving Art Museum (Beijing Shike Yishu Bowuguan) boasts over 2000 specimens of all types dating from Eastern Han through late Qing. Larger monuments are displayed outdoors behind the stupa, while several specialized exhibitions are mounted in new buildings that enclose the former temple grounds. This abundance of riches is especially deep in carvings from tombs, including grave steles of European Catholic fathers who died in the capital. The museum sees its mission as the recovery and preservation of stones from the region.

The cultural interchange between China Proper and peoples of the periphery that flourished under the Liao, Jin, and Yuan regimes intensified yet again under the Manchu Qing. Throughout Beijing today there are significant traces of the Manchu presence and of their relations with their Mongol and Tibetan dependents. In Qing times, there were forty-three Tibetan temples in the capital (Naquin, 342), as many as twenty-three of them fully funded by the Imperial Household Department. The Yonghe Gong illustrates several themes in the complex cultural and religious mixing of the last emperors and their subjects.

The story begins with two imperial successions. In 1692, the Kangxi emperor (Xuanye, r. 1654–1722) gave his fourth son, Yinzhen (1678–1735) property near Anding Men in the northeast Inner City. The Han-Chinese population of the city had been displaced, and the area with the walls divided among the Manchu Eight Banners. The northeast zone was assigned to the Bordered Yellow Banner. Yinzhen's mansion was known as the Zhen Beile Fu until 1709 when the prince was made Yong Qin Wang, a first-rank prince. At that time the property was upgraded (see Ch. 6 on the specifications for *wang fu*). Upon Kangxi's

◀ 25
Yonghe Gong

QING, 1694 AND 1744
NATIONAL REGISTER, 1961
NO. 12 YONGHE GONG
DAJIE, DONGCHENG

death in 1722, the prince assumed the throne as the Yongzheng emperor (r. 1722–35) and his former residence then became a detached palace known by the name Yonghe Gong (Palace of Harmony and Peace).

Yongzheng reigned for thirteen years, and passed away in August, 1735 while at Yuanming Yuan [31 ▶]. By custom the corpse and coffin were taken to the Forbidden City and placed in the Qianqing Gong. The new emperor, the fourth son Hongli (1711–1799), assumed the reign title Qianlong. He was inspired by his father's long association with the Yonghe Gong to honor both by having the emperor's coffin laid in state there. This necessitated upgrading the site with yellow tile, a feat accomplished in fifteen days of around-the-clock labor. After nineteen days in the palace, the coffin was transferred and remained in the former private quarters of the prince (the present Yongyou Dian) until the third month of 1737, when the remains were dispatched to the Western Qing tombs in Yixian, Hebei (see Ch. 4).

Qianlong's devotion to his father did not stop here. He has a memorial image of the deceased emperor installed in the same quarters (renamed Shen Yu Dian), and invited Tibetan monks (lamas) to participate in rites there. (Memorial offerings to Qianlong himself were regular events at Yonghe Gong in later reigns.)

The history of the site as a Tibetan Buddhist temple begins in 1744, when Qianlong re-dedicated the central and western precincts of the *wang fu* as a family temple and center for Buddhist scholarship and teaching. Major rebuilding ensued under the supervision of the emperor's companion, the "living Buddha" Rolpay Dorje of the Gelug (Yellow Hat) sect. Within a few years, the palace was transformed to its present plan (fig. 5.26).

At the south, a plaza (a) was created by a shadow wall and three large *pailou* (each about 10 m tall) that funnel foot traffic from east and west and send it north. Extending north 200 m is a processional path (b) lined by gingko trees. After Qianlong's reign, the next five Qing emperors came to the temple on his birth (8/13) and death (1/4) anniversaries and after the summer solstice ceremonies at nearby Di Tan to honor their ancestor. During such events the entourage was arrayed along this path. A new gate (c), the Zhaotai Men, was built at the north end of this alley in the style of gates in the inner court of the Forbidden City.

The front courtyard for the new temple was defined by the Yonghe Men (fig. 5.27) on the north with Bell and Drum Towers (d), twin stele pavilions (e), and paired 30 m flag poles occupying the broad space before it. Notice the wooden façade with five openings, rather than the masonry arches typical of Beijing temples. This gate (f) functions as the Heavenly Kings Hall and features both guardians and the ever-present smiling Mile Fo (Maitreya). This yard is also the venue for the so-called Demon Dances that take place after New Years.

The next yard is elevated above the grade of the first three before it. It features a square pavilion (g) that shelters Qianlong's 1792 text on "Lama Buddhism" inscribed in four languages (Chinese, Manchu, Tibetan, and Mongolian) on a monumental (6 m) four-sided stele (fig. 5.28). The text rehearses the rise of Buddhism, the importance of the Gelug sect and Dalai and Panchen lamas, and the tradition of "living Buddhas." All are viewed as essential to the security and stability of the people of the Tibetan and Mongol regions under Manchu rule. This text was composed after significant Manchu victories over Tibet.

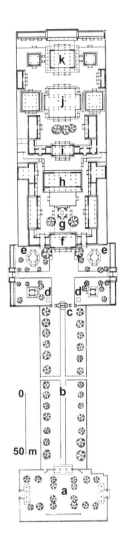

5.26
Plan of Yonghe Gong, from *Beijing gu jianzhu* (1986), 44. Diagram shows: (a) Pailou yard, (b) approach, (c) Zhaotai Men; (d) Bell and Drum Towers, (e) Stele Pavilions, (f) Yonghe Men, (g) Qianlong stele, (h) Yonghe Gong, (i) Yongyou Dian, (j) Falun Dian, (k) Wanfu Ge

5.27
Yonghe Men
(Heavenly Kings Hall) at
Yonghe Gong

The hall named Yonghe Gong (h), originally the prince's audience hall, became the temple's main image hall (fig. 5.29). It has seven bays, single eave, and hip-gable roof. Buddhas of the Three Eras (*kalpas*)—past, present, and future—are installed here. All are gilded bronze castings from the palace. Nine *lohan* (*arhat*) are arrayed along each end wall. The next yard with the Yongyou Dian (i) is again raised above the previous level. It was the prince's retiring quarters and used for Yongzheng's coffin in 1735–37. This is a five-bay hall with single eave and hip roof. Here the main image is the Buddha of Long Life (Amitayus, Wuliangshou Fo) who presides over the Western Pure Land with the Healing Buddha (Bhaisajyaguru, Yaoshi Fo) on the west and the Lion's Roar Buddha (Simhanada, Shikong Fo), thought to be incarnated by Zongkhapa, on the east. All are 2.4 m sandalwood carvings.

One step further north, the area of the former inner court became the great Falun Dian (Hall of the Dharma Wheel; fig. 5.30). This hall (j) was expanded to seven bays and given five-bay porches at front and rear for a cross-shaped plan. Five clerestories added to the roofs admit illumination for an enormous bronze image (6.1 m) of the patriarch of the Gelug sect, Zongkhapa (1357–1419). A Tibetan image of

5.28
Qianlong stele, inscribed
with essay "On Lamaism"

Sakyamuni sits before the teacher. Seats used by the
Dalai and Panchen lamas flank it on west and east,
respectively. (The 13th and 14th Dalai Lamas and the
6th, 9th, and 10th Panchen Lamas all visited Yonghe
Gong.) Cases holding the Tibetan and Mongolian
Tripitakas (Kanjur and Tanjur) fill the ends of this hall.
This hall is in use by the temple's lamas.

The climax of the temple is the Belvedere of Ten
Thousand Blessings (Wanfu Ge, k) best known for a
sandalwood Maitreya. The wood for this image,
brought from Nepal, was donated by the Seventh Dalai
Lama. The hall was constructed around the 18 m-high
image between 1748 and 1750. The building is three
levels of five bays each, with interior balconies around
open space for the image. The adjacent pavilions are
connected at the balcony level by flying bridges (fig.
5.31). A visit to Yonghe Gong should also incorporate
as many of the flanking side halls as stamina allows.

As the center of an active community of lamas,
Yonghe Gong has regular services. There are daily

5.29
Above: "Yonghe Gong"
written in Manchu,
Chinese, Tibetan, and
Mongol

5.30
Above left: Falun Dian (Hall
of the Dharma Wheel)

5.31
Wanfu Ge (Pavilion of Ten
Thousand Blessings) at
Yonghe Gong

gatherings in the Falun Dian each morning and more extensive services on the first, fifteenth, and thirtieth of each lunar month. Major seasonal ceremonies also take place during the first, fourth, sixth, ninth, and tenth lunar months.

Daoist Temples

By late imperial times, religious Daoism (as distinct from philosophical positions identified with this term) flourished under state supervision and patronage much as the Buddhist community did. In almost every way the two traditions mirrored one another. Emperors were regular patrons, although some rulers might favor one tradition over the other. Buddhist and Daoist chapels were set up on imperial property, even within the inner court. The Hall of Heavenly Peace (Qin'an Dian) of the Imperial Flower Garden (see fig. 6.22) is a rare example of a Ming structure to survive within the Forbidden City. It was dedicated to Zhenwu, the Daoist Guardian of the North. In both cases, the throne insisted on some degree of supervision by appointing a chief monk or Daoist to watch over religious practices, always a worry to imperial autocrats. The throne actively promoted publishing the canons (Tripitaka and Daozang respectively) and was deeply involved in establishing, maintaining, and restoring temples, both in the capital and at other important sites.

In Beijing, Naquin found that the most common terms for Daoist establishments—*guan* and *gong*—were far less frequent than the designations used for Buddhist sites (*si, an, chanlin*; 23). Each of the two great surviving Daoist temples were recipients of significant imperial support, and both became associated with fairs that drew enormous crowds. The Baiyun Guan (White Cloud Daoist Monastery, fig. 5.32) outside Xibian Men claims a Tang pedigree (ca. 741), and was given major support under the Jin, Yuan, Ming, and Qing. Its temple fair was held the 19th of the first month to celebrate the miraculous return of the Immortal Qiu, their patriarch. The Dong Yue Miao, on the other hand, had regular markets on the first and fif-teenth of each month, and celebrated its annual festival on the 28th of the third month. Both temples became

5.32
Baiyun Guan *pailou*

attractions for visitors and were written up in guides published in the sixteenth and seventeenth centuries.

26 ▶
Dong Yue Miao
and Beijing Folk
Museum

YUAN, MING, AND QING,
1322, 1447, AND 1698
NATIONAL REGISTER,
1996
CHAOYANG MEN WAI
DAJIE, DONGCHENG

After being occupied by the Public Security Bureau (Gong'an Ju) for almost fifty years, Dong Yue Miao was returned to the citizens of Beijing at Spring Festival (New Year) 1999. Restoration entailed years of planning and work and a budget of 20 million RMB (approaching 2.5 million USD) from Chaoyang District. Many important sites were taken over by government agencies in the early days of the People's Republic due to a dearth of facilities at that time, but few had been as vital to the city as this great Daoist institution. Today the site is a prime attraction, a popular venue for New Year celebrations, and the location of the Beijing Folk Museum in the rear courtyard.

Under the Mongols, two orders of religious Daoism attracted both the attention and the patronage of the throne. The northern, Quanzhen (Complete Perfection) order of monastic, celibate Daoists was patronized under the Jin and Yuan, with their principal temple the Baiyun Guan. Qiu Quanzhen (Qiu Chuji, d. 1227) renowned for his journeys across Central Asia and a favorite of Genghis Khan, was memorialized at Baiyun Guan. The southern order associated with Longhu Mountain in Jiangxi, the Zhengyi (Orthodox Unity) "celestial masters" who claimed a pedigree extending to the first religious Daoists of the Han (the Zhang family of Qingcheng Shan near Chengdu) was also recognized. One of their representatives, Zhang Liusun (1248–1321) held a position at the Yuan court.

In 1319, on his own initiative, Zhang bought land outside the southeast gate of Dadu (the later Chaoyang Men) for a temple dedicated to the Great Lord of Mount Tai (Dai Yue; e.g. Taishan, Shandong). After

Zhang's death (he "became a feathered immortal"), his disciple Wu Quanjie (1269–1346) began construction of a main hall and gate in 1322. Within a few years a prominent Mongol imperial princess added her support for the construction of the rear hall, completed in 1328. Zhang's efforts were commemorated by an inscription composed and written by the great Yuan calligrapher Zhao Mengfu. This stele stands within a glass case in the east half of the main yard. The good fortune of the temple continued under the Ming with the support of Yingzong, the Wanli emperor and his mother Empress Li, and various palace eunuchs. After a disastrous fire in 1698, the Kangxi emperor committed palace funds to rebuild, and by 1760 "imperially-bestowed name" status came from Qianlong. In 1900, however, Japanese soldiers looted the temple in reprisal for the Boxers, and the site declined in the twentieth century. Much of this history is rehearsed in the large collection of steles gathered in the main yard.

In its prime, the temple is said to have had its south gate about 1.5 to 2 km south of Chaoyang Men Wai Dajie at the banks of the Tonghui canal (fig. 5.33). A large masonry *paifang* with glazed tile decoration from the Qing palace workshops still marks the temple approach on the south side of the street. A rebuilt three-portal masonry gate on the north side of the street leads into a shaded yard with Drum and Bell Towers (east and west, respectively; both 1576). The former is named here the Ao Lou, a reference to the Yangzi crocodile and source of its drum head. The latter is called the Jing Lou, a reference to the whale shape of its bell-striking mallet.

The main yard of the temple is a rectangular compound contained by seventy-two bays parallel to the main axis (fig. 5.34). The yard commences with the Gazing at Mount Tai Gate (Zhan Dai Men; 1447) which houses guardian generals like the Heavenly Kings Hall of a Buddhist temple. The elevated walkway extending 60 m north is flanked by large stele pavilions built to register the donations of Kangxi (dated 1704, east) and Qianlong (dated 1761, west). The northern part of this yard is taken up with the "forest of steles." About ninety stones have been restored to their positions here.

A moon terrace fronts the Hall of Mount Tai (Dai Yue Dian, 1322). This is a five-bay hall covered by a hip roof, with porches front (three bays, hip–gable) and rear (one bay; fig. 5.35). A covered gallery connects this hall with a second, the Yude Dian directly behind. The use of a dumbbell-shaped terrace to support these two linked halls and the merging of porches with the main roofs were common among Song and Yuan buildings. The front hall houses a 4.5 m image of Dong Yue Da Di (Great Sovereign of the Eastern Holy Peak) attended by eight civil and military officials, like an outer court. The rear hall, in principle the retiring hall for the god and his consort, is now used to display the San Guan (Three Officers, in this context the Daoist

5.33
Bird's eye view of
Dong Yue Miao, from
Chen, *Dong Yue Miao*

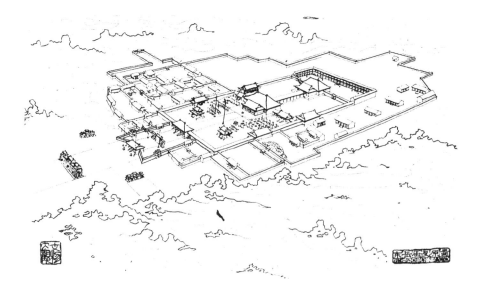

5.34
Main yard, Dong Yue Miao

Lords of Heaven at center, Earth at left, and Water at right). These are Ming images dated 1481 removed from the Daciyanfu Gong (remnants on Chaoyang Men Nei Dajie). Smaller halls on east and west (*duo dian*, "ear halls") are aligned with the front building. These memorialize three lords of the Mao Shan sect and three mountains associated with the Celestial Masters, respectively. There are also two other memorial halls, and sixty-eight chambers devoted to the seventy-six officers of hell. The image groups installed here are all recent, imaginative replacements.

5.35
Hall of Mount Tai

Passing beyond these halls, one enters the rear precinct. Two-story buildings on west, north, and east are devoted to displays narrating the history of the temple as well as the Beijing Folk Museum, with changing exhibits about the customs, festivals, and trades of the capital.

Mosques

Since the Yuan period, a significant Muslim community has resided in Beijing. At the time of Marco Polo there were said to be thirty-five mosques in Dadu serving about 10 percent of its residents. Believers came from all over Central Asia during the Pax Mongolica to serve the khans; these foreigners (not all Muslims) were known as *se mu*. They enjoyed higher status than the northern and southern Han-Chinese who submitted to the Mongols. The official in charge of the artisans who built and furnished much of Dadu and its palaces was a Muslim (possibly an Arab) named Yegdir. The term Huihui to designate this population came into use from the thirteenth century. By the Ming there were an estimated 50 to 100,000 Muslims in the capital; the census of 1938 estimated 170,000 to 200,000 (Naquin, 214). In the mid-twentieth century there were more than forty mosques in Beijing.

Chinese Mosques combine local architectural traditions with the requirements specific to their practices. Thus the Great Mosque of Xi'an, an elegant ensemble of sub-imperial architecture which was patronized by no less than the founding Ming emperor, has an uncharacteristic (for China) east-west orientation dictated by the requirement to face Mecca during prayers. Similarly, the prayer hall there is really two large structures build eave to eave in order to enhance the interior space, a plan rarely found at other sites. Today many mosques in the People's Republic in areas of Central Asia populated by non-Han communities are characterized by a different style, such as the Timurid mosques of Kashgar and other areas of Xinjiang.

The oldest and most prestigious mosque in the capital is at Niu Jie in the western half of the former Outer City. Tradition claims a founding date of 996 (the time of Liao Nanjing). However, the oldest documentary evidence preserved in steles at the site dates only from the Ming Xuande and Zhengtong reigns (1427–42), when a substantial edifice was "re-constructed" (*chong jian*) with imperial support. The imperially bestowed current name dates to 1474. The term used, *libai si*, means "temple for worship [or prayer]," a descriptive phrase for the Arabic term *masjid*, "place to prostrate [in prayer]." The other common Chinese term in use for mosques is "Temple of the Pure and True" (Qingzhen Si). This term is also applied to halal Muslim butchers and restaurants. The present buildings date to the Kangxi era (ca. 1696) although parts of several structures could be remnants from the Ming or possibly earlier. The three other great mosques of Beijing are the Dongsi Qingzhen Si in Dongcheng (early Ming), the Pushou Si of Xicheng, and the Faming Si of Dongcheng (both late Ming, Wanli era).

Niu Jie Libai Si stood outside the walls of Dadu (but within the area of Jin Zhongdu), but was incorporated into the Ming Outer City after 1553. The plot is modest, about 85 m east-west by 45 m north-south including a school at the east end. Its most notable feature is perhaps the entrance at the west end of the site on the east side of Niu Jie (Ox Street). This is marked by a simple wooden *pailou*, a stone bridge, and the two-story six-sided Moon Watching Tower (Wang Yue Lou; fig. 5.36). Entering brings the faithful to the rear of the hall of prayer. Foot traffic, therefore, is funneled

◀ 27
Niu Jie Mosque

LIAO, 996 AND MING-QING, 1442, 1696
NATIONAL REGISTER, 1988
NO. 88 EAST NIU JIE, GUANG'AN MEN NEI, XUANWU

eastward to the central yard where the minaret stands. (Visitors will be directed to the street entry at the southwest corner. Appropriate dress is required of both men and women.)

The entrance of the prayer hall is a three-bay hall (fig. 5.37) of Qing date which fronts two additional Ming halls, each five bays wide aligned north-south. Their long faces meet eave to eave moving west. The entrance area and middle hall have hip-gable roofs, while the third (west) hall has a hip roof. Surrounding the interior space is a gallery with windows along both north and south. At the west end of these three roofs stands the niche aligned with Mecca (*mihrab*), a six-sided masonry chamber called the *yao dian* (fig. 5.39), possibly Song or Jin in date. The prayer hall interior is ornately decorated with gold Arabic script on lacquer red as well as blue–green–gold floral motifs on beams and coffered ceiling. A placard over the central bay reads "Pure and true ancient teaching" (*Qing zhen gu jiao*). At the west end of the hall is a cabinet on a Mount Sumeru base dated to the founding of the mosque which holds the Holy Koran; it carries gold Arabic script on blue. (Non-Muslims may not enter the hall.)

5.37
Prayer Hall

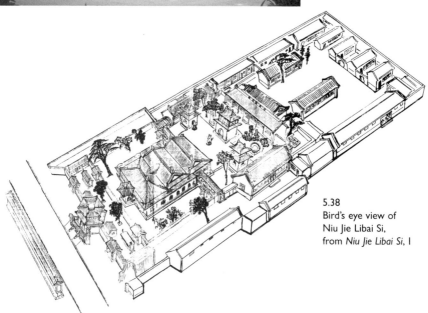

5.38
Bird's eye view of
Niu Jie Libai Si,
from *Niu Jie Libai Si*, I

5.39
Above: Niche (*mihrab*)

5.40
Above right: Minaret

The minaret (*bang ke lou, xuan li lou*) faces the hall of prayer at the center of the compound (fig. 5.40). The mosque dates it to the Song (ca. 1068–1077) with a Ming rebuilding (1496) financed by Muslim palace eunuchs. This is a two-story structure, the lower level solid gray brick with portals east and west and the second level lacquer-red timber. Flanking it on the north and south are a pair of stele pavilions also of Ming date. The seven-bay building at the east side of the central yard is a lecture hall. A second yard further east also has a seven-bay hall for gatherings; it is dated Ming (1442). The women's mosque is located to the north of the main compound but is not open to non-Muslim visitors. On the south side of the compound is a display of cultural relics associated with Niujie and an early twentieth-century ablution hall.

One of the oldest features of the mosque is a pair of tombs in the southeast corner dated 1280 and 1283 (fig. 5.41). Although recently rebuilt using black marble, their original Arabic tomb stones are mounted in the wall on the north. The eastern tomb is a teacher

5.41
Yuan tombs,
Niu Jie Libai Si

(*sheik*; *shaihai*) from Bukhara (Uzbekistan); the western tomb a teacher from Ghazni (Afghanistan).

No better treatment of this broad topic can be suggested than Susan Naquin's *Peking: Temples and City Life, 1400–1900* cited frequently above. Carefully organized and engagingly written, Naquin's text brings the city to life and at the same time has established a benchmark for Beijing scholarship.

SUGGESTED READING

SUBURBAN TEMPLES

Many of Beijing's oldest and most scenic temples are located in the suburbs west of the city. A day trip could easily incorporate a number of the sites listed below.

Fangshan County
Yunju Si (Sui-Tang)

North Pagoda (Liao)
Sutra Caves (Sui and later)

Mentougou District
Fahai Si (Ming)
Tanzhe Si (Pre-Tang)
Jietai Si (Tang)

Murals (1440s)

Ordination platform and pagodas

Western Hills (Xi Shan) and Fragrant Hills (Xiang Shan)
Wofo Si (Tang)
Biyun Si (Yuan)

Vajra Jewel Throne Stupa (Qing)

Yinshan, Changping County
Dayansheng Si (Jin)

Forest of Pagodas (Jin-Yuan)

Also recommended are J. Prip-Moller, *Chinese Buddhist Monasteries: Their Plan and Its Function as a Setting for Buddhist Monastic Life* (1937, with later printings) and Holmes Welch, *The Practice of Chinese Buddhism, 1900–1950* (1967). For the myriad contributions of Buddhism to Chinese life, see also John Kieschnick, *The Impact of Buddhism on Chinese Material Culture* (2003).

Ancient Temples in Beijing (*Beijing gu cha ming si*) published by China Esperanto Press (1993) is a handy pictorial introduction to twenty-eight temples. Nancy Steinhardt introduces Liao pagodas in her *Liao Architecture* (1997), pp. 387–97. A good introduction to Ming Buddhism is Marsha Weidner, "Buddhist Pictorial Art of the Ming Dynasty (1368–1644): Patronage, Regionalism, and Internationalism," in *Latter Days of the Law: Images of Chinese Buddhism, 850–1850* (1994), 50–87. The fiasco of Wang Zhen at Tumu is analyzed by Frederick W. Mote, "The T'u-mu Incident of 1449," in *Chinese Ways in Warfare* (1974). Patricia Berger explores Manchu involvement with Tibetan and Mongolian Buddhism in *Empires of Emptiness* (2002).

On Taoism, see the catalogue from the Art Institute of Chicago, *Taoism and the Arts of China*, ed. S. Little (1999). Also Vincent Goossaert, *The Taoists of Peking, 1800–1949: A Social History of Urban Clerics* (2007), for the Baiyun Guan.

On Sino-Muslim communities in North China, see Jonathan N. Lipman, *Familiar Strangers: A History of Muslims in Northwest China* (1997).

Residences and Gardens

6

It is always so in China. The finer the home the more care-
fully it is hidden behind high walls. Even when the front gate
is opened, the view of the house within is impeded by a Spirit
Screen which ensures additional privacy—that rare privilege
of the rich and powerful in the East—and protects from evil
influences. Our idea of a house as simply a lodging and a
shelter from weather is quite foreign to Orientals. Moreover
they value a residence rather for the size of its courtyards and
the beauty of its gardens than the height or grandeur of its
buildings.

JULIET BREDON, PEKING (1931), 71

The inhabitants of the Ming-Qing capital comprised two groups: local residents and a much smaller but more influential society, the imperial houses. Unfortunately, only estimates of their respective sizes can be suggested.

In the late Ming a total population estimated at from 600,000 to over a million included several thousand nobles and imperial family members. Several ten thousands of eunuchs and about 50,000 officials served the latter (Naquin, 126). The Ming emperor, his consorts and minor children, lived in the palace. Imperial princes of the blood, on the other hand, were dispersed to their nominal fiefs. There were about two dozen such princes in early Ming.

By contrast, with a population of perhaps a million to a million and a half, the late Qing capital was divided between Manchu bannermen in the Inner

(Northern) City and Han-Chinese residents in the Outer (Southern) City and outskirts. Estimates for the Manchu, Mongol, and Han-Chinese banners combined range around 300 to 400 thousand (Naquin, 395). The imperial line—the Aisin Gioro—numbered but a fraction of that figure. In the Qing, imperial princes remained in the capital when they reached maturity. Their abodes, the *wang fu,* form an important part of surviving pre-modern residential architecture. The Manchu presence became so strong in the capital that over time Beijing became what Mark Elliott calls a "bi-cultural" city. Chinese residents of the Outer City were probably equal in number to the Manchu banners.

Persons of property without noble status also left a legacy of residential housing. A map published in Qianlong's reign (1750) is said to show 26,000 courtyard residences. These are the *sihe yuan* for which Beijing is justly famous. Such courtyards have suffered the vicissitudes of the nineteenth and twentieth centuries most severely, and there is no doubt that a majority have disappeared, especially in the last decade as large-scale urban reconstruction accelerated. Reliable figures for the magnitude of the loss are difficult to come by, however. By one account, only some 4,000 courtyards survived at the end of the twentieth century, of which perhaps 1,000 were judged of historic value. The city government has extended protection to over five hundred courtyard residences, and 114 are enrolled on district, city, and national registers. These numbers may well change dramatically under the intense pressure of redevelopment.

Princely Mansions

Beijing had princely establishments in the Ming period, but none survive. The princes played little role in the life of the city compared to the Qing scions. An area southeast of the Imperial City east gate (Dong'an

Men) was known as "ten princely mansions" (*shi wang fu*), but the properties disappeared after 1644. Those residences presumably served a prince as temporary lodging when with permission he came to the capital from his fief. Their memory survives, however, in the name of the main north-south artery east of the Imperial City, Wangfujing ("well of the princely mansions"), a major commercial and shopping street from the early twentieth century onward. The street name became official in 1915.

The Manchus adopted their own system for dealing with princes. Four ranks were recognized: *qinwang* (first-rank), *junwang* (second-rank), *beile* (third-rank), and *beizi* (fourth-rank). None of these titles came automatically, however, as Rawski points out (392). It might be bestowed upon maturity, normally age fifteen when the prince was married and left the palace. This became a considerable preoccupation for several Qing emperors, since they had many recognized sons. (Kangxi had thirty-five sons, Qianlong seventeen, other emperors a more manageable two to sixteen.) Usually rank was given by "imperial favor," but the Qing emperors also recognized merit. The famous Eight Iron Helmets, valiant commanders of the conquest generation, all gained large mansions in the city as a reward for their service. Their descendants retained this high status over time.

Princely mansions, however, were the property of the throne, to be given or taken away as the emperor saw fit. Technically, the term *wang fu* applied only to the abodes of first- and second-rank princes and princesses, while *di* ("official residence") referred to those of the third- and fourth-rank. Properties changed hands as circumstances dictated. The titles given by the Qing emperors were empty since no territory or population came with a bestowal (a feature of the Ming system). Moreover rank did not automatically pass to male heirs. The descendants of a first-rank prince could fall to second rank and subsequently to lesser ranks unless the throne intervened (Rawski, 77). Properties that passed out of the hands of the heirs of former princes were then recycled to newly ennobled ones. Some forty-nine mansions are recorded over the span of the Qing, and a survey in Beijing conducted after 1950 counting all four ranks enumerated fifty-five sites. The detailed map of the city produced for Qianlong in 1750 shows either 37 or 42 establishments; a map dated 1921 shows 39 by my count.

Qing sumptuary regulations promulgated in 1652 and revised under Qianlong specified the architectural features of a mansion in considerable detail. The main gates of *qinwang* and *junwang* mansions featured five bays (fig. 6.1); *beile* and *beizi* gates only three bays. (The gate houses of the Forbidden City numbered either nine or seven bays.) The mansion of a *qinwang* could have three yards (*jin*) and three parallel routes (*lu*). The occupant's formal throne hall and rear chambers both were seven bays wide (fig. 6.2). For a *junwang* the size of these halls came down to five bays and for *beile* and

6.1
Gate, Prince Chun
Mansion, Hou Hai

6.2
Main hall, Fu Wang Fu,
Chaoyang Men Nei Dajie

beizi three bays. Only a first-rank prince installed a throne and screen in his reception hall. Heights of terraces and the number of flanking chambers also were specified, as was the number of gilded bosses that covered door panels. A *qinwang* had sixty-three bosses (nine rows of seven), a *junwang* forty-five (nine rows of five). (On the gates of the Forbidden City, the norm was eighty-one, nine rows of nine.) Green-glazed tile covered the roofs of halls on the main axis of princely mansions, their most readily visible feature today. Ridge ornaments followed the standard prescriptions: seven creatures rode the eaves for a first-rank prince, while only five were employed for the others (see Box, p. 140). Not all mansions matched all of these stipulations; some overshot the mark by imperial dispensation.

The Qing mansions were distributed throughout the Northern City, most in the northern portions of Dongcheng and Xicheng districts. Many today are in very imperfect condition, with a gate house, or main yard, or reception hall recognizable from the street or alley. Rear yards and secondary routes are often less intact. Most mansions that have survived with some integrity are still not available to visitors, but some may be opened in time. A prime candidate is the Fu Wang Fu on Chaoyang Men Nei Dajie (figs. 6.2, 6.3),

6.3
Stone lion,
Fu Wang Fu

which is listed on the National Register, and closely follows the formal specifications outlined above.

Today portions of four princely mansions are open, although all have been compromised. The Gong Wang Fu [28 ▶] located west of Qian Hai is well known for its extensive garden and theater. The former residence of Song Qingling, widow of Dr. Sun Yatsen, on the north side of Hou Hai, is also open. It occupies the grounds of the Chun Wang Fu gardens. The last emperor Pu Yi was born here. The Yong Wang Fu, known since 1744 as Yonghe Gong [25 ▶], retains few of the mansion's original features. Lastly, the Rui Wang Fu, palace of Dorgon (regent 1643–50) one of the Eight Iron Helmets who virtually ruled the realm after the occupation of Beijing in 1644, is now restored as Pudu Si (dedicated in 1776, the original Mahakala Temple of 1694). Only its gate and main hall survive (see p. 18).

28 ▶

Mansion and Garden of Prince Gong (Gong Wang Fu)

QING, CA. 1776 AND
1862–74
NATIONAL REGISTER,
1982
NO. A-16 LIUYIN JIE,
XICHENG

As this is written, work proceeds on refurbishing the mansion and garden to create a center for the history and culture of the imperial princes, a significant aspect of the culture of the Qing capital. In future the mansion's courtyards and garden will be open to visitors, an attraction while touring Hou Hai that can be inserted between the former residences of Guo Moruo and Mei Lanfang [29 ▶].

The detailed map of the capital commissioned by the throne in 1750 shows this area as small alleys and temples. Heshen (1750–99), a high-ranking official of Qianlong and virtually a power to himself during the emperor's declining years, assembled the property and made it his private residence. Upon Qianlong's death, Jiaqing (Yongyan, r. 1796–1820) had Heshen's vast holdings investigated on suspicion of corruption. Legend holds that the quantity of silver found in Heshen's possession was equivalent to national revenue

for a dozen years. Disgraced, Heshen committed suicide within a few weeks. The mansion then reverted
to Prince Qing, the seventeenth son of Qianlong and
brother of Jiaqing.

With the accession of the Xianfeng emperor
(Yizhu, r. 1851–61), princely holdings were reallo-
cated, and the mansion changed hands. It was
bequeathed to Prince Gong, named Yixin (1833–98),
sixth son of the Daoguang emperor and brother of
Xianfeng. The Prince played a role in the events of
1860 by negotiating with the British and French expe-
ditionary forces. John Thomson, the English photogra-
pher who took his portrait ten years later, remarked the
prince was: "Quick of apprehension, open to advice,
and comparatively liberal in his views, he is the
acknowledged leader of that small division among
Chinese politicians who are known as the party of
progress" (White, *John Thomson,* 191). When the prince
died in 1898, his second son Pu Wei retained both his
father's title and property. The prince's brother, Pu Ru
(best known as Pu Xinyu), lived in the garden for a
time while gaining a reputation as one of the foremost
painters of the day. By ca. 1937, the property was sold
to Furen University, which had previously built a modern campus nearby (fig. 7.16). After 1949, a parcel originally stables became the home first of Song Qingling
and then Guo Moruo.

The mansion conformed to most of the
perquisites of a first-rank prince. Being situated near
Qian Hai, a water channel (since covered over) ran
from the reservoirs and wrapped around the property
on west and south (fig. 6.4). This channel sustained a
large water feature in the rear garden, a great rarity in
the capital except at imperial properties. The buildings
were laid out along three parallel north-south axes.
The central ensemble began with a three-bay gate

6.4
Plan of Gong Wang Fu,
from Zhou, *Gudian yuanlin*,
293. Diagram shows:
(a) garden gate, (b) Feilai
Shi, (c) Anle Tang, (d) Fu
Ting, (e) Yu Guan, (f) Guan
Yu Tai, (g) theater

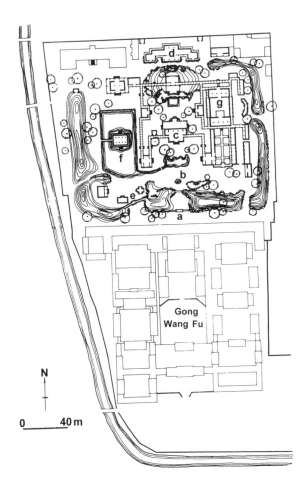

6.4
Plan of Gong Wang Fu, from Zhou, *Gudian yuanlin*, 293. Diagram shows: (a) garden gate, (b) Feilai Shi, (c) Anle Tang, (d) Fu Ting, (e) Yu Guan, (f) Guan Yu Tai, (g) theater

fronted by stone lions and a second, five-bay gate that delimited the front yard. This area burned to the ground in 1921. A rear yard survived, however, and includes the "Jia Le Tang" (Hall of Happiness), a name first associated with the notorious Heshen. These buildings use green-glazed roof tiles. The east axis retains two yards with main and flanking halls of five bays. The front yard is said to be where Prince Gong negotiated with the British and French; the rear was used as his residence. The west axis also has front and rear yards with five- and seven-bay halls, respectively. The latter was found during Heshen's inquisition to be constructed and furnished with precious hardwoods. The former master confessed under interrogation that he had not stolen building materials from the imperial stores as alleged, but had copied the Ningshou Gong (Qianlong's retirement palace), an instance of *lèse majesté*. Across the rear of the site runs a two-story structure of fifty bays with high windows looking down on the garden.

If parts of the present mansion were already standing by Heshen's time, Prince Gong seems to have created the garden while in residence (ca. 1862–74). Known as the Garden of Assembled Splendors (Cuijin Yuan), it occupies a plot about 170 m wide by 150 m deep with thirty named pavilions, galleries, and halls. This area was larger than any of the four imperial gardens within the Forbidden City (see p. 274). Like the mansion, it too is organized around three parallel axes. The interior is screened by man-made hills adorned with Taihu rocks around the east, south, and west. The gateway (a) on the south (fig. 6.5) has an arched portal imitating the European buildings of Yuanming Yuan [31 ▶]. Passing through one negotiates a gap in the rockeries to each side and confronts a 5 m-tall Taihu rock (b) called Dule Feng or Feilai Shi (fig. 6.6). Beyond this guardian lies a small pond in the shape of

6.6
Feilai Shi, a Taihu garden rock at Gong Wang Fu

6.5
Gate, Gong Wang Fu

a bat (*fu,* a homonym for the character meaning "prosperity") and an elevated hall (c) with galleries running to either side. The sequence then repeats with variations moving north: more rockeries and elevated pavilions with wings and galleries. Look for the grotto with a stone bearing the character *fu* (prosperity) written by the hand of the Kangxi emperor. The eastern route divides between the front area, a formal yard for lotuses, and the rear dominated by a large theater (g). The western side, by contrast, is entered after strolling through an imitation pass in the Great Wall (e) called Yu Guan, "Elm Pass." The main feature is a rectangular water tank with a five-bay pavilion (f), the Fish Watching Terrace (Guan Yu Tai) at center. Throughout the garden are placards naming twenty scenic views derived from verses written by the son of Prince Gong. For readers of *The Story of the Stone* (also know as *Dream of Red Mansions*), this garden will be highly evocative.

Courtyard Houses

Unlike the Yuan capital, whose northern districts were never fully occupied, the area within the walls of the Ming and Qing Inner (or Northern) City became densely settled residential wards. The Outer (or Southern) City remained rustic, with vegetable plots and fish ponds until the twentieth century. The total area within the combined Inner and Outer City walls was 62 square kilometers. A high proportion of this area was under the imperial house in various guises: the Forbidden City and Imperial City, the Altar to Heaven, the many Qing princely mansions, plus granaries, depots, and so on. The courtyard residences for which Beijing is famous filled in the remainder.

Courtyard houses from the Yuan period have been excavated along the path of the early Ming north wall, literally built over residential sections of Dadu (see Ch. 1). The best preserved residential site from the Yuan was at Houyingfang, a hutong near Xizhi Men. Although only areas under the superimposed wall remained (fig. 6.8 and see fig. 1.14), this was clearly part of a large household (or two?) with two parallel routes and several yards. The largest terrace carried a hall three bays wide and deep flanked by side rooms, while a somewhat smaller building on the east, set slightly to the north, had the dumbbell-shaped terrace noted above in discussions of Yuan palaces and temples. Here, front and rear halls of three bays were flanked by side chambers facing inward, a precursor of the classic Ming and Qing courtyard plan. The side rooms of this house were built with the heated platforms (*kang*)

HUTONG

The Yuan city had major thoroughfares emanating from the principal gates and running parallel to the walls (see fig. 1.8). Narrower streets and alleys filled in the cells created by the intersection of the former. This grid survived in Ming and Qing times. Even today many east-west alleys north of Chang'an Avenue on the east side of the city can be taken back to the Mongol era (fig. 6.7). These alleys measure 9 m wide, half the width of secondary roads (18 m) and a quarter that of the major arteries (37 m). Studies of hutong have become an indoor sport among Beijing scholar-residents. One expert claims that 1316 streets, lanes, and alleys use the term hutong (based on data from the early 1980s; Weng 9). Many do not conform to the hypothetical dimensions established in the Yuan period.

The Mongol word designating these residential alleys was *hottog*, meaning originally "water well." It may also have signified an encampment of *gir* (better known as yurts) or a residential area. In Beijing speech, the word became hutong, rendered with many different Chinese graphs. While prominent in Beijing vocabulary, the term can be found throughout North China. Many hutong take their names from nearby sites, as for example Lumicang hutong, location of Zhihua Si [22 ▶]. Others designate vanished features of the city's life or history, a market, imperial warehouse, or temple such as Hou Yuan'ensi hutong, where Mao Dun's residence is found [29 ▶].

6.7 Dong Si Liutiao

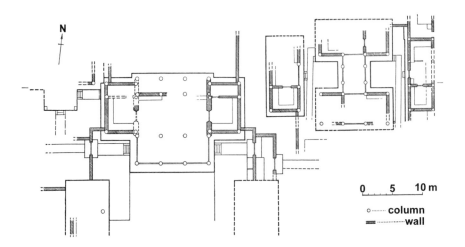

0　　5　　10 m

○ ······· **column**
■ ··············· **wall**

6.8
Plan of Yuan houses at
Houyingfang (cf. Fig. 1.14),
from *Kaogu* 1972.6: 3

typical of North China. Impressions of wooden door and window panels could be seen captured in the pounded earth fill of the Ming wall.

Under both the Ming and Qing, sumptuary ordinances dictated many features of a city dweller's private residence. Domestic halls could not be more than three bays in width, no bracket clusters were to be employed under the eaves, and the polychrome decorative painting typical of the palace was outlawed. Gray roof tile was the order of the day. Wealthy residents manifested their good fortune by the size of their properties, the elaboration of yards and routes. Gardens amid these plots were another outlet for the aspirations of the rich and famous. The consistency of these residences, the strength of a local tradition maintained by artisans for five hundred years strikes one forcefully. One can predict with considerable accuracy the features of a "classic" Beijing courtyard house (*sihe yuan*). We need a vocabulary to describe this classic type.

Courtyard houses were built on either the north or south side of those hutong running east-west. Whichever position the house occupied, the plan remained the same. If a house was north of the alley (fig. 6.9), the entrance gate (*da men*) was invariably at the southeast corner. A gate (a) here allows one to enter the east end of a shallow but wide yard running from side to side. By placing the entrance at the corner of the property, the family enhanced their privacy. No one passing by could see into the inner yard and chambers from the public hutong. The street side of this yard had chambers (b), perhaps with a few high windows onto the alley, used for a variety of practical purposes. They might, for example, store a sedan chair or coffin. The Chinese name for this area, *daozuo fang,* literally "reversed chambers," registers their orientation: the front wall faces north, the opposite of rooms across the axis. When a house was built on the south side of an alley, the gate was positioned at its northwest corner, and one reached the "front" (south) courtyard via a long corridor along the west side of the house.

The inner side of this south yard had a wall with an elaborate gateway at the center (e), the true entrance to the household (fig. 6.10). This gate to the living space of the family was on axis and often given special architectural decoration as a "falling flower" (*chui hua*) or "festooned" gateway. Steps leading up to

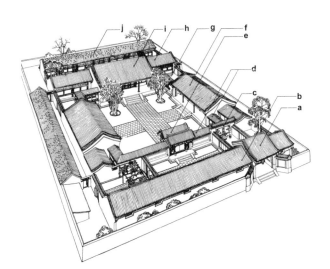

6.9
Plan of *sihe yuan*, from *Beijing gu jianzhu* (1986), 35. Diagram shows: (a) entrance, (b) reversed chambers, (c) screen wall, (d) covered galleries, (e) "festooned" gateway, (f) side chambers, (g) corridor, (h) ear room, (i) main hall, (j) rear covered chambers

the threshold were sheltered by overhanging eaves, which were carried without prohibited brackets by posts that appear to hang in thin air (fig. 6.11). The gate was the interface of the larger public world and the private inner sphere of the residents. Some business was transacted at the alley gate, some in the front yard outside this inner gate.

Courtyards are common to vernacular buildings all over present-day China, but they vary by region and climate. In the south, it is often said the yard is a "sky well" (*tian jing*) for admitting light while also shielding the residents from the oppressive heat. In southern houses, buildings and their eaves are closely set, even linked, and a sharp contrast of bright and dark

6.10
Inner gate,
Mei Lanfang
residence

6.11
"Falling flower" gateway
(*chuihua men*), from Ma,
Muzuo yingzao jishu, 96

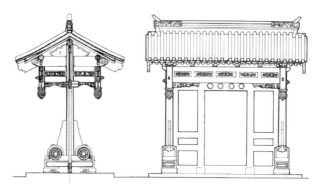

areas results. In the north, where the warmth of the sun is much sought after in the cold season, surrounding buildings are set back and apart from each other. The yard is wider and more open. This yard became the main stage for many family activities, from servant's work or relaxation of master and mistress to family rituals like weddings and funerals. In Beijing the yard is crossed by walkways that connect the gate with the main hall opposite and link this path in turn to side chambers. Fruit trees were often favored here as well (fig. 6.12). Covered galleries (*chaoshou youlang*) running around the margins linked the front gate to side chambers (d), and the latter to the main hall. They provided shelter in inclement weather and alternative paths so that lesser persons did not intrude.

The term "four-sided courtyard" (*sihe yuan*) signifies the placement of buildings facing inward on all sides of the walled property. For the plan described above to qualify, one must count the reversed chamber as the fourth member of the set in addition to the main hall (*zheng fang*) and side chambers (*xiang fang*). The main hall (i) is the most important space within the household and thus was devoted to the ancestors and senior generation, progenitors of the ideal "five

6.12
Courtyard,
Guo Muoro residence

6.13
Large gate
(*guangliang men*)

6.14
Small gate
(*manzi men*)

generation family under one roof." The elders enjoyed the best sunlight and warmth, as well as the optimum vantage point from which to enjoy the central yard and observe the rest of the family. By the same logic, married sons should occupy the side chambers (f), the senior son at the parental right hand (west). Both the main hall and the side chambers might also have appended rooms (*er fang*, "ear rooms") for other purposes. Ear rooms (h) placed at the rear corners might enjoy an intimate yard as their private space. A courtyard residence might also have a rear yard with rooms built against the back wall (j), the "rear covered chambers" (*hou zhao fang*).

Given the large number of well-to-do bannermen and imperial officials resident in the capital, many courtyard houses exceeded the essential elements sketched above. The virtue of the courtyard unit is that it can be replicated in both dimensions: by additional steps on axis from front to back and by parallel routes as seen also in temples and the Forbidden City. To the outside world, however, it was the entrance gates that signaled degrees of status and wealth. Several types of gates are recognized. The *guang liang* ("broad and bright") and *jin zhu* ("golden column") *da men* each consist of a single bay. Roomy covered areas are sheltered beneath a roof elevated above adjacent walls (fig. 6.13). Door panels were installed at the columns under the ridge with equal space to each side in the former. The latter had the door set forward. *Manzi* and *ruyi* gates, by contrast, have smaller dimensions and door panels installed in frames under the exterior eave, affording little shelter (fig. 6.14).

Large and small gates feature several kinds of decoration. Round "drum stones" (*bao gu shi*; fig. 6.15) anchor many door jambs. Escutcheons for affixing the door pulls were usually given the shape of Chinese

6.15
Drum stone (*bao gu shi*) at door jamb

6.16
Carved brick, decorating sides of doorways

cymbals. Carved beams extending from the lintel (called *can*, "hairpins") might carry auspicious characters like "long life" as do door panels. Carved bricks with a variety of floral motifs decorate areas flanking the doorways (fig. 6.16)

Prime example of large, well-preserved *sihe yuan* are not yet open for visitors in Beijing, although placards designating them are fairly common on some alleys (fig. 6.17). In Dongcheng district, for which we have a thorough survey of historic architecture, there are more than eighty courtyard residences from before the twentieth century, many city- or district-level protected sites. About two dozen have several axes of several yards each; some also have gardens. Most of the larger properties are occupied by government agencies; many others are residential, but in all cases they are not open.

◀ 29

Homes of the Famous

VARIOUS LOCATIONS

6.17
Sihe yuan placard

One can well imagine a center for domestic architecture being created at one of the sites above, for example the former residence of Chong Li at Nos. 63–65 Dong Si Liutiao, Dongcheng, which is listed on the national register (see fig. 6.7). This large property, over 10,000 square meters, has three axes with several yards each. It is a private residence.

For now the curious visitor can visit one of the "former residences" (*gu ju*) of historic notables to experience this residential environment. The following list is by no means complete, but all the houses have been open on a regular basis in recent years. One can buy a ticket for admission to all five at a discount.

*Former Residence
of Mao Dun*
SHEN DEHONG
(1896–1981)

―――――――――

NO. 13 HOU YUAN'ENSI
HUTONG,
NEAR JIAODAO KOU,
DONGCHENG

This residence is the modest but comfortable dwelling where the writer lived from 1974. Mao Dun was active both in the progressive New Culture movement of the 1920s and as a leftist writer in the 1930s; he served as Minister of Culture after 1949. The front yard (fig. 6.18) is a traditional *sihe yuan* now used for displays, while the rear has furnished modernized rooms. The plaque inside the gate is the calligraphy of Deng Yingzhao, wife of Zhou Enlai.

Even more modest, this house was occupied by the writer from 1950 until his suicide during the Cultural Revolution. It became a Memorial Hall in 1999. A single yard with modernized facilities, the emphasis here is on exhibits showing the author's career and literary output. Best know for his novel *Rickshaw Boy,* Lao She was active during the Second World War and spent time abroad. A bookstore devoted to Beijing topics complements the house.

Former Residence of Lao She
SHU QINGCHUN
(1899–1966)

NO. 19 FENGFU HUTONG, DENGSHIKOU, DONGCHENG

The largest among this group, Guo's estate occupies grounds used for stables of the Prince Gong mansion [28 ▶]. Before 1963 when Guo moved in, it was the residence of Song Qingling, widow of Dr. Sun Yatsen. (Her subsequent residence was the garden of the former Chun Wang Fu, on the north side of Hou Hai. It is also protected and open to the public.) Guo's residence features a garden and modernized and quite spacious rooms with furnishings from the 1960s and 70s as well as exhibits highlighting his successful scholarly and literary careers.

Former Residence of Guo Moruo
(1892–1978)

NO. 18 QIAN HAI XI JIE, WEST OF SHISHA HAI, XICHENG

6.18
Mao Dun residence

Former Residence of Lu Xun

ZHOU SHUREN

(1881–1936)

NO. 19 GONGMENKOU ERTIAO, FUCHENG MEN NEI, XICHENG

Lu Xun's literary career played out in many places including four different addresses in the northern capital. His actual residence here lasted only from 1924 to 1926, but it was one of his most productive periods. Lu Xun bought and remodeled the property for his mother and first wife. Both lived on here after his death. The house is exceedingly modest, but claims a few original furnishings. The Lu Xun Museum Exhibition Hall within the same compound has informative displays covering the writer's entire life.

Former Residence of Mei Lanfang

(1894–1961)

NO. 9 HUGUO SI JIE, XICHENG

One of the great figures of twentieth-century Peking Opera, Mei (fig. 6.19) was lionized both before and after 1949, and attained an international reputation. Mei's family residence and birth place in Xuanwu district is also protected but not open; Mei lived here after 1949. The attractive yard and handsome furnishings reflect the actor's comfortable life.

Sihe Yuan Hotels

Several traditional residences now function as hotels. These include (asterisks denote registered historic sites):

Lu Song Yuan Guest House
    No. 22 Banchang hutong, Dongcheng
Hao Yuan Guest House*
    No. 53 Shijia hutong, Dongcheng
Red Capital Residence
    No. 9 Dongsi Shitiao, Dongcheng
Hejingfu Guest House*
    No. 7 Zhang Zizhong Road, Dongcheng
Huadu Hotel*
    No. A-28 Wangzhima hutong, Dongcheng
Zhuyuan Guest Hotel
    No. 24 Xiaoshiqiao, Jiugulou Street, Xicheng
Dayuan Guest Hotel
    No. A-1 Fuyuan Men, Haidian

6.19
Bust of Mei Lanfang, at his former residence

Europe must be quite a small and miserable country, since there is not enough land to expand cities,
and they are obliged to live in the air.

ATTRIBUTED TO QIANLONG IN M. ADAM,
*YUEN MING YUEN, L'OEUVRE ARCHITECTURALE DES
ANCIENT JESUITES AU XVIIIe SIECLE* (1936), 10

Gardens for the Emperors

The encounter with China changed European garden
design, but China experienced a reverse impact as
well, as hinted by Qianlong's observation (see
Yuanming Yuan [31 ▶]). What at first seemed strange
and marvelous about Chinese gardens to European
visitors we now take for granted. Most of the features
we think of as typical and classical, however, were
habits, even fads of the late Ming and Qing periods.
This is especially true of Beijing, where all imperial
gardens are either creations from the reign of
Qianlong (r. 1736–99) or were heavily edited during
that period.

Whether classified as imperial, private, or temple, a Chinese garden was appended to a residential
area, be it the palace, a private dwelling, or monks'
quarters. Whatever its scale and specific features, the
owners experienced the garden regularly as an
adjunct to their life. A garden was space to relax, to
enjoy fine weather, to take shelter in inclement conditions, to celebrate the seasons and traditional festivals. Gardens were always as much "man-made" as
"natural" in the sense that: (1) a large proportion of
the space and expense was devoted to architectural
elements, and (2) the overall design was the product
of human labor, from water features and hills to
rockeries and plantings. No one entered a Chinese
garden in Ming and Qing times with the intention of
experiencing unvarnished nature, a setting as found.
Rather the garden would take advantage of whatever
plot was available, large or small, and compress into

that space as many features and experiences as possible for the enjoyment of the owners.

A vocabulary of natural elements employed to create "scenic views" (*jing*) became the common coin of late imperial garden design. Vantage points to be enjoyed for their distant prospect, perhaps a "borrowed" one, seasonal plantings, or a setting to observe the moon all feature prominently in gardens. In Qing times, and especially under Qianlong, scenic views were self-consciously enumerated and illustrated via poetry, pictorial albums, and scrolls. The physical garden replicated the ideal compositions of the poet-painter, as at the garden of the Gong Wang Fu [28 ▶]. Many views evoked scenic areas such as West Lake in Hangzhou or the scholar gardens of Suzhou. A knowing visitor was likely to recognize the allusions. Other creations might evoke historic places or events for which there may have been no physical prototype. Upon arriving at a pavilion with its placard hanging, a visitor read the title and grasped the aesthetic or historical context. These aspects of garden design were within the purview of scholars, but were often devised by specialists. One of the most famous was Ji Cheng, known for his treatise "The Craft of Gardens" (*Yuan ye*, ca. 1634).

The views were created from a limited menu: walls and gates, pavilions, galleries, and more elaborate structures, water features, rockeries created from the strangely shaped Lake Tai limestone, patterns for window lattice and pebble pathways, and of course flowers, bushes, and trees, many associated with seasonal pleasures. In spite of the southern origins both of garden aesthetics and these natural components, imperial gardens in Beijing utilized the same elements, to be enjoyed with a dusting of snow more often than would be expected in Hangzhou or Suzhou.

The Forbidden City came to incorporate four gardens (see the table below), but only two are now open. The oldest is the Imperial Flower Garden (Yuhua Yuan) at the north end of the central axis, the final area astride the center line of the Inner Court (fig. 6.20). This was an original feature of the Ming residential quarters, known then as the "rear palace garden" (Gong Hou Yuan). In this period the garden was integral to the empresses' residential palace. It was also accessible to residents of the Six East and Six West Palaces [12▶] via gates at the southeast and southwest corners. In Qing times a gate was built behind the Kunning Gong to restrict access. At 12,000 sq m, this is the largest garden in the palace, but less than two percent of the area within the walls of the Forbidden City.

Symmetrical in plan, a balanced array of buildings flank the central area of trees and elevated flower beds (fig. 6.21). A rare Ming building within the palace occupies the center of the garden at the rear. The Hall

Gardens in the Forbidden City

6.20
Plan of the Imperial Flower Garden (Yuhua Yuan), from Yu, *Zijincheng*, 197. Diagram shows: (a) main gate, (b) east and west gates, (c) Red Snow Pavilion, (d) Spiritual Cultivation Studio, (e) Ten Thousand Springs Pavilion, (f) One Thousand Autumns Pavilion, (g) Jade-Green Floating Pavilion, (h) Auspicious Clarity Pavilion, (i) Imperial Prospect Pavilion, (j) rear gates

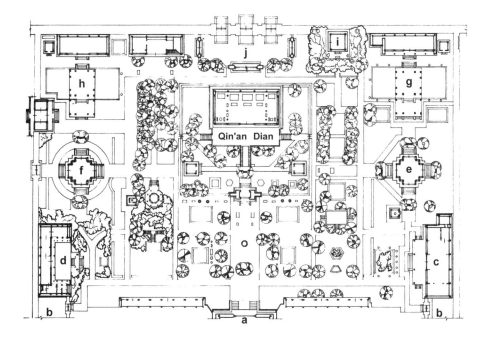

Qin'an Dian

6.21
Ten Thousand Springs
Pavilion, Imperial Flower
Garden (Yuhua Yuan)

6.22
Hall of Heavenly Peace
(Qin'an Dian)

of Imperial Peace (Qin'an Dian, 1535), a five-bay hall on a raised terrace, is dedicated to Zhenwu, the Daoist protective deity of the north (fig. 6.22). The hall was refurbished recently, and a porch of five bays recreated across the front. Multi-story chambers line up against the rear, north wall. An artificial rockery (*jia shan*), the Hill of Piled Excellence (Tuixiu Shan) was added in the Wanli era (1583) and is well-suited for moon gazing (fig. 6.23). The Imperial Prospect Pavilion (Yu Jing Ting) on top was one of the few places in the Forbidden City where one could see the wider world. In Ming times it was often enjoyed on the Double Ninth Festival, and is furnished with a throne (i). The last emperor, Pu Yi, allowed his tutor Reginald

Johnston to live in the Studio of Spiritual Cultivation (Yangxing Zhai) at the southwest corner of the garden (d). Although often crowded, this garden today offers several welcome amenities, including a café, restrooms, bookstore, and shops.

The Cining Gong Flower Garden, south of the palace of the same name, also dates to the Ming. This palace and garden precinct were occupied by empresses after the demise of their emperor and change in status. If the empress was the birth mother of the new reigning emperor, they were entitled to deluxe accommodations and regular visits by their son. This garden is somewhat more than half the area of the Imperial Flower Garden used by the reigning empress and her ladies, but had far fewer buildings. Again the plan is symmetrical, with a simple two-step, open courtyard plan. At this writing both palace and garden are being restored.

The most notorious of the palace gardens is the Flower Garden of the Palace for the Establishment of Happiness (Jianfu Gong) built ca. 1740 by a young Qianlong on the site of his princely residence. Known initially as the West Flower Garden (Xi Hua Yuan), it is divided into two zones: a long narrow strip of three steps incorporating the palace halls, and a wider area centered on a larger hall (the Yanchun Ge, the same name as Khubilai Khan's rear palace) fronted by an immense rockery in the fashion of the day.

The garden's notoriety stems from an incident in 1923, after the palace collections of Qianlong had been gathered. When Pu Yi demanded an inventory of his holdings in response to rumors of pilfering by eunuchs, a mysterious fire broke out on June 27, making a reckoning impossible. The incident is dramatized in Bertolucci's film *The Last Emperor*. Through private funding (US$4 million), this garden was rebuilt and restored in 2000 to 2006. It is now used by the Palace Museum for receptions and other gatherings but is not generally open to visitors.

The final palace garden is now the focus of long-term restoration supported by the World Monuments Fund. The so-called "Qianlong's flower garden" fills

Palace Gardens			
Name	**Date**	**Area**	**Area of Buildings**
Yuhua Yuan	Ming	130 x 90 m; 12,000 sq m	1/3rd
Cining Gong	Ming	50 x 130 m; 6500 sq m	1/5th
Jianfu Gong	1742	4000 sq m	1/2
Ningshou Gong	1771-76	40 x 160 m; 6400 sq m	1/2

Source: Yu, *Zijincheng jianzhu yanjiu* (1995), 189–90

the western side of the emperor's retirement quarters, the Palace of Tranquil Longevity (Ningshou Gong). This compound had been used in the Ming period for elderly palace ladies. Kangxi turned it into quarters for his mother and grandmother in 1689. Qianlong's project defied convention because no previous emperor had declared himself "retired"; an emperor normally died on the throne. The budget amounted to 1,290,000 ounces of "white silver," an astounding sum for superior materials and craft. The southern courtyard featured the Hall of Imperial Supremacy (Huangji Dian), an outer court at reduced scale. Behind it, the emperor's quarters, the Hall of Spiritual Cultivation (Yangxing Dian), were modeled on the Yangxin Dian but used precious Nanmu and Zitanmu dark hardwoods (compare Heshen's grand garden estate, p. 257). To the rear, another pair of halls modeled on the suburban Changchun Yuan (see below) also featured hardwoods in the manner of the prosperous cities of Jiangnan. A theater pavilion as well as library and Buddha Hall occupied the east axis. The west route remained for the garden. Altogether Ningshou Gong was very much a "palace within the palace."

The garden occupies a long strip about 40 m wide and four times that in length (fig. 6.26). The eastern edge is irregular, dictated by the footprint of the main axis palaces, while a straight-line wall 8 m high defines the western limit. Subdivided into four steps, each section differs in plan. All are filled with structures to afford a variety of covered interior spaces from which to enjoy the garden's many features. The first yard is not symmetrical, although the open hall at the rear (c) is centered (fig. 6.25); an open pavilion (b) with a water channel in its floor faces east. This contrivance commemorates the custom of floating cups of wine on a winding stream on the 3rd day of the 3rd month.

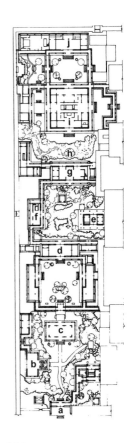

6.24
Plan of Qianlong's flower garden (Ningshou Gong), from Yu, *Zijincheng*, 200. Diagram shows: (a) Spreading Happiness Gate, (b) Cup Floating Stream, Ceremony of Purification Pavilion, (c) Ancient Flowers Pavilion, (d) Active Retirement Hall, (e) Three Friends Pavilion, (f) Tower of Extended Delight, (g) Lush Scenery Tower, (h) Jade-green Conch Pavilion, (i) Anticipation of Good Fortune Belvedere, (j) Peaceful Old Age Study

QIANLONG REMAKES THE CAPITAL

The three early Qing sovereigns—Kangxi, Yongzheng, and Qianlong (ca. 1662–1795)—showed themselves to be indefatigable, in garden building no less than in other pursuits. Both Yongzheng and Qianlong were also filial, much in awe of their father and grandfather, respectively. All three emperors invested themselves in renovating the old and in creating anew. Their efforts transformed the late Ming capital and palace defining the look of historic Beijing today (fig. 6.25). Ever attentive to what it meant to be both a (Chinese) Son of Heaven and Manchu ruler, they created environments that augmented imperial majesty and power. Consider Qianlong's major projects (opposite):

6.25 Jing Shan (Coal Hill) This hill was erected over the site of the Yuan rear palace precincts ostensibly to suppress the charisma of the Mongol rulers, and renamed Wansui ("ten thousand years") Hill by the Ming. The last Ming emperor committed suicide here. It became Prospect Hill after 1655, but was more commonly known to foreign visitors as "Coal Hill." The five pavilions are improvements of the Qianlong emperor, ca. 1750.

Calendar	Era Year	Site
1736–39	QL 1–4	Tai Miao [14 ▶]
1737	QL 2	Guozijian and Kong Miao [17 ▶]; Yuanming Yuan
1740	QL 5	Jianfu Gong garden; Anyou Gong (*YMY)
1742	QL 7	Xian Can Tang (BH)
1744	QL 9	Yong *wang fu* (Yonghe Gong) [25 ▶]; Ancient Observatory [7 ▶]
1745	QL 10	Jingyi Yuan, Xiang Shan (destroyed 1860)
1747–51	QL 12–16	European palaces (YMY) [31 ▶]
1746	QL 11	Chanfu Si (BH)
1747	QL 12	Zhong Lou [6 ▶]
1748	QL 13	Biyun Si, Xiang Shan
1749	QL 14	Changlang (YHY)
1750	QL 15	Wanfu Ge (Yonghe Gong) [25 ▶]; pavilions, Jingshan; Jingming Yuan, Yuquan Shan; Qi Nian Dian (AH) [16 ▶]
1750–64	QL 15–29	Qingyi Yuan (YHY, destroyed 1860)
1751	QL 16	Changchun Yuan (YMY); Xie Chu Yuan (YHY)
1752	QL 17	Huang Qiong Yu (AH) [16 ▶]
1753	QL 18	European palaces (YMY) [31 ▶]
1756	QL 21	Nine Dragon wall (BH); She Ji Tan [13 ▶]
1757	QL 22	Haopu Jian (BH); Jingqing Zhai (BH); Xumi Lingjing (YHY)
1758	QL 23	Foxiang Ge (YHY)
1759	QL 24	Huafang Zhai, Xi Tian Fan Jing (BH)
1760	QL 25	Ziguang Ge, Zhong Hai
1771	QL 36	Yan Lou, Xiao Xi Tian (BH)
1771–76	QL 36–41	Ningshou Gong garden
1772	QL 37	Qichun Yuan (YMY)
1774–83	QL 39–48	Libraries: Palace, Yuanming Yuan
1780	QL 45	Zongjing Dazhao temple, Jingyi Yuan
1782	QL 47	Xi Huang Si stupa

* Abbreviations: AH = Altar to Heaven; BH = Bei Hai;
YHY = Yihe Yuan; YMY = Yuanming Yuan

Source: Fang Xianfu, "Qianlong shiqi de jianzhu huodong," *Gujian yuanlin* 5 (1984)

6.26
Ancient Flowers Pavilion,
Qianlong's flower
garden (Ningshou Gong)

Immortalized by the most famous of all calligraphic works, the "Lanting Preface" of Wang Xizhi, the custom surely appealed to Qianlong, a great admirer of Wang. The second yard by contrast is an elegant *sanhe yuan,* a courtyard with three flanking chambers. The third yard lacks obvious symmetry and has the least area under cover (e, f, g). The fourth yard begins with a huge rockery (h), like the Jianfu Gong, and has a large forward hall (i) and open yard at rear surrounded by arcades.

The two rear sections of this garden, more than half, have been closed as restoration work proceeds. Visitors to the Zhenbao Guan, the palace treasure displays, should check to see which parts of this garden are open.

30 ▶
Bei Hai

QING, CA. 1741–71
NATIONAL REGISTER,
1961
XICHENG

For most of its history Bei Hai (Northern Sea; fig. 6.27) shared some characteristics with a modern public park: it was set aside for pleasure and recreation and tended like a garden to fine tune its appearance. However, before the twentieth century visitors were restricted to intimates of the imperial court. Most of the first modern parks in Beijing had been imperial sites: for example, Tai Miao [14 ▶], Sheji Tan [13 ▶], Di Tan, and Tian Tan [16 ▶]. Few were as well suited for this modern transformation as Bei Hai.

In the Liao period, the area was a marshy lake, a natural reservoir along an ancient bed of the Yongding River. The lake was improved with construction of the Daning Palace in 1179, a detached palace for the Jin rulers. The island, called Qionghua (Jasper Flowers, the name in use today) and surmounted by the Guanghan Dian, was enhanced with a collection of fantastic Lake Tai rocks purloined from the sacked Northern Song capital at modern Kaifeng,

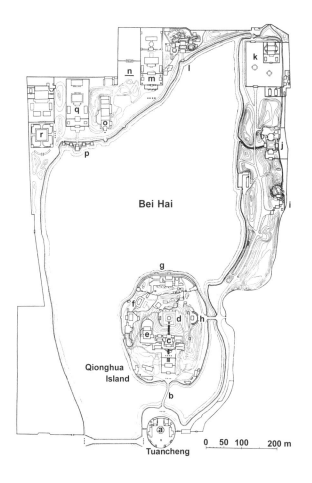

6.27
Plan of Bei Hai, from *Beijing gu jianzhu* (1986), 30. Diagram shows: (a) Hall for Receiving Light, (b) Nine-arch Bridge and *pailou*; (c) Temple of Eternal Peace, (d) White Dagoba, (e) Hall of the Contented Heart, (f) Tower for Reading the Classics, (g) Fangshan Restaurant, (h) Qianlong stele; (i) Hao and Pu Brooks, (j) Painted Pleasure Boat Studio, (k) Altar to Sericulture; (l) Studio of Mirror-like Clarity, (m) *Paifang*, Western Paradise, (n) Nine Dragon Wall, (o) Kuaixue Hall, (p) Five Dragon Pavilions, (q) Revealing Happiness Temple, (r) Little Western Paradise and World of Bliss

the Genyue garden of Emperor Huizong (r. 1101–26). Some of these stones are said to remain among the extensive rockeries. The Mongols camped on this island, perhaps enjoying the abandoned hall, after the destruction of Zhongdu. In 1262 Khubilai Khan and his advisors decided to establish their new capital, Dadu, with island and lake as part of its imperial core (see fig. 1.8). The lake was renamed Taiye Pond (an allusion to the Tang) and the isle became Wanshou or Wansui Shan (Longevity Hill). This area may be what Marco Polo called Green Isle.

As a practical matter, Bei Hai formed part of the system of vital reservoirs for water brought from the Western Hills to the capital. The system began with the Jishui Tan, which extended in an arc toward the northern limits of the Imperial City. It collected water entering through the west wall just north of Heyi Men (Xizhi Men). These lakes north of the Imperial City (modern Hou Hai) became a major market within the capital in Marco Polo's day. Taiye Pond, in turn, flanked the khan's palace and separated it from those for the heir and empress dowager on the west. Its area approximated modern Bei Hai and Zhong Hai. Other channels connected the lakes to the palace moat and canals serving the city.

When Yongle began serious work on his new capital, he expanded the lakes to create the three-part division we recognize today. The new lake bed excavated at the south, extending to the southern limits of the Imperial City (modern Chang'an Avenue), became Nan Hai. A small island immediately south of Qionghua was also transformed in the Ming. With a nine-arch stone bridge (b) connecting the two and a surrounding brick wall, it is today's Tuancheng. The Ming north city wall cut off parts of the former Jishui Tan (see fig. 2.7) while the lakes north of the Imperial

city (Hou Hai or Shi Sha Hai, Ten Temples Lake)
changed shape. The Ming reworking of the city also
put the canal connected to markets north of the
Imperial City inside the east wall of the latter, ending
canal boat traffic.

In Ming times, the area of Bei Hai was known
simply as the Western Park (Xi Yuan). While off limits
to most residents of the capital, it nonetheless became
well known. The Jiajing emperor (Zhu Houcong, r.
1522–66) resided in the Xi Yuan for twenty-five years,
but more often the lakes and gardens became settings
for ad hoc imperial entertainment and recreation.
Scholars favored with an invitation eagerly described
its features to their friends. Craig Clunas suggests their
accounts thereby played a role in garden design in
Jiangnan, where the so-called classic or scholar garden
was then taking shape. An altar for the cult of sericulture used by the empress and court ladies was built in
the northwest corner of Bei Hai, presumably because
it was more convenient than locations outside imperial precincts.

The Qing renovation of Bei Hai began with construction of a Tibetan Buddhist temple (c, d) atop
Qionghua Island by Shunzhi in 1651. In Qianlong's
reign this was renamed Temple of Eternal Peace
(Yong'an Si). The emperor's attentions extended over
thirty years, ca. 1741–71. He reworked the eastern and
northern shores of the lake and the slopes of the main
island to create what Naquin calls the "community
center of the palace and well known symbol of the
capital" (308). The projects ranged from small-scale
gardens to several temples, Buddhist and Tibetan,
along the north shore. The area known as Zhong Hai
was equally part of the emperor's designs: the
Belvedere of Purple Brightness (Ziguang Ge) was
used to celebrate military victories, and portraits of

heroic commanders were installed in the hall. The emperor feasted tributaries here, and reviewed military examinations and archery contests. Court paintings show bannermen on ice skates demonstrating their proficiency for an imperial audience.

Today Bei Hai is the only portion of the imperial parks that can be visited. Zhong Hai and Nan Hai, recently added to the National Register, are closed to the public for reasons of "security and preservation." Since the republican governments of the nineteen-teens, this area has been co-opted by the national government. The first Presidential Palace (Zongtong fu) of the Republic took up quarters here. Juliet Bredon's *Peking* (1931) describes a visit to this area ("The Sea Palaces and the Mongol Throne," pp. 133–55). After 1949, the lakeside real estate became residential and office facilities for the leaders of the party and government.

A walking tour of the gardens within Bei Hai can proceed from the south at Tuancheng, just northwest of the Forbidden City, or alternatively from the north gate on Di'an Men Xi Dajie. The attractions are clustered in

6.28
"The Pei-hai winter
Palace, Peiping"
Anonymous post card

three separate areas: Tuancheng and Qionghua Island, the eastern shore, and the northern shore. To incorporate the latter, some backtracking will be required.

To visit Tuancheng and Qionghua Island, one can start from the gate and parking area on Jing Shan Xi Dajie. Enter Tuancheng on its north side or skirt around to cross the marble bridge (b) to Qionghua Isle directly (fig. 6.28).

Once a small island in the lake, the area of Tuancheng was enlarged in the Jin period, and walled at that time. Some of the oldest trees seen today may date to this period. Once connected by a wooden bridge to the eastern shore, the area was filled in as Yongle built his capital. The focus of Tuancheng now is the Hall for Receiving Light (Chengguang Dian, 1690; fig. 6.29), an elaborate structure with four wings and gables (a). It houses a large white jade Buddha, a donation by a Chinese monk in 1898. The jade Buddha is from Burma, and akin to another example now in Shanghai.

A stone pavilion (*ting*) built by Qianlong in 1746 houses an immense jade boulder 5 m in diameter

6.29
Hall for Receiving Light,
Tuancheng, Bei Hai

6.30
Yong'an Si dagoba,
Bei Hai

dated to the Yuan period (ca. 1265). Legend says it was once housed atop the larger isle to hold drink for banqueting Mongols. Its original base is held by Fayuan Si. The buildings that surround the main hall have good displays on the history of Bei Hai. Tuancheng also offers views of the bridge crossing the water to the west and parts of Zhong Hai.

The southern slopes of Qionghua Isle are occupied by the Temple of Eternal Peace (Yong'an Si, 1743), a series of yards (c) that climb the hill on axis with the north end of the bridge. They ascend toward the summit (d) with its White Dagoba (1651, elevation 82 m above sea level; fig. 6.30). To the west of the temple axis, the Hall of the Contented Heart (Yuexin Dian) has a moon terrace and palatial halls (e) with views of the three great lakes. A higher position near the dagoba affords views of the Forbidden City, Jing Shan, and even the Western Hills on a clear day. The rockeries around the slopes are said to include Huizong's garden rocks from Kaifeng.

Wandering to the west one arrives at the Tower for Reading the Classics (Yuegu Lou, 1753), a two-story structure (f) with a semi-circular plan. The tower houses 500 rubbings of Qianlong's favorite calligraphy specimens: the *Sanxi Tang fatie* (*Model Calligraphy of the Three Rarities Studio*). A covered two-story gallery of sixty bays (300 m long), the Yanlou Arcade (1771), extends along the northern shore, home to the Fangshan Restaurant. Paths amid the rockeries climb the slope back toward the dagoba, each turn offering a new vista of the water, palace, or city. On the eastern side of the island stands Qianlong's stele "Spring Clouds on Jasper Flower Island" (1751), one of the "Eight Views of Yanshan" (see fig. 1.6; Box, p. 50).

A short bridge on the east side of Qionghua Island leads to Bei Hai's eastern shore, where three

attractions await. Coming from the south the first is
the Hao and Pu Brooks (Haopu Jian, 1757), a twisting
path that ascends eastward featuring a zigzag stone
bridge across a water tank (i). An enclosed tank
became a favorite device of eighteenth-century
designers and can be found at several Qianlong gardens around the capital. Further north is the Painted
Pleasure Boat Studio (Huafang Zhai, 1757), a four-
sided courtyard (j) also with water at the center. These
two compounds were built after Qianlong's first
southern journey, when he personally experienced the
scholar gardens of Jiangnan. This visit would seem to
have been a vector carrying fresh design ideas back to
the capital from the sophisticates of the southeast. At
the north end of the eastern shore lies the Altar to

6.31
"Scene in the Imperial City,
Peking," postcard by
Camera Craft, Peking

Sericulture (Xian Can Tan), rebuilt by Qianlong in 1742 to replace the neglected Ming altar at the north-west corner (k). Like the Painted Pleasure Boat Studio, it is closed at present.

Six parallel compounds fill the northern shore of Bei Hai. They begin on the east inside the north gate with the Studio of Mirror-like Clarity (Jingqing Zhai, 1757; later renamed Jingxin Zhai), a "garden within the garden" (l) notable for its rear hall facing the lake and a rockery (9 m high) across the north (fig. 6.31). This is usually a crowded venue, but well worth a visit.

Several temple precincts lie to the west. The first is the Western Paradise (Xi Tian Fan Jing, 1759) with its glazed tile *paifang*. The temple's first two yards (m) are open, with a very impressive main hall of Nanmu construction housing bronze images (Wanli era). The rear yards are closed. On a parallel axis to the west is the Nine Dragon Wall (Jiulong Bi, 1756), a full 25 m in length and 6 m in height (n). The temple compound on the north for which the wall was installed is closed. It once housed the blocks used to print the Buddhist canon.

The next compound, originally the Gazing at Water Hall (Chengguan Tang), was built on the site of the original Ming sericulture altar (o). It was renamed the Kuaixue Tang in 1779 after a specimen of calligraphy and is now used for shops. Next west is the Revealing Happiness Temple (Chanfu Si, 1746), which offers modern peony and rose gardens; the original halls (q) are lost. The Five Dragon Pavilions (Wu Long Ting) opposite perch at water's edge (p), artfully placed to offers prime views of the broad expanse of lake and distant Qionghua Island. Finally at the western end is the Little Western Paradise World of Bliss (Xi Tian Jile Shijie). This temple is a square compound (r) with *pailou* gates and corner towers enclosing a moat. The main hall at the center is a square pavilion occupied by an enormous Mount Sumeru populated with pavilions, stupas, and 262 Buddha images. Disassembled in 1953, the present version was restored in 1992.

Garden-Palaces

Ming emperors spent most of their time while in the capital within the Forbidden City or the Western Park nearby. The court did develop Xiang Shan and the Western Hills, however. This attractive scenery had been appreciated in Liao and Jin times and temples and retreats were built even then. In the Hongzhi and Zhengde reigns (ca. 1488–1521), the Hao Yuan, an imperial garden, was built on an old temple site; this location ultimately became the Summer Palace (Yihe Yuan) of recent times (see below). Wealthy capital officials also began to build private gardens northwest of the city in Haidian District, now the campuses of Peking and Qinghua (Tsinghua) universities.

The early Qing rulers, however, initiated the building of large-scale gardens in these areas (fig. 6.32). Kangxi built his Garden (or Villa) of Joyful Springtime (Changchun Yuan) on the site of a famous private Ming garden (a). Kangxi also gave his heir, the future Yongzheng emperor, a small garden north of his retreat. This garden (d), known ultimately as Yuanming Yuan (Garden of Perfect Brightness) became three huge linked garden establishments under Yongzheng, Qianlong, and Jiaqing. For much of the Qing the emperors preferred these gardens over the Forbidden City. Its demise in 1860 resulted from this role. Had the Forbidden City been the regular locus of power for the throne, it instead might have been looted and torched by the British and French forces. Recognizing the long-term residence of the emperors in these gardens, Naquin prefers to call them "villas," while other sites visited for the short term she calls "parks" (312).

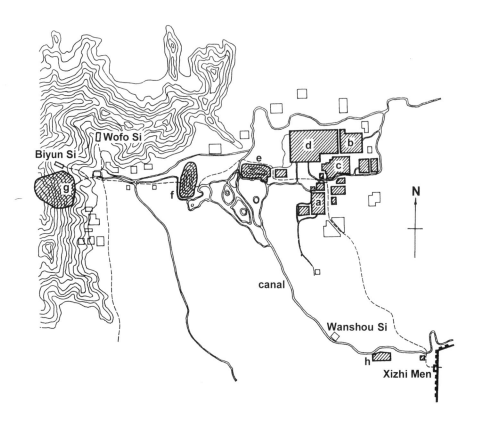

6.32
Qing garden-palaces and gardens, from Zhou, *Gudian yuanlin*, 185. Diagram shows: (a) Changchun Yuan (Joyful Spring); (b) Changchun Yuan (Eternal Spring); (c) Qichun Yuan (Variegated Spring); (d) Yuan Ming Yuan (Perfect Brightness); (e) Qingyi Yuan (Clear Ripples) at Longevity Hill, later Yihe Yuan; (f) Jingming Yuan (Tranquil Brightness) at Jade Spring Hill; (g) Jingyi Yuan (Peace and Harmony) at Fragrant Hills; (h) Leshan Yuan (Benevolent Goodness), later the Beijing Zoo

Yuanming Yuan exemplifies a new type of imperial project, a kind of "garden-palace." Extensive imperial parks located outside the capital walls were built as early as the Qin and Han, and the most important Tang palace from the late seventh century onwards, the Daming Gong, incorporated park-like rear areas around a man-made lake. Hence, an emperor's use of garden and park-like settings as adjuncts to his palace life had ancient precedents. The Qing inherited the Forbidden City with its modest gardens as well as the convenient Western Park and Jing Shan annexes. By creating suburban gardens outside the city walls with court halls and support facilities to accommodate the regular business of the throne, a new kind of palace took shape. Yongzheng seems to have taken the lead in this development, spending long periods in his garden and insisting that important affairs be managed on a regular schedule without returning to the Forbidden City. His son, the future Qianlong, grew up with his own garden within Yuanming Yuan, and in due course developed the complex even more. When Lord Macartney wanted to present his gifts, they were assembled in Yuanming Yuan for the emperor's delectation, not within the Forbidden City.

After due mourning for his father Yongzheng, Qianlong began expansion of Yuanming Yuan in 1737. Rather than increase the area of the garden, by 1744 his renovations added twelve new scenic views for a total of forty. Court artists were ordered to make paintings that complemented imperially brushed verse. Ultimately words and images were produced as a printed palace edition. In spite of promises to curb his enthusiasms, Qianlong almost immediately began work on a new garden on the east (b), the Garden of Eternal Spring (Changchun Yuan), rationalizing it at the time as his future retirement retreat. In fact, he was not to retire for another fifty years. When he did so he confined himself to the Ningshou Gong, rebuilt for the purpose in the northeast corner of the Forbidden City.

It was during this period European-style fountains and palaces under Jesuit direction [31 ▶] were begun. A third garden complex was added by 1772, known initially as the Garden of Variegated Spring (Qichun Yuan) and later as Ten Thousand Springs (Wanchun). It was a pastiche created by assembling smaller garden plots (c). This garden was extended even more under Qianlong's successor, Jiaqing (Yongyan, r. 1796–1820), between 1801 and 1810. These multi-generational efforts created a vast garden complex (b, c, d) occupying 350 hectares inside a wall system that ran for 10 km.

About half of the area was dedicated to water features, and the remainder given over to 123 architectural ensembles with carefully chosen poetic names evoking their harmonious assemblages of water, hills, and pavilions.

The myriad steps and considerable budget needed to create and fine tune Yuanming Yuan did not exclude other projects. At the same time garden villas (or parks) were being developed elsewhere: to the west at Weng Shan (Qingyi Yuan [e], the Villa of Clear Ripples, from 1745, later Cixi's Summer Palace); on Jade Spring Hill (Jingming Yuan [f], the Villa of Tranquil Brightness, from 1753); and further west still on Xiang Shan (Jingyi Yuan [g], the Villa of Peace and Harmony, 1745).

31 ▶
European Palaces
of Yuanming Yuan

QING, CA. 1747–68
NATIONAL REGISTER,
1988
HAIDIAN

Christian missionaries from several Catholic orders arrived in Beijing in the late Ming period. The best known, Matteo Ricci (1552–1610), took up residence by 1601. The missionaries had limited success both at court and among the general population during the late Ming. Christianity was indulged and proscribed by the early Qing rulers. Kangxi favored several Catholic fathers by employing them in the imperial court on calendrical calculations, cartography, cannon production, and astronomy (see p. 94). Yongzheng, on the other hand, demolished the first churches built in the capital (see Ch. 7) and eschewed association with Europeans. Qianlong, however, again favored the Jesuits, inducting a number into his court for their artistic and scientific skills. The most famous was the nimble Italian painter Giuseppe Castiglione (1688–1766), known also by his Chinese name, Lang Shining. Qianlong's curiosity about water fountains depicted in engravings shown him by the Jesuits led to an unusual commission: a suite of fountains and buildings to be erected across the north of his Garden of Eternal Spring, by then a part of Yuanming Yuan (fig. 6.32, b).

These "European–style buildings" (*xiyang lou*) became the most well-known feature of those gardens, although in their day they seem to have been little more than a short-lived imperial enthusiasm. They occupied a very small portion of the immense garden tracts. Their fame derives from their later history and relative preservation. Built from more durable materials than most architecture in the gardens, they survived the great conflagration of October, 1860 somewhat better than the myriad timber pavilions and halls. As scenic ruins, several generations of visitors to the capital came to see and photograph them (fig. 6.33). Today the Yuanming Yuan is under state protection, and the European ruins have become an especially popular destination.

Their story begins in 1747 with Qianlong's order to Castiglione, who took overall responsibility for the project. Jean-Dénis Attiret (1702–68) and Ignatius Sichelbarth (1708–80) were charged with the plans and elevations for the palace buildings, while Michel Benoist (1715–74) supervised construction of the several fountains. Work started at the west end with an

6.33
Ruins of Calm Sea Hall (Haiyan Tang), Yuanming Yuan, from Fu, *Historical Photos*, 121

6.34
Calm Sea Hall (Haiyan
Tang) fountain ruins,
Yuanming Yuan

ensemble consisting of the Palace of the Delights of Harmony (Xieqi Chu) on the north flanked by a Water Storage Hall (Xushui Lou) on the west and an Aviary (Yangque Long) on the east (ca. 1747–51). This suite has been compared to the now lost Trianon de Porcelaine of Versailles (ca. 1670). An extensive maze filled the north portion of the plot, which has been rebuilt as a tourist attraction.

The largest portion of the project was a strip extending west to east about 770 m by 60 m with the Belvedere (Fangwai Guan) and Calm Sea Hall (Haiyan Tang). Both were elevated structures complemented by fountains. The latter had a fountain on the west side (fig. 6.34) with water spouts in the form of twelve bronze animal heads, one for each two-hour division of the day (or zodiac) as a water clock. These animal heads disappeared, resurfaced on the auction market, and were acquired by the Poly Museum (near the Dongsi Shitiao Overpass) in recent memory. To the east the Great Fountain (Da Shuifa) was complemented by a viewing area opposite for the imperial throne (Guan Shuifa).

About a decade later, another large palace was constructed to display a set of Beauvais tapestries given to Qianlong by the French king. These were installed in the Observatory of Distant Waters (Yuanying Guan). The culmination of this series of palaces and fountains was a large water feature backed by a perspectival array called the Painting East of the Lake (Hudong Xianfa Hua), a kind of stage set with walls in echelon to create a deep vista. If one enters today through the east gate, this is the first major site encountered.

These pseudo-European palaces nonetheless utilized traditional construction: pounded earth platforms carried the halls and tanks for the fountains. Wooden skeletons framed the halls and glazed tiles covered the roofs. However, infill walls of brick with plaster and carved stone ornament at corners and around doors and windows set these structures apart. These ponderous stone carvings now litter much of the site. The lower floors of each hall had fictive façades masking the earthen platforms. All interiors consisted of single-story spaces, without stairs and second floors, which seem to have been unappreciated by the patron (see Qianlong's quote, p. 269). The fountains that were the inspiration for the project did not long function. Pumps designed by Benoist broke down. In later years palace eunuchs were required to carry buckets of water to fill the tanks prior to imperial visits. The entire project has been likened to stage design by Michele Pirazzoli-t'Serstevens, an apt comparison.

A visit to the ruins is certainly worthwhile, but the status of the site has been contested since its "rediscovery" in the late 1970s. Its meaning and value have been much debated: as a symbol of national shame, as a ruin to be maintained, as a platform for thoroughgoing reconstruction and commercial exploitation. Over the last several decades, both careful excavations and kitschy adaptive reuse have taken place. This heritage site will no doubt continue to evolve.

The Summer Palace (Yihe Yuan)

The most extensive portion of the Qianlong emperor's grand designs to survive is the garden known in English as the Summer Palace (fig. 6.35). Located west of Yuanming Yuan, in the emperor's lifetime this was the Villa of Clear Ripples (Qingyi Yuan, 1750–64). At 290 hectares it is almost as large as Yuanming Yuan in its prime. Three-quarters of the area is devoted to three lakes which act as reservoirs for the capital, linked by channels to feed Bei Hai and the Forbidden City. Construction began in 1750 in commemoration of the emperor's mother's sixtieth birthday. The embankments that run north-south call to mind West Lake in Hangzhou. The hill that rises across the north was devoted to temples and palace courtyards, and like Yuanming Yuan was laid waste in 1860.

By the 1880s, the Empress Dowager Cixi (1834–1908) undertook reconstruction, making the garden her long-term residence. The ruined Yuanming Yuan nearby became a source of building materials; not all the damage sustained there can be laid at the feet of the British and French. Only during this phase was a complete circuit of walls constructed and proper halls for court business and residence added on the east. Cixi's new name, Yihe Yuan, is variously translated: Garden to Nurture Harmony (Rawski) or Villa of Smiling Harmony (Naquin).

A visit to the four principal areas is a major undertaking: (1) the court and residential complex inside the main east gate; (2) the long corridor and many compounds and temple precincts on the south slope of the hill; (3) additional features including Suzhou Street across the north side (rear) of the hill; and (4) the south and west lakes running along the west side of the site with their bridges and pavilions. Some time should also be spent on the water. The crowds are often very

large, especially in the court complex inside the east gate and the long gallery. Across the water and at the rear, the ambiance may be calmer.

6.35
Kunming Lake,
Summary Palace

SUGGESTED READING

For an overview of domestic architecture, see Ronald G. Knapp, *Chinese Houses: The Architectural Heritage of a Nation* (2005). The former residence of Mei Lanfang is profiled on pp. 100–111. An album with many photos of pre-modern houses is Zhang Zhan, *Beijing ming ju* (*Celebrated Residences of Old Beijing*) (2005). A telling analysis of life within the household is Francesca Bray, *Technology and Gender: Fabrics of Power in Late Imperial China* (1997), pp. 50–172. Nancy Berliner, *Yin Yu Tang: The Architecture and Daily Life of a Chinese House* (2003) examines a single family and its house in Anhui over several centuries. This dwelling is now reconstructed at the Peabody-Essex Museum in Salem, Massachusetts.

Two volumes offer glimpses into Peking life during the early twentieth century: H.Y. Lowe, *The Adventures of Wu: the Life Cycle of a Peking Man* (1983) and Tun Li-chen, trans. Derk Bodde, *Annual Customs and Festivals in Peking* (1936). For an expatriate account, see George N. Kates, *The Years That Were Fat: Peking, 1933–1940* (1952).

˜ General introductions to gardens include Maggie Keswick, *The Chinese Garden: History, Art, and Architecture* (2nd edition 2003) and Craig Clunas, *Fruitful Sites: Garden Culture in Ming Dynasty China* (1996), a rethinking of many received notions. The classic text by Ji Cheng on garden design has been published as *The Craft of Gardens*, trans. Alison Hardie (1988).

Carroll Brown Malone, *History of the Peking Summer Palaces under the Ch'ing Dynasty* (1934) and Hope Danby, *The Garden of Perfect Brightness* (1950) are early studies of the Qing garden-palaces. Young-tsu Wong, *A Paradise Lost: the Imperial Garden Yuanmingyuan* (2001) is more up-to-date.

The European palace ruins have been the focus of much attention. A good introduction is Geremie Barmé, "The Garden of Perfect Brightness, a Life in Ruins," *East Asian History* 11 (June, 1996): 111–58. See also Régine Thiriez, *Barbarian Lens: Western Photographers of the Qianlong Emperor's European Palaces* (1998) for fascinating glimpses of the ruins before they reached their present state.

The Early Twentieth Century

7

Before the events of 1900 the Diplomatic Quarter, as such, did not exist, though most of the Legations were situated on or near the Chiao Min Hsiang [Jiaomin Xiang] (Street of Intercourse With the People), so named because here, under the Manchu rule, tribute-bearing envoys like the Koreans, Mongols and Thibetans were given lodgment. However unflattering, it is a fact that the Manchu sovereigns long persisted in regarding Western diplomats in the same category as these messengers from tributary states.

JULIET BREDON, *PEKING* (1931), 37

The city that intrigued Juliet Bredon and other authors of early guides and memoirs will never return. The goal of this chapter is to assess the most significant impacts of early twentieth century modernization on the Ming and Qing capital in order to understand the surviving monuments introduced above.

Beijing experienced several foreign occupations in the century before the Second World War. After the Second Opium War, the British and French decided in the fall of 1860 to "teach the Manchu Qing court a lesson." The Xianfeng emperor (Yizhu, r. 1851–61) and his court fled the palace, and for a short time the European military controlled the city. The so-called Summer Palaces, the Yuanming Yuan [31 ▶] and others, were looted and then burned. This catastrophe was the prelude to establishing the first European diplomatic legations, an event that promoted penetration of the Qing domain by foreign powers. In 1900, after Empress Dowager Cixi and a duplicitous court threw their support to the Boxers, the city was first ravaged by the famous siege of the legations and then liberated by the eight Allied Armies in August of that year. For a time the palace was empty again and freely visited by foreign soldiers and tourists. The suburban palaces and gardens once again suffered heavy damage. The city itself, especially around Qian Men, the legations, and Beitang (North Church) saw considerable destruction. With the resolution of this crisis, a proper Legation Quarter [32 ▶], a "country within a country" in the view of most Chinese writers, was established in the capital. After 1900 the pace of change picked up, and the first scars on the historic city appeared.

In retrospect, the transformation of Peking into a modern city unfolded unevenly across the first four decades of the twentieth century prior to the third occupation by the Japanese in 1937. However, the Japanese takeover was peaceful when compared to the events of 1860 and 1900. The city avoided protracted fighting during the war years, much less the bombings that devastated Tokyo and Berlin. The city literally dodged the bullet.

The peaceful transfer of the imperial palaces to the Republic after 1911 and the fall of city to the PLA (People's Liberation Army) authorities in 1949, moreover, preserved the past. So too did the determination of the people's government to preserve "cultural relics." The first decade of the new People's Republic of China witnessed many important decisions and grand projects that have left their mark on the city and seriously harmed its historic fabric in the eyes of many. Historic Beijing weathered another crisis in the 1960s and 70s, the years of the Great Proletarian Cultural Revolution. Locked up behind its walls and gates, the palace emerged unscathed, although the general population and other sites could not make that claim. By the end of that turbulent decade and more, the walls and gates were gone, an irreparable loss (see Ch. 2).

Long before the disaster of 1860, a foreign presence had grown slowly on Beijing soil since the arrival of Matteo Ricci (1552–1610) in 1601. There had been some knowledge of Christianity even earlier under the Mongol Khans. Two churches were founded ca. 1299–1305 by Giovanni di Monte Covino at a location corresponding to today's Xinhua Men, the south gate to Nan Hai on West Chang'an Avenue. But the first lasting Christian churches were established during the seventeenth century. From 1650 to 1652, Adam Schall built on the site that became the Nan Tang (South Church) near Xuanwu Men. In 1655, another plot east of the palace was given to two fathers. This became the Dong Tang (East Church, St. Josephs) on Wangfujing. In 1703, the Qiushi Tang, precursor to the Bei Tang (North Church) was established inside the Imperial City. In 1723, the Xi Tang (West Church) was established. Each of these four churches went though three to six episodes of building including repairs or reconstruction after 1900. All of these Catholic churches survive today in their Gothic, Renaissance, or Baroque guises. The Bei Tang, the Cathedral of Our Savior (fig. 7.1) and the largest Catholic congregation in the city, serves as the seat of the bishop of Beijing. It was rededicated in 1985. Thus a whiff of European architecture has been present in Beijing since the seventeenth century.

A short-lived vogue for western things appeared at court in the late nineteenth century. Sheet glass was installed in the palace windows and electric lights were in use by 1890. The marble steamboat, the

Turn of the Century Beginnings

Qingyan Fang, at Yihe Yuan is notorious. Empress Dowager Cixi had western-style buildings constructed in Zhong-Nan Hai as a reception hall for diplomatic occasions (the Haiyan Tang, 1904; destroyed 1960s) and also as a resting palace on the canal leading to the Summer Palace outside Xizhi Men (the Changguan Lou at Leshan Yuan, 1898; now part of the Beijing Zoo). There is even a western folly in the Forbidden City, the Palace of Prolonged Happiness (Yanxi Gong), one of the Six Eastern Palaces [12 ▶]. Today only a hollow shell of bronze and stone in a tank meant to be filled with fish can be seen (fig. 7.2).

7.2
"Crystal Palace" (Yanxi Gong), Eastern Six Palaces (1909)

Neither European architectural styles nor advanced construction techniques inspired modernization. Rather the practical need for better infrastructure, especially transportation, ruled the day. Rail lines connecting the city to Hankou (the south), Fengtian (the northeast), Tongzhou (the east), and Zhangjiakou (the northwest) appeared between 1896 and 1909. This demanded puncturing the Outer City walls and building stations near Qian Men. The Jing-Feng Railroad Station (1903) serving the Beijing to Fengtian (now Shenyang) line immediately southeast of Tian'an Men Square features a fine Victorian clock tower. It is now a shopping center.

Zhu Qiqian (1871–1964), as de facto administrator of Beijing, initiated more radical steps to improve transportation. The authorities tore down the walls that tied the Arrow Tower to Qian Men (see fig. 2.2), and sliced through five other city gates and two corners of the Inner City wall (fig. 7.3) so an urban rail line could wrap around from the south to the northwest. Fifteen stations were built between Qian Men and Xizhi Men, Beijing's first mass transit.

Creating new gates and streets, paving them with macadam, as well as introducing water, electricity, and telephone services, also constituted part of Zhu's

agenda. By 1922, the east, north, and west walls of the Imperial City had been leveled, leaving its eastern and western gates standing in isolation. Arched openings in the south wall of the Imperial City were created at Nan Chizi (fig. 7.4) and Nan Chang Jie, north-south streets on the east and west sides of the palace respectively. The city's grid began the painful process of rationalization that continues today. The walls surrounding the approach to Tian'an Men were taken down, as were the walls at both east and west Chang'an Jie (the ends of the T). This was the birth of today's Chang'an Avenue. By 1937 this artery emerged from the city by gaps in the wall at both ends (Jianguo Men and Fuxing Men). Additional east-west cross

7.4
Nan Chizi traffic opening,
Imperial City wall,
Chang'an Avenue (1922)

town links were created by opening the corridor between the palace and Jing Shan across the Bei Hai bridge to Xi'an Men (connecting Dong Si and Xi Si).

With Pu Yi's eviction from the palace in 1924 came a surge of adapting imperial properties to public spaces and institutions. The Palace Museum (Box, p. 122) opened in 1925 in the inner court, the Historical Museum set up in the area from Duan Men to Wu Men by 1928, She Ji Tan became first Central Park (1914) and then Zhongshan Park (1928) in honor of Sun Yatsen whose remains had lain in repose in the sacrificial hall there [13 ▶]. Meanwhile, Zhong-Nan Hai became the Presidential Palace (Zongtong Fu), and Bei Hai [30 ▶] another park. Until the Nationalist capital was formally moved to Nanjing in 1928, the city and national governments invested in new buildings for a variety of agencies and civic institutions, from a national assembly (unrealized) to a model prison. Some of these projects also took over imperial sites: the Examination Hall (Gong Yuan) was leveled for the assembly. Leshan Yuan became an Agricultural Station (later Zoo). The Army was ensconced in a magnificent European-style complex (fig. 7.5) that had once been the He Qin Wang Fu.

A growing number of western buildings transformed other parts of the city, many intended to serve an international clientele, whether resident or tourist. The Peking Hotel (established 1903) moved to its present location, then north of the Legation Quarter, with a handsome French-style seven-story edifice (1907, 1917; fig. 7.6). It boasted 105 rooms with baths and a rooftop bar and terrace for dancing. Wangfujing Dajie became known for Dong'an Shichang, a market on the site of the present-day Dongfang Mall, as well as shops and restaurants. By 1934, 136 stores had joined the merchants association. (For a time the street was renamed in honor of George Ernest Morrison, long-

7.5
Former site of Duan Qirui
Government (Qing Army
Headquarters, ca. 1906), at
No. 3 Zhang Zizhong Road

7.6
Peking Hotel (Raffles), at
No. 33 Chang'an Avenue
(Brossard Mopin, 1917,
1931)

time Peking correspondent and onetime advisor to
Yuan Shikai. Foreign visitors often used this name.)
The north–south avenue starting from Chongwen Men
(or Hata Men) served as a commercial strip, as did lanes
around Qian Men in the Outer City, an area badly
damaged in 1900. Dashalan flourished with tea houses
and theaters. Their owners embraced eclectic architecture blending *pailou* facades and western ornament. The
near-total redevelopment of this area (for which read,
destruction) goes forward as this is written.

After 1900 the most thorough modernization of any part of Beijing took place when the area southeast of the Imperial City was formally recognized as the Legation Quarter (Shi Guan Jie). In the time of Dadu, this area (outside the wall) had been where rice and other commodities from the south arrived by canal boat. An alley running east-west became known as Jiang Mi Xiang (*jiang* signifies south of the Yangzi, hence "southern rice alley"). When the Ming pushed the Inner City wall south, agencies managing tribute and visiting embassies (the Siyi Guan and Huitong Guan) were established, convenient to the Ministry of Rites and translation bureau east of Tian'an Men. In the Qing, both the Macartney (1792) and Amherst (1816) missions took up residence here. Sometime in the Qing, the name of the alley changed to the similar sounding Jiaomin Xiang ("mixing people alley"), recorded by 1897. Early on, Russian priests had been ensconced in a hostel in this district. Their facilities grew steadily over the eighteenth century to include even an Orthodox Church chapel.

The history of the Legation Quarter, however, begins on the heels of the British and French occupation of 1860. The following year, the British took over a *wang fu* (fig. 7.7) on the west side of the Jade Canal (Yuhe, now Zhengyi Road) running south from the southeast corner of the Imperial City. The French occupied another mansion further east on Taijichang. They were joined by nine other nations between 1862 and 1873: Russia (upgrading its hostel), the United States, Germany, Belgium, Spain, Italy, Austria-Hungary, Japan, and Holland. The Chinese Imperial Customs, operated by the British under the renowned Sir Robert Hart, and a local population also inhabited these alleys. When the Boxer siege began in early summer of 1900, the larger legations, especially the

◀ 32
Legation Quarter

AFTER 1900
NATIONAL REGISTER, 2001
DONG JIAOMIN XIANG, DONGCHENG

7.7
"British Legation"
(Liang Gong Wang Fu),
postcard by
Th. Culty, Peking

British, became a refuge for resident foreigners and some Chinese Christians. After an 80-day struggle, the foreigners were liberated by the eight Allied Armies. More precisely, gallant Sepoys of the 1st Sikhs slogged in through the Water Gate (Sluice Gate) that ran under the city wall. Chinese Christians and French fathers were also besieged at the Bei Tang, the only Christian church not destroyed in the events. The fighting before, during, and after the siege took a considerable toll on the city: large areas around Qian Men as well as the gate house itself leveled, the corner towers badly damaged, and many foreigner's houses and several churches burned.

Rising from the ashes after 1900 was a new, expanded Legation Quarter stretching from Dong Chang'an Jie on the north to the Inner City wall on the south and from Chongwen Men on the east to the ministries flanking Tian'an Men on the west (fig. 7.8). A walled and gated precinct (fig. 7.9) with military barracks and an international police force emerged. Wide-open drill fields on three sides protected the margins. The quarter became a "semi-colonial" realm:

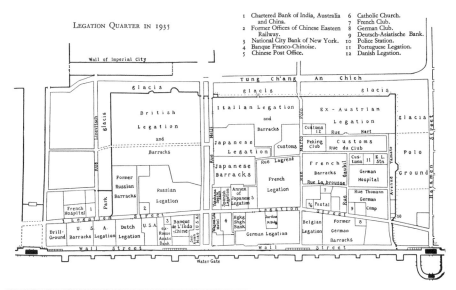

LEGATION QUARTER IN 1935

1 Chartered Bank of India, Australia and China.
2 Former Offices of Chinese Eastern Railway.
3 National City Bank of New York.
4 Banque Franco-Chinoise.
5 Chinese Post Office.
6 Catholic Church.
7 French Club.
8 German Club.
9 Deutsch-Asiatische Bank.
10 Police Station.
11 Portuguese Legation.
12 Danish Legation.

7.8
Above: Map of Legation Quarter, ca. 1935, from Arlington and Lewisohn, *In Search* (1935), opposite p. 5

7.9
Left: "Entrance to the Legation Quarter" (Dong Jiaomin Xiang), postcard, anonymous

international residents exempt from Chinese laws, Chinese excluded. Streets acquired new names: Jiaomin Xiang became Legation Street. The road running along the Yuhe (fig. 7.10) became Rue Meiji (now Zhengyi Road). All of the legations rebuilt and all but Spain enlarged their holdings. The only substantial structure built prior to 1900 to survive is a portion of the Japanese legation from 1884 to 1886. By the teens and twenties, the quarter had eleven modern legation compounds, as well as eight barracks,

7.10
"Legation Street" [sic]
(Jade Canal from south),
postcard by S.Yamamoto,
Peking

six banks, three hospitals, two clubs, two post offices, two churches, one hotel, and many merchants.

The quarter makes a fine walking tour, especially because traffic is restricted during rush hours. The sights are limited to the historic gates of the legations and a few early commercial buildings, many now on the National Register as a group designation. Walking down Zhengyi Road (the former Rue Meiji), one encounters the severe gate of the British Legation on the west (fig. 7.11) and the more grand twin gate houses of the Japanese Legation on the east (fig. 7.12) now the Beijing City government. At the crossing of Dong Jiaomin Xiang and Zhengyi Road is the imposing Yokohama Shokin (Specie) Bank (1910) on the northeast corner, a fine essay in Beaux Arts red brick and

7.11
British Legation,
Zhengyi Road

stone. Wandering west will bring one to the former
International Banking Corporation (H.K. Murphy,
1917–20; now the Beijing Police Museum). The gate of
the Netherlands (1909) and the Russian legations survive, but not the U.S. embassy gate (now being developed). Strolling east from the same intersection offers
the French Post Office (fig. 7.13), more gates and compounds for snooping (the French and Belgian) and St.
Michael's Church. North up Taijichang (Rue Marco
Polo in its day) toward Chang'an Avenue is the handsome Italian embassy. Many of these compounds have
been occupied by governmental agencies or hotels.
Guards as a rule do not permit idlers to enter and some
will wave away photographers.

7.12
Japanese Legation, No. 2
Zhengyi Road (1907–09)

7.13
French Post Office, No. 19
Dong Jiaomin Xiang

The Twenties and Thirties

For Beijing the two decades between the end of the First World War and the Japanese occupation (1937) mixed growth and development with repeated crises. Most importantly, in 1928 Beijing lost its status as national capital when the Nationalist government established itself in Nanjing. Control of the city changed hands a dozen times, and from 1931 the specter of Japanese aggression also loomed. In spite of these challenges, projects in city planning, capital construction, and historic preservation went forward.

The first significant projects designed by named architects, both Chinese and foreign, were realized. The Chinese architects were in almost all cases trained abroad, especially at the University of Pennsylvania as it happens. The impact of their education appeared in banks, theaters, and university campuses. Representative of this period would be the Zhenguang Theater (1920, now the Children's Theater) on Donghua Men Dajie by Shen Liyuan, and the Continent Bank (1924, now Bank of China; fig. 7.14) on the west side of the Chairman Mao Memorial Hall by Zhu Lin (1896–1971). Both manifest Beaux-Arts style.

7.14
Former Continent Bank (now Bank of China), Xi Jiaomin Xiang (Zhu Lin, 1924)

More prominent, however, were several large projects undertaken by institutions utilizing foreign architects. Foremost among these were the campus of the Peking Union Medical College (1917–28), the campus of Yanjing University (ca. 1926, now Peking University), Furen University (1930), and the National Library (1931). These buildings share an attempt to blend elements from a traditional Chinese architectural idiom with modern, western construction. Some critics see this as a traditional revival, distinct from more eclectic contemporary styles also in evidence during the period.

The Peking Union Medical College was built on the site of the Yu Wang Fu, and retained its gate on the south. To announce its Chinese identity as a vanguard institution promoting western medical science, the fourteen buildings constructed by Shattuck and Hussey between 1912 and 1921 combined traditional green-glazed tile roofs (echoing the original *wang fu*) and white stone platforms with solid, low-rise gray masonry masses harmonious with the fabric of the city. Both the college entrance on the south and the hospital entrance on the west opened onto courtyards (fig. 7.15). However, these yards were composed of large buildings of similar mass and status, rather than following the hierarchy implicit in a palace or *sihe yuan*.

Furen University built an oversized courtyard with a prominent main gate house (fig. 7.16) and even corner towers, like a palace. But here too no main hall stood opposite the entrance as traditional plans would predict. The National Library design took the emulation of the past even further by creating an ersatz palatial hall with a façade rich in columns, lattice doors and windows, and other details

7.15
Peking Union Medical
College, No. 9 Dong Dan
Santiao (Shattuck and
Hussey, 1919–21, 1925)

This decade marks the beginnings of modern scholarly studies of China's architectural heritage, and the first restorations of historic structures. The modernizer of Beijing, Zhu Qiqian, patronized the Society for the Study of Chinese Architecture (Zhongguo Yingzao Xueshe) from 1930. It was staffed with western- and Japanese-trained architects, the most famous being Liang Sicheng (1901–72) and Liu Dunzhen (1897–1968). These scholars and their students pioneered the discipline of architectural history in China combining analysis of traditional sources with field investigations of extant structures. Liang held forth at Qinghua University, while Liu was professor at Nanjing. Their younger associates—including Chen Mingda, Liu Zhiping, Luo Zhewen, Mo Zongjiang, Shan Shiyuan to name only a few—went on to create present-day knowledge of this field and of historic Beijing. Liang and Liu's cohort was put to work on restoration projects ca. 1935–37: the Southeast Corner

7.16
Main Entrance, Furen
University (Adelbert
Gresnigt, 1930)

Tower [5▶], the Altar to Heaven [16▶], the Changling in the Ming Valley [18▶], Zhihua Si [22▶], Tianning Si pagoda [21▶], Wu Ta Si [24▶], and Yihe Yuan, among sites featured in this volume.

For modernization throughout China, see Joseph W. Esherick, ed., *Remaking the Chinese City: Modernity and National Identity, 1900–1950* (2000). For the Legation Quarter, see Michael J. Moser and Yeone Wei-Chih Moser, *Foreigners Within the Gates: the Legations at Beijing* (1993).

Sidney D. Gamble, *Peking: A Social Survey* (1921) offers a fascinating look at the real life of Peking peo-

SUGGESTED READING

ple in the early twentieth century. David Strand, *Rickshaw Beijing: City People and Politics in the 1920s* (1989) and Madeleine Yue Dong, *Republican Beijing: The City and Its Histories* (2003) both cover the Nationalist era (1928–37). Jeffrey W. Cody, *Building in China: Henry K. Murphy's "Adaptive Architecture," 1914–1935* (2001) chronicles the career of one of the most prominent of non-Chinese architects active in this period.

Appendixes
Walking the City

Because it is so flat, Beijing invites walking or riding a bicycle. No hilly areas or heights interrupt the regular grid. And with the exception of two artificial hills, Jing Shan (see fig. 6.25) and Jasper Flower Island at Bei Hai (see fig. 6.28), vistas are unobstructed. Major avenues have shaded sidewalks and lanes for slow traffic, shielding the pedestrian or bicyclist from the sun and from exhaust. All major intersections have traffic police energetically waving commands and blowing whistles.

Caution: Whether on foot or bicycle, pay attention to traffic at all times, even when on sidewalks and especially when crossing with the light. Turning vehicles do not stop!

The ten walking tours outlined feature two dozen entries in parts of the city where several sites can be conveniently visited. Interesting side streets and alleys as well as other attractions will enhance your exploration. Distances between sites are generally moderate. Be sure to bring along a good street map of the area.

Caution: A full day walking in heat, pollution, and noise can wear down even the fittest.

Wear sturdy shoes, protect yourself with a hat or sunblock, and always carry water. Regular breaks in the shade of a courtyard are highly recommended.

Sooner or later you may be unable to find what you are looking for. You can then have one of the best experiences Beijing has to offer: being an outsider asking directions. Note that the "outsider" designation is not limited to foreign nationals; *wai di ren* signifies anyone who does not call Beijing home.

Older residents of a neighborhood resting on a stoop are more likely to know the way than younger people or anyone just passing through. (They are probably lost too!) Vignettes of Beijing alley life are a part of getting lost and, of course, present photo opportunities. So relax and enjoy your meandering.

Street Signs

Large streets (*jie, da jie*) have signage in white on blue that gives both Chinese characters and *pinyin*, the standard rendering in Roman letters, and a handy system for visitors to learn. Many avenues are named after the former city gates (see example below and Box, p. 83) or a landmark like the Bell Tower [6▶], for example. This kind of name will be modified by the terms *nei* (inside) or *wai* (outside) indicating position in relation to the old wall (now the Second Ring Road). Street names are also modified by directions: *bei* (north), *dong* (east), *xi* (west), or *nan* (south). Arrows at each end of the sign point out the directions.

On the other hand, alley (hutong) signs may or may not be labeled in pinyin (opposite above). Their names often allude to the history of the neighborhood, for example former markets or trades or temples. The names of hutong (Box, p. 259) will often be unknown to city residents who are not from the neighborhood. Alleys run parallel and perpendicular to main arteries, but some wind and some are dead ends. They invite wandering.

Street sign reading Jianguo Men Nei Dajie, literally "Founding Country Gate Inner Great Street." Smaller characters and arrows indicate east and west directions.

Street sign reading Mao'er hutong, literally "Hat Lane," one of many interesting back streets of Beijing.

ASCENDING THE HEIGHTS

Scaling a gate, tower, wall, or hill affords a vista of the surrounding areas and on a clear day a distant prospect, as the view from Jing Shan (Coal Hill, see below and fig. 6.25). This is surely one of the best ways to learn the city and to put its parts together. Many examples are featured in this guide: Zhengyang Men [4 ▶], Southeast Corner Tower [5 ▶], Bell and Drum Towers [6 ▶], Observatory [7 ▶], Tian'an Men [8 ▶], Wu Men [10 ▶], Jing Shan, and the Bei Hai White Dagoba [30 ▶]. Three of these sites are recommended: the Bell and Drum Towers (for the northern Inner City), Jing Shan (for areas surrounding the Forbidden City), and the White Dagoba atop Jasper Flower Island in Bei Hai.

Both Jing Shan and the Bell and Drum Towers give a dramatic sense of the city's main axis. In Ming and Qing times, the entire capital was transfixed by a straight line extending from Yongding Men, the south central gate of the Outer City (recently rebuilt) to the Bell and Drum Towers, a distance usually computed as 7.8 km. The palace straddles this axis, so that its north and south gates and the elevated terraces of the Outer and Inner Courts also participate in this grand design. When Liang Sicheng proclaimed historic Peking a "masterpiece" of urban design, he emphasized the rigor of its heroic, walled, axial plan.

Vista from Jing Shan

Walking Tours

TOUR 1

TIAN'AN MEN SQUARE AND THE LEGATION QUARTER

References: Ch. 2, Walls and Gates; Ch. 3, Palaces; Ch. 7, Twentieth Century

Highlights: Front Gate and Arrow Tower [4▶]; Gate of Heavenly Peace [8▶]; Tian'an Men Square with Martyrs Monument, Great Hall of the People, National Museum, Chairman Mao Memorial; Legation Quarter [32▶; fig. 7.8] with Zhengyi Lu, Dong Jiaomin Xiang, Peking Hotel

TOUR 2

FORBIDDEN CITY (fig. 3.16)

References: Ch. 3, Palaces [10▶–12▶]; Ch. 6, Gardens

TOUR 3

SOUTHEAST QUADRANT, IMPERIAL CITY

References: Ch. 3, Palaces; Ch. 4, Altars

Highlights: Imperial City Wall (Strip Park), Imperial City Art Gallery, Huangshi Cheng [9], She Ji Tan and Tai Miao [13▶–14▶], Pudu Si, Lao She Residence [29▶]

TOUR 4

BEI HAI (fig. 6.27)

Reference: Ch. 6, Gardens [30▶]

TOUR 5

SOUTHEAST QUADRANT, INNER CITY

References: Ch. 2, Walls and Gates; Ch. 5, Temples

Highlights: Ming-Qing City Wall Park, Corner Tower [5▶], Observatory [7▶], Zhihua Si [22▶]

TOUR 6
NORTHEAST QUADRANT, INNER CITY

References: Ch. 4, Altars; Ch. 5, Temples

Highlights: Confucian Temple [17 ▶] and Guozijian Street, Yonghe Gong [25 ▶], Di Tan, Bailin Si, Nan Xin Cang

TOUR 7
NORTH INNER CITY

References: Ch. 2, Walls and Gates; Ch. 6, Residences

Highlights: Bell and Drum Towers [6 ▶], Prince Gong Mansion and Garden [28 ▶], and Guo Moruo and Mei Lanfang Residences [29]

TOUR 8
WEST INNER CITY

References: Ch. 4, Altars; Ch. 5, Temples

Highlights: Lu Xun Museum [29 ▶], Bai Ta Si [23 ▶], Lidai Diwang Miao [15 ▶], Guangji Si, Bei Tang

TOUR 9
TIAN TAN (fig. 4.15) AND XIAN NONG TAN

Reference: Ch. 4, Altars

Highlights: Altar to Heaven [16 ▶], Agriculture Altar and Ancient Architecture Museum

TOUR 10
SOUTHWEST OUTER CITY

Reference: Ch. 5, Temples

Highlights: Baiyun Guan, Tianning Si [21 ▶], Niujie Mosque [27 ▶], Fayuan Si [20 ▶]

Site Index

19 ▸ **Dingling**
Ming Shisan ling, Changping

20 ▸ **Fayuan Si**
Fayuan Si Qian Jie No. 7, Xuanwu

21 ▸ **Tianning Si Pagoda**
Tianning Si Qian Jie, Xuanwu

22 ▸ **Zhihua Si**
Lumicang hutong No. 5, Dongcheng

23 ▸ **Bai Ta Si (Miaoying Si)**
Fucheng Men Nei Dajie, Xicheng

24 ▸ **Wu Ta Si (Beijing Shike Yishu Bowuguan)**
Wu Ta Si No. 24, Baishi Qiao, Haidian

25 ▸ **Yonghe Gong**
Yonghe Gong Dajie No. 12, Dongcheng

26 ▸ **Dong Yue Miao**
Chaoyang Men Wai Dajie, Dongcheng

27 ▸ **Niu Jie Mosque**
Dong Niu Jie No. 88, Guang'an Men Nei, Xuanwu

28 ▸ **Mansion and Garden of Prince Gong**
Liuyin Jie No. 16A, Xicheng

29 ▸ **Former Residence of Mao Dun**
Hou Yuan'en Si hutong No. 13, Jiaodaokou, Dongcheng
Former Residence of Lao She
Fengfu hutong No. 19, Dengshikou, Dongcheng
Former Residence of Guo Moruo
Qian Hai Xi Jie No. 18, Xicheng
Former Residence of Lu Xun
Gongmenkou Ertiao No. 19, Fucheng Men Nei, Xicheng
Former Residence of Mei Lanfang
Huguo Si Jie No. 9, Xicheng

30 ▸ **Bei Hai**
Xicheng

31 ▸ **Yuanming Yuan, European Palaces**
Haidian

32 ▸ **Legation Quarter**
Dong Jiaomin Xiang, Dongcheng

Bibliography

Aisin Gioro Puyi. *From Emperor to Citizen*. Translated by W.J.F. Jenner. Hong Kong: Oxford University Press, 1987.

Aldrich, M.A. *The Search for a Vanishing Beijing: A Guide to China's Capital Through the Ages*. Hong Kong: Hong Kong University Press, 2006.

Ancient Temples in Beijing (Beijing gu cha ming si). Beijing: China Esperanto Press, 1993.

Arlington, L.C. and William Lewisohn. *In Search of Old Peking*. Peking: Henry Vetch, 1935.

Barmé, Geremie. "The Garden of Perfect Brightness, a Life in Ruins." *East Asian History* 11 (June, 1996): 111–58.

Becker, Jasper. *The City of Heavenly Tranquility: Peking in the History of China*. Hong Kong: Oxford University Press, 2008.

Belsky, Richard. *Localities at the Center: Native Place, Space, and Power in Late Imperial Beijing*. Cambridge: Harvard East Asia Center, 2005.

Berger, Patricia. *Empires of Emptiness*. Honolulu: University of Hawaii Press, 2002.

Berliner, Nancy. *Yin Yu Tang: The Architecture and Daily Life of a Chinese House*. Boston: Tuttle, 2003.

Bray, Francesca. *Technology and Gender: Fabrics of Power in Late Imperial China*. Berkeley: University of California Press, 1997.

Bredon, Juliet. *Peking: A Historical and Intimate Description of Its Chief Places of Interest*. Shanghai: Kelly & Walsh, 1931.

Bretschneider, Emil. *Archaeological and Historical Researches on Peking and Its Environs*. Shanghai: American Presbyterian Mission Press, 1876.

Cameron, Nigel and Brian Brake. *Peking: A Tale of Three Cities*. Tokyo and New York: Weatherhill, 1965.

Cameron, Nigel. *Barbarians and Mandarins: Thirteen Centuries of Western Travelers in China*. Tokyo and New York: Weatherhill, 1970.

Chan, Hok-lam. "A Mongolian Legend of the Building of Peking." *Asia Major*, 3rd series, 3.2 (1990): 63-93.

Chang, Sen-dou. "The Morphology of Walled Capitals." In *The City in Late Imperial China.* Edited by G.W. Skinner. Stanford: Stanford University Press, 1977.

Clunas, Craig. *Fruitful Sites: Garden Culture in Ming Dynasty China.* Durham, N.C.: Duke University Press, 1996.

Cody, Jeffrey W. *Building in China: Henry K. Murphy's "Adaptive Architecture," 1914–1935.* Hong Kong: University of Hong Kong Press, 2001.

Danby, Hope. *The Garden of Perfect Brightness: The History of the Yuan Ming Yuan and of the Emperors Who Lived There.* London: Williams and Norgate, 1950.

Dong, Madeleine Yue. *Republican Beijing: The City and Its Histories.* Berkeley: University of California Press, 2003.

Dorn, Frank. *The Forbidden City: the Biography of a Palace.* New York: Scribner's, 1970.

Elliott, Mark C. *The Manchu Way: The Eight Banners and Ethnic Identity in Late Imperial China.* Stanford: Stanford University Press, 2001.

Elman, Benjamin A. *A Cultural History of Civil Examinations in Late Imperial China.* Berkeley: University of California Press, 2000.

Esherick, Joseph W., ed. *Remaking the Chinese City: Modernity and National Identity, 1900–1950.* Honolulu: University of Hawaii Press, 2000.

Franke, Herbert. "Consecration of the 'White Stupa' in 1279." *Asia Major,* 3rd series, 7.2 (1994): 155–84.

Fu Gongyue, et al eds. *Historical Photos of Old Beijing (Jiu jing shi zhao).* Beijing: Beijing Press, 1996.

Fu Xinian, et al. *Chinese Architecture.* Edited by Nancy S. Steinhardt. New Haven: Yale University Press, 2002.

Gamble, Sidney D. *Peking: A Social Survey.* New York: Doran, 1921.

Goossaert, Vincent. *The Taoists of Peking, 1800–1949: A Social History of Urban Clerics.* Cambridge: Harvard University Press, 2007.

Harris, David. *Of Beauty and Battle: Felice Beato's Photographs of China.* Santa Barbara: Santa Barbara Museum of Art, 1999.

Hevia, James L. *Cherishing Men from Afar: Qing Guest Ritual and the Macartney Embassy of 1793.* Durham, N.C.: Duke University Press, 1995.

Huang, Ray. *1587: A Year of No Significance, the Ming Dynasty in Decline.* New Haven: Yale University Press, 1981.

Ji Cheng. *The Craft of Gardens.* Translated by Alison Hardie. London: Yale University Press, 1988.

Johnston, Reginald F. *Twilight in the Forbidden City.* 1934; reprint Hong Kong: Oxford University Press, 1985.

Kates, George N. *The Years That Were Fat: Peking, 1933–1940.* New York: Harper and Row, 1952.

Keswick, Maggie. *The Chinese Garden: History, Art, and Architecture.* New York: Rizzoli, 2003.

Kieschnick, John. *The Impact of Buddhism on Chinese Material Culture.* Princeton: Princeton University Press, 2003.

Knapp, Ronald G. *Chinese Houses: The Architectural Heritage of a Nation.* Boston: Tuttle, 2005.

Larner, John. *Marco Polo and the Discovery of the World.* London: Yale University Press, 1999.

Li, Lillian M., Alison J. Dray-Novey, and Haili Kong. *Beijing: From Imperial Capital to Olympic City.* New York: Palgrave Macmillan, 2007.

Lipman, Jonathan N. *Familiar Strangers: A History of Muslims in Northwest China.* Seattle: University of Washington Press, 1997.

Little, Stephen. *Taoism and the Arts of China.* Berkeley: University of California Press, 2000.

Lowe, H.Y. (Liu Xinyao). *The Adventures of Wu: the Life Cycle of a Peking Man.* Princeton: Princeton University Press, 1983.

Malone, Carroll Brown. "History of the Peking Summer Palaces under the Ch'ing Dynasty." *Bulletin of the University of Illinois,* 31.41 (1934).

Marco Polo: the Travels. Translated by Ronald Latham. Harmondsworth: Penguin, 1958.

Meyer, Jeffrey F. *The Dragons of Tiananmen: Beijing as a Sacred City.* Columbia, S.C.: University of South Carolina Press, 1991.

Moser, Michael J. and Yeone Wei-Chih Moser. *Foreigners Within the Gates: the Legations at Beijing.* Hong Kong: Oxford University Press, 1993.

Mote, Frederick W. "The T'u-mu Incident of 1449." In *Chinese Ways in Warfare.* Edited by Frank A. Kierman and John K. Fairbank. Cambridge: Harvard University Press, 1974.

Naquin, Susan. *Peking: Temples and City Life, 1400–1900*. Berkeley: University of California Press, 2000.

Paludan, Ann. *The Imperial Ming Tombs*. New Haven: Yale University Press, 1981.

Prip-Moller, J. *Chinese Buddhist Monasteries: Their Plan and Its Function as a Setting for Buddhist Monastic Life*. 1937; reprint Hong Kong: Hong Kong University Press, 1967.

Ratchnevsky, Paul. *Genghis Khan: His Life and Legacy*. Oxford: Blackwell, 1991.

Rawski, Evelyn S. *The Last Emperors: A Social History of Qing Imperial Institutions*. Berkeley: University of California Press, 1998.

_____. "The Imperial Way of Death: Ming and Ch'ing Emperors and Death Ritual." In *Death Ritual in Late Imperial and Modern China*. Edited by James L. Watson and Evelyn Rawski. Berkeley: University of California Press, 1988.

Rawski, Evelyn S. and Jessica Rawson, eds. *China: The Three Emperors, 1662–1795*. London: Royal Academy of Arts, 2006.

Rennie, D. F. *Peking and the Pekingese during the First Year of the British Embassy at Peking*. 2 vols. London: John Murray, 1865.

Rossabi, Morris. *Khubilai Khan: His Life and Times*. Berkeley: University of California Press, 1988.

Ruitenbeek, Klaas. *Carpentry and Building in Late Imperial China: A Study of the Fifteen-century Carpenter's Manual* Lu Ban jing. Leiden: E. J. Brill, 1993.

Shi Mingzheng. "From Imperial Gardens to Public Parks: The Transformation of Urban Space in Early Twentieth Century Beijing." *Modern China* 24.3 (July, 1988): 219–54.

_____. "Rebuilding the Chinese Capital: Beijing in the Early Twentieth Century." *Urban History* 25.1 (1998): 60-81.

Spence, Jonathan. *Emperor of China: Self-Portrait of K'ang-hsi*. New York: Knopf, 1974.

Steinhardt, Nancy Shatzman. *Chinese Imperial City Planning*. Honolulu: University of Hawaii Press, 1990.

_____. *Liao Architecture*. Honolulu: University of Hawaii Press, 1997.

Strand, David. *Rickshaw Beijing: City People and Politics in the 1920s*. Berkeley: University of California Press, 1989.

Thiriez, Régine. *Barbarian Lens: Western Photographers of the Qianlong Emperor's European Palaces.* New York: Gordon and Breach, 1998.

Thorp, Robert L. *Visiting China's Past: A Guide to Sites and Resources.* Warren, CT.: Floating World, 2006.

Tun Li-chen. *Annual Customs and Festivals in Peking.* Translated by Derk Bodde. Peking: Henri Vetch, 1936.

Tung, Anthony M. *Preserving the World's Great Cities: The Destruction and Renewal of the Historic Metropolis.* New York: Clarkson Potter, 2001.

Waldron, Arthur. *The Great Wall of China: from History to Myth.* Cambridge: Cambridge University Press, 1990.

Wan Yi, Wang Shuqing, and Lu Yanzhen, eds. *Daily Life in the Forbidden City: The Qing Dynasty, 1644–1912.* Translated by Rosemary Scott and Erica Shipley. Harmondsworth: Penguin, 1988.

Weidner, Marsha. "Buddhist Pictorial Art of the Ming Dynasty (1368–1644): Patronage, Regionalism, and Internationalism." In *Latter Days of the Law: Images of Chinese Buddhism, 850–1850.* Honolulu: University of Hawaii Press, 1994.

Welch, Holmes. *The Practice of Chinese Buddhism, 1900–1950.* Cambridge: Harvard University Press, 1967.

Wong, Young-tsu. *A Paradise Lost: the Imperial Garden Yuanmingyuan.* Honolulu: University of Hawaii Press, 2001.

Wood, Frances. *Did Marco Polo Go to China?* Boulder, Colo.: Westview, 1996.

Wright, Arthur F. "The Cosmology of the Chinese City." In *The City in Late Imperial China.* Edited by G. W. Skinner. Stanford: Stanford University Press, 1977.

Wu Hong. *Remaking Beijing: Tiananmen Square and the Creation of a Political Space.* Chicago: University of Chicago Press, 2005.

Wu Liangyong. *Rehabilitating the Old City of Beijing: A Project in the Ju'er Hutong Neighborhood.* Urbanization in Asia. Vancouver: University of British Columbia Press, 1999.

Yu Zhuoyun and Graham Hutt. *Palaces of the Forbidden City.* New York: Viking, 1984.

Zito, Angela. *Of Body and Brush: Grand Sacrifice as Text/Performance in Eighteenth-Century China.* Chicago: University of Chicago Press, 1997.

Chinese Sources by Chapter

Unless otherwise noted, city of publication is Beijing.

Introduction

Beijing Municipal City Planning Commission, ed. *Beijing lishi wenhua ming cheng Beijing Huang cheng baohu guihua.* Zhongguo jianzhu gongye, 2004.

_____. *Beijing jiu cheng lishi wenhua baohu chu shi zheng jichu sheshi guihua yanjiu.* Zhongguo jianzhu gongye, 2006.

Dong Guangqi. *Gu du Beijing wu shi nian yanbian lu.* Nanjing: Dongnan daxue, 2006.

Shan Jixiang. *Chengshihua fazhan yu wenhua yichan baohu.* Tianjin: Tianjin daxue, 2006.

Liu Dunzhen, et al. *Zhongguo gudai jianzhu shi.* 2nd ed. Zhongguo jianzhu gongye, 1984.

Feng Jiren. "Zhongguo gudai mugou jianzhu de kaoguxue duandai." *Wenwu* 1995.10: 43–68.

Liang Sicheng. *Qing-shi yingzao zeli.* Qinghua daxue, 2006.

_____. *Qing Gong Bu "Gongcheng zuofa zeli" tu jie.* Qinghua daxue, 2006.

Ch. 1: Before the Ming

General

Hou Renzhi, ed. *Beijing lishi ditu ji.* Beijing chubanshe, 1988.

Zhu Zuxi. *Ying guo jiang yi: Gu du Beijing de guihua jianshe ji qi wenhua yuanyuan.* Beijing wenhua shi. Zhonghua shuju, 2007.

Early Cities

Zhao Qichang. "Jicheng de tanyuan." In *Beijing shi yanjiu,* 37–51. Beijing shi shehui kexue, 1986.

Su Bai. "Sui Tang cheng zhi leixing chutan (tigang)." In *Jinian Beijing Daxue Kaogu zhuanye sanshi zhounian lunwenji, 1952–1982,* 279–85. Wenwu, 1990.

Jin Zhongdu

Beijing Liao-Jin City Walls Museum. *Jin Zhongdu shui guan yizhi kaolan.* Beijing Yanshan, 2001.

Beijing Cultural Relics Institute. *Beijing Jindai huang ling.* Wenwu, 2006.

Luo Zhewen, Yu Jie, Wu Menglin, and Ma Xigui. "Lue tan Lugou Qiao de lishi yu jianzhu." *Wenwu* 1975.10: 71–83.

Liang Xinli. *Beijing gu qiao.* Beijing tushuguan, 2007.

Yuan Dadu

Zhu Xie. "Yuan Dadu gongdian tu kao." In *Xi ri jing hua,* 1–49 (original 1936). Tianjin: Baihua wenyi, 2005.

Capital Museum. *Yuan Dadu,* Zhang Ning and Zhao Qichang, eds. Beijing Yanshan, 1989.

Hou Renzhi. "Yuan Dadu cheng." In *Zhongguo gudai jianzhu jishu shi,* edited by Zhang Yuhuan, 437–43. Kexue, 1985.

Fu Xinian. *Zhongguo gudai chengshi guihua jianzhu qun buju ji jianzhu sheji fangfa yanjiu.* Zhongguo jianzhu gongye, 2001.

_____. "Yuan Dadu Danei gongdian fuyuan yanjiu." In *Fu Xinian jianzhu shi lunwenji,* 326–56. Wenwu, 1998.

Su Bai. "Juyong Guan guojie ta kao gao." *Wenwu* 1964.4: 13–29; reprinted in *Zangchuan Fojiao siyuan kaogu,* 338–64. Wenwu, 1996.

Ch. 2: Walls and Gates

Nanjing

Li Weiran. "Ming Nanjing cheng." In *Zhongguo gudai jianzhu jishu shi,* 443–48. Kexue, 1985.

Wei Zhengjin, et al. *Chengyuan cangsang: Nanjing chengqiang lishi tulu.* Wenwu, 2003.

Construction of Ming Beijing

Beijing Cultural Relics Institute. *Beijing kaogu sishi nian.* Beijing Yanshan, 1990.

Xu Pingfang, ed. *Ming Qing Beijing cheng tu.* Kaoguxue zhuankan, Series B, No. 23. Ditu chubanshe, 1986.

Hou Renzhi. "Ming Qing Beijing cheng." In *Zhongguo gudai jianzhu jishu shi,* 448–53. Kexue, 1985.

Wei Yuqing. "Yingjian Changling yu qian du Beijing." In *Zhongguo Zijincheng xuehui lunwenji* 1. Edited by Shan Shiyuan and Yu Zhuoyun, 104–08. Zijincheng, 1997.

Li Xieping. *Mingdai Beijing ducheng yingjian congkao.* Zijincheng, 2006.

Song Lei. "Ming shisan ling jianzhu yong zhuan kao." In *Zijincheng xuehui lunwenji* 1, 263–68.

Monuments

Dongcheng District People's Government. *Beijing Dongcheng wenwu jianzhu.* Chaohua, 1997.

Chen Ping and Wang Shiren, eds. *Dong Hua tuzhi: Beijing Dongcheng shiji lu.* 2 vols. Tianjin: Tianjin guji, 2005.

Xiao Mo. *Weiwei di du: Beijing lishi jianzhu.* Qinghua, 2006.

Walls and Gates

Zhang Xiande. "Ming Qing Beijing chengyuan he cheng men." *Gujian yuanlin jishu* 8 (1985): 49–52 and 9 (1985): 45–47.

Fu Gongyue, ed. *Beijing lao cheng men.* Beijing Meishu Sheying, 2002.

Beijing News (*Xinjing Bao*), ed. *Gu du cheng men.* Zhongguo luyou, 2007.

He Baoshan. "Ming Shizu zeng jian Beijing wai cheng." *Gu Gong bowuyuan yuankan* 1986.4: 47-48.

Chen Xiaosu. "Cong Ming dai Beijing de jingji fazhan kan Beijing waicheng de xiujian." *Beijing wenwu yu kaogu* 2 (1991): 280–87.

Zhu Yingli and Zeng Yixuan. *Beijing Zhong Gu lou* (*Beijing Bell and Drum Towers*). Beijing Meishu Sheying, 2003.

Jiang Zhongyi. "Beijing Guanxiang Tai de kaocha." *Kaogu* 1983.6: 526–30.

Beijing Observatory, ed. *Zhongguo gudai tianwenxue chengjiu.* Beijing kexue jishu, 1987.

Yu Jie and Yi Shitong. "Beijing gu Guanxiang Tai." In *Zhongguo gudai tianwen wenwu lunji,* edited by Institute of Archaeology, 409–14. Wenwu, 1989.

Great Wall

Wenwu Editorial Committee, ed. *Zhongguo changcheng yiji diaocha baogao ji.* Wenwu, 1981.

Luo Zhewen. "Wanli chang cheng." In *Luo Zhewen gu jianzhu wenji,* 102–07. Wenwu, 1998.

Wu Yuanzhen and Wu Menglin. "Beijing Huairou xian Mutianyu Guan changcheng diaocha." *Wenwu* 1990.12: 66–79.

Ch. 3: Emperors and Palaces

Imperial City

Zheng Lianzhang. "Wansui shan de shezhi yu Zijin cheng weizhi kao." In *Zijincheng jianzhu yanjiu yu baohu: Gu Gong bowuyuan jianyuan 70 zhounian huigu*, edited by Yu Zhuoyun, 240–48. Zijincheng, 1995.

Zheng Zhihai. "Zijincheng de wu zhong men." In *Zijincheng xuehui lunwenji* 1, 123–27.

Zhang Chengyou. "Tian'an men chenglou ji Tian'an men guangchang." *Gujian yuanlin jishu* 11 (1986): 55–60, 64.

Li Pengnian. "Huangshi Cheng: Wo guo gulao de dang'an ku." *Gu Gong bowuyuan yuankan* 1979.4: 11–15.

Forbidden City

Shan Shiyuan. "Ming dai yingjian Beijing de sige shiqi." In *Zijincheng jianzhu yanjiu yu baohu*, 3–8.

Pan Guxi and Chen Wei. "Ming dai Nanjing gongdian yu Beijing gongdian de xingzhi guanxi." In *Zijin cheng xuehui lunwenji* 1, 85–92.

Fu Xinian. "Guanyu Mingdai gongdian tanmiao deng da jianzhu qun zongti guihua shoufa de chubu tantao." In *Fu Xinian jianzhu shi lunwenji*, 357–78.

———. "Zhongguo gudai yuanluo buzhi shoufa chutan." *Wenwu* 1999.3: 66–83.

———. "Zhongguo gudai jianzhu waiguan sheji shoufa chutan." *Wenwu* 2001.1: 74–89.

Zhou Suqin. *Zijincheng jianzhu*. Zijincheng, 2006.

Construction

Shi Zhimin and Chen Yinghua. "Zijincheng hu cheng he ji weifang yange kao." In *Zijincheng jianzhu yanjiu yu baohu*, 229–39.

Shi Zhimin. "Gu Gong diji jichu zonghe kancha." In *Zijincheng jianzhu yanjiu yu baohu*, 273–85.

Bai Lijun and Wang Jingfu. "Gu Gong jianzhu jichu de diaocha yanjiu." *Ibid* 286–315.

———. "Beijing Gu Gong jianzhu jichu." In *Zijincheng xuehui lunwenji* 1, 238–52.

Wu Menglin and Liu Jingyi. "Fangshan Dashiwo yu Beijing Ming dai gong dian ling qin cai shi: jian tan Beijing lichao yingjian yong shi." *Ibid* 253–62.

Piao Xuelin. "Gongting jinzhuan yu qingzhuan de chengzao ji kanman." In *Zijincheng jianzhu yanjiu yu baohu*, 391–97.

Yu Zhuoyun. "Gu Gong san da dian xingzhi tanyuan," "Gu Gong san da dian," "Gu Gong Taihe Dian," "Taihe Men de kongjian zhuhe yishu." In *Zhongguo gongdian jianzhu lunwenji*, 20–39, 40–52, 53–60, 84–90. Zijincheng, 2002.

Zhou Suqin. "Shixi Zijincheng Dong Xi Liu Gong de pingmian buju." In *Zijincheng jianzhu yanjiu yu baohu*, 132–41.

Zheng Lianzhang, "Zijincheng Zhongcui Gong jianzao niandai kaoshi." *Ibid*, 142–59.

Jiang Shunyuan. "Ming Qing Dong chao Dong gong dui Zijincheng jianzhu de yingxiang." In *Zijincheng xuehui lunwenji* 1, 109–22.

Fu Lianzhong. "Qingdai Yangxin Dian shinei zhuangxiu ji shiyong qingkuang." *Gu Gong bowuyuan yuankan* 1986.2: 41–48.

Zhuankan: Gu Gong Bowuyuan 80 nian. Zijincheng 132 (May, 2005).

Ch. 4: Altars and Tombs

Wan Yi, Wang Shuqing, and Lu Yanzhen, eds. *Qingdai gong ting shenghuo.* Hong Kong: Shangwu, 1985.

Shan Shiyuan. "Mingdai yingzao shiliao: Mingdai She Ji Tan." *Zhongguo yingzao xueshe huikan* 5.2 (December, 1934): 116–26.

Fu Gongyue. "Qingdai de Tai Miao." *Gu Gong bowuyuan yuankan* 1986.3: 73–79, 86.

Shan Shiyuan. "Mingdai yingzao shiliao: Tian Tan." *Zhongguo yingzao xueshe huikan* 5.3 (March, 1935): 110–38.

Li Yuanlong. *Tian Tan.* Chaohua, 1988.

Yu Zhuoyun. "Tian Tan de jianzhu xingzhi yu xiangzheng yishu." In *Zhongguo gongdian jianzhu lunwenji*, 214–25.

Qi Xin. *Beijing Kong Miao.* Wenwu, 1983.

Ming and Qing Tombs

Liu Dunzhen. "Ming Changling." In *Liu Dunzhen wenji* vol. 1, 261–86. Zhongguo jianzhu gongye, 1982.

Institute of Archaeology. *Dingling,* 2 vols. Wenwu, 1990.

Liu Dunzhen. "Yi xian Qing xi ling." In *Liu Dunzhen wenji*, vol. 2, 74–144.

Ch. 5: Temples for Gods and Buddhas

Fu Xinian. *Beijing gu jianzhu.* Wenwu, 1986.

Wang Shiren, ed. *Xuan Nan hong xue tuzhi.* Zhongguo jianzhu gongye, 1997.

Li Hongwu. *Miao hui.* Beijing difang zhi Fengwu tuzhi congshu. Beijing chubanshe, 2005.

Buddhist Temples

Fu Xinian. "Beijing Fayuan Si de jianzhu." In *Fu Xinian jianzhu shi lunwenji,* 264–68.

Liang Sicheng and Lin Huiyin. "Ping jiao jianzhu zalu (xu)." In *Liang Sicheng wenji* vol. 1, 353–67. Zhongguo jianzhu gongye, 1982.

Liu Dunzhen. "Beiping Zhihua Si Rulai Dian diaocha ji." In *Liu Dunzhen wenji,* vol. 1, 61–128.

Xu Huili. *Gu cha gui bao: Zhihua Si.* Beijing Yanshan, 1990.

Tibetan Buddhist Temples

Bai Ta Si Protection Agency. *Miaoying Si Bai Ta.* Wenwu, 1985.

Yang Yi and Chen Xiaosu. *Miaoying Si Bai Ta shiliao.* Beijing Yanshan, 1996.

Su Bai. "Yuan Dadu 'Sheng zhi tejian Shijia sheli ling tong zhi ta bei wen.'" In *Zangchuan Fojiao siyuan kaogu,* 322–37. Wenwu, 1996.

Luo Zhewen. "Zhenjue Si Jingang baozuo ta," *Wenwu* 1979.9: 86–89.

Daoist Temples

Beijing Dong Yue Miao. Chaoyang Cultural Relics Bureau, 1999.

Chen Bali. *Dong Yue Miao.* Zhongguo shudian, 2002.

Mosques

Liu Zhiping. *Zhongguo Yisilanjiao jianzhu.* Urumqi: Xinjiang Renmin, 1985.

Beijing Niu Jie Libai Si (996–1996). Jinri Zhongguo, 1996.

Ch. 6: Residences and Gardens

Residences

Zhang Zhan. *Beijing ming ju (Celebrated residences of old Beijing).* Beijing guji, 2005.

Wang Xin. *Wang fu.* Beijing difang zhi Fengwu tuzhi congshu. Beijing chubanshe, 2005.

Ma Bingjian. *Zhongguo gu jianzhu muzuo yingzao jishu.* Kexue, 1991.

_____. *Beijing sihe yuan (Quadrangles of Beijing).* Beijing Meishu sheying, 1993.

Weng Li. *Beijing de hutong.* Beijing Yanshan, 1992.

Gardens

Zhou Weichuan. *Zhongguo gudian yuanlin shi.* Qinghua daxue, 1990.

Fang Xianfu, "Qianlong shiqi de jianzhu huodong yu chengjiu," *Gujian yuanlin jishu* 5 (1984): 47–54.

Huang Ximing. "Zijincheng gongting yuanlin de jianzhu tese." In *Zijincheng jianzhu yanjiu yu baohu,* 189–201.

Wang Puzi. "Gu Gong Yuhua Yuan." *Ibid,* 202–07.

Fu Lianxing and Bai Lijuan. "Jianfu Gong hua yuan yizhi." *Ibid,* 206–12.

Ru Jinghua and Zheng Lianzhang. "Cining Gong hua yuan." *Ibid,* 224–28.

Yu Zhuoyun and Fu Lianxing. "Qianlong hua yuan de zaoyuan yishu." In *Zhongguo gongdian jianzhu lunwenji,* 70–83.

Sun Dazhang. "Qingdai Zijincheng Ningshou Gong de gaijian ji Qianlong de gongting jianzhu yijiang." In *Zhongguo Zijincheng xuehui lunwenji* 1, 289–96.

Ch. 7: The Early Twentieth Century

Wang Shiren et al, eds. *Zhongguo jindai jianzhu zonglan: Beijing (The Architectural Heritage of Modern China: Beijing).* Zhongguo jianzhu gongye, 1993.

Zhang Fuhe. *Beijing jindai jianzhu shi (The Modern Architectural History of Beijing from the End of the 19th Century to 1930s).* Qinghua daxue, 2004.

Wang Jun. *Cheng ji.* Sanlian, 2003.

Fu Gongyue, ed. *Jiu jing daguan (Old Beijing in Panorama).* Renmin Zhongguo, 1992.

Hu Piyun and Fu Gongyue, eds. *Jiu jing shi zhao (Historical Photos of Old Beijing).* Beijing chubanshe, 1996.

Satellite view of
Beijing metropolitan area
taken by Chinese-American
astronaut Leroy Chiao,
February 2005, from
Ni Hao, No. 5, 2005: 25

Floating World Editions publishes books that contribute to a
deeper understanding of Asian cultures. Editorial supervision:
Ray Furse. Book and cover design: Liz Trovato. Production
supervision: Bill Rose. Printing and binding: Malloy
Incorporated. The typefaces used are Bembo and Gill Sans.